FORBIDDEN

FORBIDDEN

WRITTEN BY DIAMOND SPEAKS

Sherell Highsmith
Forbidden
All rights reserved
Copyright © 2024 by Sherell Highsmith

Published by Spines
ISBN: 979-8-89383-900-5

CONTENTS

INTRODUCTION

Philadelphia is the City of Brotherly Love. In the light of day, it is filled with tourists visiting the Liberty Bell, buying soft pretzels, and scoffing down cheesesteaks. But, when night falls, the streets of the city become deadly, filled with crime, sex, deceit, and murder. Forbidden takes you on a journey of four lives that become intertwined as they each realize they are just pawns in a web full of lies, drugs and money. No one is safe, and only the strong will survive. They each will learn that the past is never forgotten, no matter how hard you try to cover it up, and when you're from the streets, you learn some things are truly FORBIDDEN...

Regina regained consciousness on the clammy, dampened concrete floor, and her thoughts were racing. She opened her eyes and tried to focus. They felt like tiny chips of glass had cut into them. The old, dilapidated room encased her as she tried to visualize her surroundings. When she looked up, she could see that the floor had caved in on her as broken wood and marble tiles still fell from above. She had fallen a whole floor down. The distinctive odor of rats and rusty nails filled her nostrils as she started to inhale frantically. A shudder and chill went from her feet up to her head. She was panicking as her body started to tremble with fear. She wanted to get up and run but felt paralyzed. A tight knot formed deep in her throat from the smoke that filled the room. It all seemed surreal to her. She needed to know what was going on, where Clayton was, and if anyone else was still alive. She tried to collect her thoughts and make sense of everything that happened. She couldn't see anything in the dark room, and the only light that shone in was from the upper-level ball-room. Where was everyone? She thought. Her vision was still blurred from the dust, but she could smell a ghastly stench in the air.

It was eerily silent except for the crackling of wood burning and the sirens of an ambulance in the far distance, and she silently prayed it was on its way to save her. She thought of the explosion and how it had been so strong the floor caved in. Everything had happened so fast. The party was so beautiful, she thought, and then they showed up. How in the hell did they know she would be there, how to find her, and how on earth did they know Clayton and Mr. Price? How did those bastards get to her? She could not believe how lucky she was to still be alive. She lay still, trying to listen for any human sound. There was nothing but flames nearby, so she assumed she was alone. She moved her arm slowly and could feel the shard of glass beneath it. It cut into her skin like a razor, and she felt a warm liquid flow down her arm. She knew it was her blood. She lay listening for a few more seconds before deciding to try and sit up again. Her body quivered violently. As she pressed her palms into the glass and rubble on the ground, she winced while pushing herself into an upright position. Her head started spinning, and a sharp pain shot up the right side of her body. She was disoriented and confused as she squinted her eyes and looked around.

Her head was throbbing, and her heart was pounding out of control. She reached down to feel her legs and realized she was covered with broken pieces of glass, debris, and the same warm liquid that ran down her arm. Oh God, she cried, realizing she was covered in blood. Was it hers? Someone else's? She could not gather her thoughts to remember. As she sat there, panic overcame her smoke-filled lungs quickly, and she knew she had to find an escape. "I got to get outta here," she kept repeating over and over in her head as she felt tears forming in her eyes. She tried standing but was in so much pain she couldn't. She had no idea if her legs were broken from the fall and the wood and glass that lay on top of her, but she knew she couldn't stand on her feet. She was in excruciating pain. She began feeling around the floor for something, anything she could use as a crutch to stand.

The streetlight did not provide enough light to help her see. Salty tears ran down her cheeks as she crawled around, and she felt her body growing weaker. She frantically searched the floor with her hands when she came across a large bulky object that felt like a body. It scared the hell out of her, and she fell back onto the floor and screamed. "Hello, please, somebody help me, please," she yelled at the top of her lungs into the darkness. Please, God, somebody help me she repeated as she began to scream louder. Oh my God, oh my God, who could this be? She thought, terrified and shaking feverishly. Regina felt sick to her stomach. She reached over again to feel the lifeless body of a man she knew had to be dead." How did this happen?" Regina cried out as she tried to sit up again but couldn't.

She slumped back down into the trash and debris and began to cry harder as she tried to make sense of everything that happened. Why did this happen to her!!! How did she get caught? She had tried so hard to play everything right, but the devil had caught up to her. She finally began to accept the fact that she just could not escape. Her body was getting weaker from losing so much blood; the smoke seemed to get thicker each time she inhaled, and she saw no way out. Her head was spinning, and as she drifted in and out of consciousness, her thoughts went to her daughter. How would she survive? She knew there was nothing she could do to help her now, so all she could do was wait for her fatal demise and silently pray her daughter would be safe…

1

REGINA AND CLAYTON

Shit! Regina said aloud as she looked at the run in her stockings. She reached for her worn-out coach bag and hoped she had remembered to put her clear nail polish inside. When she looked in, she saw Clayton's business card: "Tailored To You Full-Service salon, where we make your dreams a beautiful reality." Regina smiled to herself as she thought about Clayton. They had met a few months before, but he already had Regina hooked. How was she so lucky to have met such a great man like him? She would never know, she thought, as her mind drifted back to the first day they met.

Clayton Taylor owned and operated one of the largest beauty and full-service salons in Philly and had recently expanded his businesses to Washington, New York, and Atlanta. He was the top business mogul in beauty, servicing the biggest stars in the Entertainment industry. He came to Price and Associates to obtain an attorney at the law firm where Regina was employed and hired Ethan Price, her boss, to represent him in his mergers. When she first saw him walk through the double doors, she was instantly put off guard by his smile. Hello, beautiful Clayton said, flashing a gorgeous set of pearly white teeth. Regina's heart fluttered as she tried not to stutter when she asked, "How can I help you"? She tried to keep her composure as he looked at her. "I have an appointment with Mr. Price," Clayton said in a cool and relaxed tone.

"Sure, and may I ask your name, please?" Regina said, hoping he didn't see her heart starting to beat in her chest through her silk blouse. "I am Clayton Taylor; he is expecting me," he said, flashing that beautiful smile again. Regina watched as his full lips moved and wondered how they would feel on hers. She had never fantasized about a man like this before, but it was something about the way he was looking at her that sparked a flame that had not been lit in years. She hadn't felt the touch of a man in so long and was in desperate need of one." Oh, ok, have a seat while I page Mr. Price and let him know you are here," Regina said with her voice shaky as she stared into his gorgeous hazel eyes.

When she picked up the phone to call Mr. Price, she noticed Clayton looking around the office, admiring the pictures and degrees that decorated the ivory-colored walls, and she couldn't help but see how sexy and alluring he looked in his well-tailored Armani suit and freshly shined Balenciaga shoes. He had an air of class and confidence that turned Regina on immediately. She had never seen a man like him before. All she was used to was the rough, rouged men from the south or the thug wanna-be gangsters she had met at the clubs or hookah bars in Philly. But Clayton was different. He exulted style. He was 6'3 with broad shoulders, his hair was jet black, and his waves were on spin. His skin was smooth and dark like chocolate, and his beard was trimmed perfectly.

"He will be with you momentarily, Mr. Taylor. May I show you to the conference room?" Regina asked as she rose from her desk. "Yes, of course," Clayton responded as he watched her walk towards him. Seeing her up close, he realized how attractive she really was. Regina stood 5'7 with curvy hips and a plump ass that made you look twice, given the right outfit. She had a beautiful round face with deep-set brown eyes and luscious lips that she adorned with red lipstick. Her hair was a natural sandy brown that she wore in a curly style, and her breasts stood perky and full as he could tell she was not wearing a bra underneath her top. Her skin was the color of a new bronze penny, and she looked younger than her 38 years, but her clothes and demeanor were modest, simple, yet tasteful. As Clayton stared at her, he envisioned how beautiful she would look after a makeover at his salon. He made a mental note to give her an invitation when he was done with Mr. Price. Regina led Clayton to a large set of glass doors to an elegant study filled with antique books and plush leather sofas that surrounded a marble table with beverages and fresh fruit. "Please make yourself comfortable, Mr. Taylor. Mr. Price will be with you shortly."

"May I offer you some coffee, tea, or water?" Regina asked as she placed some writing utensils and a notepad on Mr. Price's desk next to the intercom. "No, thank you," he paused as he realized he had not asked her name. "Regina," she said shyly as she blushed, knowing he was finally paying her some atten-tion. "No, thank you, Regina, I'm fine," he said in a flirting tone. "Yes, Lawd, you are fine," Regina said in a low whisper as she made her way to the doors. "What did you say?" Clayton asked, quickly turning around in her direction. "Oh, nothing, Mr. Taylor. If you need anything else before Mr. Price joins, you just push the intercom located on the table," she said as she hurried out of the room.

When Regina got back to her desk, she drank a bottle of water. Suddenly, she was extremely hot and sweaty. She knew it was Clayton, and she was excited to feel so aroused by a man again. Regina had been single for four years since she came back to Philly from North Carolina, and the dating pool in this city was shallow. She had been on a few dates but always ended up with jerks. She was careful about who she dated because she was a single mom of a 15-year-old and refused to bring just anyone around her daughter Nyla. She was her pride and joy, and she would do anything to protect her. She began to calm her nerves and get back to work. She convinced herself how silly she was being, daydreaming about a man she had just met and would never give her the time of day. But as she tried to finish the papers, she was proofing to her boss she could not keep her mind off the handsome stranger she had just laid eyes on. She found herself fantasizing about him, imagining what it would be like to be held in his arms and made love too. She felt her mouth getting dry again and sweat starting to form on her brow, and she felt moist between her legs just as her desk phone rang and snapped her back to reality.

"Good afternoon. Price and Associates, how can I help you?" Regina answered the phone, slightly out of breath. "Hey girl, why does it sound like you just got done running a marathon or having some freaky ass sex!!!" Monica said, busting out laughing. Monica was Regina's cousin and the only family she had left in Philly, and she looked in on Nyla when Regina worked late. "You are so silly, girl. I am working as usual; my mind was just preoccupied, that's all," Regina said, looking at the clock on her desk and trying to change the conversation. "What's up with you calling me this early in the day? Shouldn't you be out stalking your man?" Regina said, annoyed she had called and interrupted her thoughts.

"No honey, I just got through whipping this good stuff on Kenny, and he is knocked out," she said, laughing at her own raunchy comment. Monica could be so tacky at times. "I called to see if you wanted to go out to Rose Lounge tonight. Kenny gave me 2 VIP wristbands to the club, and of course, I'm asking you first since you are my bestie," Monica said in her ghetto girl voice, "Mo, you just want me to go so that you can have a reason to spy on Kenny. You know I do not like going out to those clubs anymore because there is nothing but hood rats and weed heads there!" Regina said, getting frustrated with her cousin. "Whatever, Regina," she said, knowing she couldn't convince her to go out with her again. She tried to hang out with her cousin a few times, but every time they would go out, Monica ended up leaving her for some guy she just met. She had asked her many times after that to go out and have some fun for a change, promising she would not abandon her, but every time she turned her down. She was tired of the club scene; besides, she knew she would never find a good man there. "Call me later if you change your mind. You need to stop being so boring and corny and go out and have a little fun sometimes. You might even get lucky and get a stiff one!" Monica said, laughing, and hung up the phone.

Regina was agitated by Mo's call, but she knew she meant well. She was a sweet girl, beautiful and full of potential, but, to Regina, she had her priorities all wrong. She was 27, had her own apartment, a college degree from one of the top black colleges in the country and made a pretty decent living, but she was lazy as hell. She was a massage therapist at the local sports arena, and all she dated were men who were drug dealers' athletes and thugs. Monica felt that while she still had it to flaunt, she would use it to her advantage. She had a killer body and a phat ass that would make any man stand at attention, and she didn't have a problem wearing revealing, sometimes downright slutty outfits to show it. Her current beau, Kenny, was a 30-year-old waste of time. Mo had met him one night at a concert they attended in Fairmount Park. He had two baby mamas and always kept Monica in some type of drama. He was the owner of a jazz and Hookah club in the Center City, and that was his chick trap to pick up women. He slept with half his staff and about two-thirds of his patrons, but Monica thought she was his one and only main Jawn.

She knew he cheated sometimes but always felt like those other chicks meant nothing to him. She was very self-conscious, but she would never admit it, so every time she got the chance, she would go down to the club to make sure she was the one he left with at the end of the night. Regina tried convincing her she could do better, but she said he treated her real good and fucked her even better, so for now he was there to stay. Just as Regina was about to get back to work, the phone buzzed again, but this time it was Mr. Price. "Regina, can you please come in and take some notes for me?" He asked in his usual cheerful voice. "Yes sir, Mr. Price, right away," she said, thrilled she got to sit in on the meeting with her fantasy man.

She rushed down the hall and got a look at herself in the mirror. Not bad, she thought to herself as she adjusted her pencil skirt and fluffed her curls. But as she entered the study, she suddenly felt out of place. She instantly did not like the outfit she had chosen that day, but she did not know she was going to meet such an attractive guy. Regina wore a cream satin top with no bra that could have used good ironing and a straight skirt that did nothing for her figure. She did not have many clothes, but she knew she could have looked a bit more presentable. She suddenly felt embarrassed and hoped Mr. Price hadn't noticed. Her boss was a kind man who always gave her the utmost respect and praise for being a great paralegal, and he never crossed the line with Regina. He was married to a powerful and beautiful woman that he adored, and she knew he would never cheat on her, so Regina never felt the need to look extra special at work. Not that she would even consider an affair with Mr. Price. He was nice-looking, but he was not her type. She was always presentable but nothing incredibly special. Besides, his clients were usually old, rich white men, married or gay anyway, so she never worried about any of them finding her attractive. But today, she wished her appearance were a lot better. In her three years there, she had never seen a client come into the office that sent her heart racing, and the first thing she noticed was his finger did not have a ring on it, so she silently prayed he was single, but for the life of her, she could not understand why he would be. He may have been a player or a gigolo, she thought, but she really didn't care. All she knew was that he was making her feel ways she had not felt in an awfully long time. As she took a seat across from Mr. Price, she could feel Clayton staring at her. Chills started to cover her, and she kept adjusting herself in her chair and hoped she did not appear too nervous.

She sat and took notes of the meeting and found out that Clayton's businesses were worth millions and that he was hiring Mr. Price to oversee all his legal contracts pertaining to his company." Ms. Allen, can you please make sure we handle Mr. Taylor's matters delicately and with urgency? He said to Regina. "And Mr. Taylor, please feel free to contact Ms. Allen with any concerns or issues that may arise, and she will be sure to forward me all information needed," Mr. Price said, pleased with Clayton and the outcome of the meeting. "Will do, Mr. Price," Regina replied as she got up to leave. "Excuse me, Regina," Clayton said in a very seductive voice, "will you be available to take all my demands needed at my request?" "I don't think that would be a problem, Mr. Taylor, as long as I am made aware in a timely manner. We are here to assist you 24 hours a day," Regina said as she flashed a seductive smile at him and nodded to Mr. Price before leaving the room. She could feel her nipples starting to harden through her blouse, and she felt mortified. She had to get back to her desk immediately; she was starting to feel sweat running down her body. A few minutes later, Clayton was standing in front of her, smiling. "Ms. Allen, is it?" He said, knowing she was slightly uncomfortable in his presence. "It's Regina," she said, trying not to make direct eye contact with him as she shuffled papers around on her desk. "Well, Regina, I would like for you to make a reservation to come by my Salon and see exactly who I am and who you will be representing. Oh, and enjoy a complimentary spa day." Clayton said, finding himself intrigued by her. "Mr. Taylor, I couldn't accept such a gift," Regina said, surprised at his offer. "It's Clayton, and of course you can. Here is my card call; speak to my assistant. Geneva, and she will take care of the rest," Clayton said as he placed the beautiful linen business card into Regina's hand. She sat there elated, not knowing what to do, so she simply took the card and said thank you. Clayton then unexpectedly took her hand, kissed it gently and said, "It was truly a pleasure meeting you, Ms. Regina Allen, and I look forward to seeing you again soon," and then he left the office.

Regina watched him walk away, and she felt tears well up in her eyes. In her entire life, no man had ever made her feel like this. She had never felt more beautiful and alive than she did at that very moment, and she wished this feeling could last forever.

2

ETHAN AND EVELYN

As Ethan Price sat in his office, he smiled with satisfaction. He had just landed the biggest legal deal of his career, and he was finally able to make the last payment to the loan sharks he borrowed money from three years prior to starting his firm. He felt good, and the first thing he wanted to do was surprise his lovely wife with an expensive gift and take her out to dinner to celebrate. It had taken Ethan twenty of his forty-nine years to finally make it big in the city, and he felt on top of the world. Ethan picked up his iPhone to call Evelyn as he looked at their wedding photo on his desk. The phone rang two times before she answered, "Hello darling," Evelyn said in a soft, seductive voice. "Hi there, beautiful," Ethan said happily smiling. "How is your day so far, my love?" she said, slightly out of breath as she ran on the treadmill in their 5000 square feet home. Ethan reclined back in his leather chair and grinned as he listened to his wife's sexy voice. "Well, I have fantastic news, and I want to go out and celebrate tonight, so get dressed and be ready for dinner at eight and wear something hot because you know I love showing you off," Ethan said as he pictured her in sexy lingerie from Victoria's Secret. He made a mental note to have Regina run out and pick up something nice for his lovely bride.

"That sounds delightful, dear. What are we celebrating?" She said, sounding excited. "It's a surprise, but I will tell you this: we will never have to worry about money again after today," he said, feeling proud of his accomplishments. "Wow, ok baby, I am excited, and I will be ready at eight. Will you be sending a car, or would you like me to meet you?" Evelyn asked, starting to feel anxious about the planned evening.

"I'm going to send a driver. We are going to be doing a lot of celebrating and drinking tonight, so we will definitely need a car, baby," Ethan said, feeling good about spending time with his wife. It had been a long time for them to just go out and spend a romantic evening alone together. He was always working, trying to be successful, and he felt like he was neglecting her. She was a beautiful woman, and he knew he was the luckiest man on earth to be married to her. When he hung up from their call, he started to reminisce about the first time he saw her.

They had met eight years ago at a dinner party for one of his colleagues at the firm where he was a junior partner, and for Ethan, it was love at first sight. He watched her all evening as she glided across the room, and he knew he had to meet her. "Hey, Richard, who is that lovely lady over by the fountain?" Ethan asked his friend at the party. "Oh, that's Miss Evelyn St. James. She is a big supporter of equal rights for women, and she contributes generously to our firm for pro bono work for battered woman cases," Richard said, eyeing Evelyn with lust in his voice. "She is a bitch, but she's a beautiful one and loaded," he said sarcastically as he downed his scotch. "She doesn't look that intimidating," Ethan said, staying focused on her every move. "Go for it, man! She has already turned down every guy in here tonight; you just might get lucky," he said with a chuckle, knowing every man had struck out with her so far." I think I just might do that," he said, as he turned to the bartender and ordered two glasses of Prosecco. As Ethan walked over to her, Evelyn noticed him and turned away. He continued over, not feeling intimidated by her gesture, and asked her if she could hold his drinks while he tied his shoes. She looked down and saw he didn't have laces, and she laughed as if he had told her a very funny joke. "That is a highly creative way to meet someone," she said when she finished laughing. "I couldn't think of another way to approach you," he replied calmly as he looked into her beautiful blue eyes. "Well, you succeeded, Mr..." Evelyn waited for him to say his name. "It's Ethan, Ethan Price," he answered proudly. "I'm Evelyn," she responded back hesitantly.

Evelyn had very striking features. She was mixed with Cherokee Indian and African American and had the face of an angel. She was very fair-skinned with deep sea blue eyes and lovely long black hair that she wore in an updo for the evening to show off her gleaming diamond necklace. Everything about her screamed elegance. She had a slim, thick hourglass shape with a perfect size D cup. She stood 5'8 with beautiful, shapely long legs and a discreet thigh gap. She was indeed a vision to look at a class-A lady, to say the least, and Ethan was drawn in immediately. They began talking, and

Evelyn shared with him that she was from Queens, New York, and was raised by her wealthy grandparents after her mother and father were killed in a plane crash. She was an only child and, after their deaths, inherited their fortune. She was a very guarded woman and liked to be in charge. She hired escorts because she didn't want to get too involved with anyone seriously, and she was an advocate for women's rights. She had never been married and had no desire for children, and she loved fine art and music. She was 36 years old and was considered one of the wealthiest women in Philadelphia. She owned several companies and invested her money wisely. Everything about her fascinated Ethan, and the more they spoke, the more he wanted to know. They had taken their conversation out to the balcony, and before they knew it, they were being told the party was over. By the end of the night, they both knew they were meant to be together. He had escorted Evelyn home that night, and from then on, they were inseparable.

Ethan, at the time, was a 39-year-old lawyer and junior partner at a low-key law firm in Bucks County, concentrating on mergers and acquisitions, but kept his head down and worked diligently to one day own his own Corporate and Criminal case law firm. He had a good client base but could not save enough to start out on his own. He made good connections but never found anyone willing to invest or take a chance with him. He won several cases and was a beast in the courtroom, but that never was enough. Ethan was making a name for himself, focusing on business and corporate law, but criminal cases were always his passion.

He stood 6'1 at two hundred and sixteen pounds. He had hazel green eyes and oval-shaped lips. He wore his hair short with tapered sides. He was quite an attractive man and had a way with the ladies. He could charm just about anyone and always worked hard for the prize. When they started dating, he and Evelyn would talk for hours, and he told her how much he wanted to one day own his own law firm. After discussing his dreams with her, Evelyn wanted to open a firm for him. She had the means and could easily afford it because she believed in him and knew how talented he was, but he refused to accept any handouts from her because he wanted to prove he was his own man and could make it big on his own. He worked hard and showed Evelyn he was worthy of her hand in marriage, and six months later, they wed, and she made Ethan the happiest man alive. He continued to strive at work, saving for his own firm, and one day, while working for Davis and Shultz, he met two clients that would make Ethan an offer he could not refuse, changing his life forever.

As Evelyn hung up the phone, she started to think about what she would wear tonight for her special evening with her husband. She was excited and could not wait to find out his exciting news. She knew he was working on some big cases and just assumed he had won a big settlement for a client and wanted to celebrate. Ethan had been so preoccupied lately, but he always spoiled her every chance he could. Buying her expensive jewelry and furs and sending her on fabulous trips whenever she wanted to travel. He was not as financially stable as she was, but he was well respected and was building a small fortune with his firm. She was incredibly supportive of him, and she loved him deeply.

He was a naive, sweet man who didn't really pry into her past. He was so in love with her that he never really cared how she became so wealthy and who or where the rest of her family was. To him, none of that mattered as long as she was with him. Evelyn had many secrets, none of which her husband knew, and she planned to keep it that way. She had buried that part of her life long ago, and being with Ethan made her feel safe. She had long since forgotten about her past, but in the back of her mind, she knew she would destroy anyone who tried to dig up old skeletons, even the ones she loved.

3

REGINA

When Regina got home, she was exhausted. She had worked three extra hours for Mr. Price and had to make a shopping run to buy a gift for his wife. She enjoyed making trips for him because she got the chance to go into high-end stores and purchase expensive things as if they were for her. She had never met Mrs. Price, but from the pictures her husband had all around his office, she got a sense of what her style was. Besides, she never knew Regina was her husband's personal shopper, and Mr. Price never complained about what she bought. They both were around the same size, and he liked Regina's taste. She was not too upset anyway about the additional hours she had worked that day because Mr. Price had given her a sizable bonus for landing the new client, Clayton Taylor. She felt good she had some extra money in her pocket and she was finally home to rest in peace. Or so she thought. Just as she took off her shoes and put her feet up on the coffee table to fantasize about Clayton, Nyla walked in, talking nonstop about her day. "Hey, moms, how are you? I missed you today," Nyla exclaimed as she planted a big, wet kiss on Regina's cheek. "I'm good, sweetie, just really tired. I had a long day." Regina replied as she looked at her beautiful daughter.

As much as she wanted her thoughts to be about Clayton, she directed her attention to Nyla. She went on about her day and told her she had gotten a solo part in the school musical. Nyla had a beautiful voice, and she hoped she would be famous one day, like the talented woman she had posted on her bedroom wall. "So, missy, I know you are excited about the show and all, but have you finished your homework and cleaned your room?" Regina asked her as she started to go through the mail on the living room table. "Of course I did, Mother," Nyla said, aggravated that her mom asked the same questions every night she came home from work. "Watch your tone, young lady," Regina replied as she watched Nyla roll her eyes and huff away out of the living room into the kitchen.

"Teenagers," Regina said out loud but to herself. Nyla was a good kid, always respectful and obedient, but lately, Regina had been sensing she was changing. The groans and eye-rolling were becoming more consistent, and Regina assumed it was puberty, or so she hoped. All she could think about was that when she started the sassing off at the mouth, it was because of a boy. She could hear her own mother's voice in her head saying, "Don't you start getting too grown just because you're smelling yourself." Regina chuckled because, as a teenage girl, she never understood what that meant, but when she became a mom, a lot of her own mother's advice started to make so much sense. She had hoped Nyla had not started liking boys yet because she wasn't sure if she could handle that right now. "Hey, mamma, you hungry?" Nyla asked as she looked in the fridge for a snack. "No, baby, get you something. I already ate," Regina said, smiling at her daughter.

She had just started to feel comfortable being back in Philly, and it was feeling like home again. She had been through a lot, moving from state to state trying to survive on the little money she had saved. She was only a child herself when she had Nyla and had endured so much abuse from her baby daddy she just wanted to settle down and try to live a normal life. She still had nightmares of the time she spent with him and knew that if she did not get away from him, her life would be over, and so would her child's. It was hard to do because every time she thought she had escaped him, he would always find her, but so far, not this time; she finally felt like she would be ok. When she arrived in Philly, she had just twenty dollars left in her name, and Monica had taken Nyla and her in. She had nowhere else to go, so she helped her get on her feet.

Monica had a nice 2-bedroom apartment in Queens Village, a lively, upbeat section of the city, and she welcomed them with open arms. It wasn't a lot of space, but they made it work. Monica knew about some of Regina's struggles, but she had no idea all she had gone through. She was simply happy to help her favorite cousin. Regina was so thankful and made a point to look after Mo as much as she could when she landed a job. She was the older cousin, but she felt like she was her big sister. Mo had also helped her land the job at Price and Associates through one of her past conquests she was fucking at the time. She had been involved with a guy who had two open murder cases and had just caught a drug charge a few months prior. He was being represented by Mr. Price, and when she went with Mo to pay another installment of his retainer fee, she met her future boss. He was just starting out on his own and mentioned he was looking for a paralegal to help with his caseload.

Regina jumped at the opportunity to let him know her qualifications since she did have an online degree in law. She studied hard for six years, working odd jobs and living in cheesy motels while she was in hiding. That part she left out, not wanting to scare him off. Mr. Price was impressed by Regina's demeanor and qualifications and offered her the job a few days later. When they left Mr. Price's office, Regina could not wait to tell her cousin how she felt. She was excited about landing a fantastic job but irked by the circumstances in which she got it. "Monica, why do you insist on messing with these thug ass niggas?" Regina asked her on the train ride to the Center City that afternoon. "Because they take care of me financially and sexually, and I get to look good and have loads of money in my pocket," Mo said in a cocky tone. "But you are so smart and have a good head on your shoulders. You deserve so much better," Regina said, feeling sorry for her. "You are ruining your life, and take my word, dealing with these street dudes is going to land you in a world of trouble," Regina said, concerned about her cousin.

Monica rolled her eyes at her and began checking her Instagram account on her iPhone, ignoring what she was saying. "You should be grateful to my thug ass man. Because of him, you got a job," she said, never looking up from her phone. She knew about some of Regina's troubles and felt bad for her, but she knew that it was her demons to face, not hers. She didn't have a clue about the horror she had gone through, but she was not gonna let Regina make her feel guilty about her choices. A lot of the dudes she kicked it with were bums, but they gave her what she needed, and that was just fine by her. Regina sat back and huffed as she realized Mo was ignoring what she was saying, and her mind drifted to the terrible moments she endured some time ago. Things had gone so wrong in North Carolina, Regina thought to herself. She had seen too much and knew too much, and the thing that frightened her most was if her past ever found her, the first thing it would do was shut her up permanently.

Regina was just 15 when she met the man who would be her daughter's father. He was an identical twin, but he and his brother had hugely different personalities. The Spears brothers were definitely men to be admired but very much feared. Jacob was the playful and friendlier one, while James was quiet and mysterious. She met them one Labor Day weekend while visiting her grandparents and cousin in Fayetteville, NC. She lived in Philly with her mother, who worked all the time, so she was alone most days. When she was given the opportunity to go the four hundred and fifty miles to visit on holidays, she jumped at the chance. There wasn't much to do there in the south, but that didn't bother Regina. Her grandma and grandpa had a big house with a farm out back, and if she only got to feed the chickens, that was all right with her. Her auntie stayed at the house as well with her daughter Val, who was close to Regina's age and when she visited, there was always some trouble for them to get into. It was the holiday weekend, and Regina was excited.

It was a beautiful night, and she was so happy no one fused or complained about her being out with her favorite cousin. Val was seventeen, and what the older people called a fast-tail child because she drank beer and smoked cigarettes, and she had already had sex three times and to Regina, that was a world record. Her reputation was scarred, but Val could care less what those old bitches had to say about her in this hick of a town. Her mom was a junkie that got caught up in the drug epidemic that started to plague the country in the early 80s, and she never cared where Val was as long as she brought her home a few dollars every now and then to support her habit. They moved in with her parents so that Val could at least have some type of stability and supervision. She never knew who Val's dad was, and it was rumored that Auntie slept with a guy for some drugs one night and got pregnant with Val, but when he found out she was knocked up, he left town quickly. Val was a big-boned, pretty girl with short, curly hair and a chubby, round face, and at seventeen, she could easily have passed for an older woman in her twenties. She had a sharp tongue and a feisty attitude to match. She loved hanging out in the streets and flirting., She would go into town and charge the teenage boys in the neighborhood fifty cents to look up her dress and rub on her breasts for five minutes, and that's the way she made a few dollars to drink and smoke. For Regina, being younger and naive, she fascinated her! She thought Val was the coolest person on earth! She exposed her to things she had never seen or even heard of in her fifteen years.

On that warm Monday night in September, the two girls went into town to cause some mischief. They were hanging out in front of the local nightclub so that they could see who was sneaking with whose husband or wife, and they could shake them down for some money to go to the Waffle House to eat. As they stood there talking, the biggest, longest black Cadillac Regina had ever seen in her life pulled up to the curb with the words Black Bullet written across the top window shield. It looked like something straight out of a movie, and it shone like it had been waxed minutes ago. Val and Regina stood there staring, waiting to see if a movie star would emerge. They watched the door fly open, and out stepped a woman dressed head to toe in a see-through catsuit and rhinestone-studded high heels. She wore a blond wig that was slanted on her head, and her face was covered with cheap makeup that looked as if she had applied it in the dark. "I know one thing, bitch: if my money ain't right tonight, I'm gonna put your ass in the hospital tomorrow. I promise you that!" A man yelled from the driver's side of the black hog. You could not see his face through the dark tinted windows, but his voice was harsh and mean and sent a chill up Regina's spine when he spoke. "Ok, daddy, but I told you shit is slow out here tonight," the whore said in a slow childlike voice.

"I don't give a fuck. You had better make it fast," the man shouted back before speeding off from the curb, leaving the door to slam shut from the speed. The woman looked pissed as she removed a cigarette from her handbag. "Hey, big Val, give me a light," she called out to my cousin, who was laughing at the scene that had just taken place. It was obvious Val knew her, and Regina was dying to know how. She had never seen a hoe in real life, just on TV or from what she heard the kids talk about in school, so this excited her the most. "I ain't got no light, Candy, but I'll get you one if you give me a port," Val said, eager to get a smoke. "OK, but hurry up. If Twin swings back around and sees me still standing here, he is gonna kick my ass for sure," she said, looking up and down the street to make sure he was gone.

While Val ran into the alley behind the bar to look for a book of matches, Regina just stood there, not able to speak or move. She was still trying to process the fact that this woman was a whore, selling her body for money. Not the childish stuff Val did for 50 cents, but actually letting men screw her for cash. Val was back in less than a minute. "Here you go, Candy," she said as she handed her a lighter she had found in the ally. "Thanks, small stuff," the woman said, lighting her cigarette and handing Val hers for the trade. "What you doing out here tonight, and who's the skinny bumpkin you got with you?" Candy said in a gritty tone as she gestured over at Regina. "Oh, that's my cousin, she cool," Val replied, "We just trying to come up with a few dollars to go over to the Waffle House and get something to eat."

"Well, listen here, that's where twin is now, waiting on me to make some money," Candy said, annoyed that she had to turn a trick tonight because she came up short with her pimp's money that morning. She was supposed to have the night off and go out to celebrate Labor Day, but she needed to get her drug fix the night before, so she smoked away the money and twin was pissed. He told her she had to make double tonight, but she was just not in the mood.

"Hey, how's about I give you and cornball over there five dollars apiece to go sit in the Waffle House and eat, but when you see Twin get up to leave, you page me, and I can come back on the corner like I'm still trying to get a trick," Candy asked hoping she could convince the girls to be her lookout so she could go in the Club and relax for a while. "What do you say?" Candy asked again, hoping they would take the bait. "Hell, yeah, Candy. We don't have a problem helping you out," Val said, happy that she and Regina didn't have to keep standing outside the club like they were trying to pick up a date. Candy reached into her DD bosom and pulled out a 10-dollar bill, along with a card with her pager number on it and handed it to Val. "Now, listen, you call me as soon as you see him about to leave. Don't let me down, small stuff; I'm depending on you," Candy said over her shoulder as she sashayed in the club.

As the whole scene transpired, Regina was stuck in one spot. She couldn't believe what she had just witnessed. "Val, is you insane? Why would you take her money and tell her we would be her lookout out?" She shouted as Val walked back in her direction, waving the ten-dollar bill. "Girl, please, I always help out Candy and some of the other hoes from time to time. They pay me for my services, and I don't have to lay on my back for it," she said as she laughed aloud. "Come on, Chile, and let's go get some waffles. You look like you starving," Val said as she yanked Regina by the arm and led her toward the Waffle House two blocks away.

When they walked through the doors of the brightly lit restaurant, Regina thought she had double vision. Sitting in a booth near the back of the diner were two men who shared the same face. Both were clad in big gold chains and diamond rings on each finger. Each one had a distinct style of fashion. You could see their clothes were expensive, and you could tell they both were getting money. One was dressed like he had a Clyde's Dale tied up outside. He wore a huge cowboy hat and a pair of ponyhair boots. The other was a bit more subtle. He wore a baseball cap, a pair of denim jeans and a cashmere sweater. But both had on a ton of jewelry. Val and Regina walked in and took a seat a few tables over so they could hear their conversation clearly. "Man, I'm so mad right now," the twin in the big cowboy hat said to the other. "That hoe, Candy, must think I'm stupid. That bitch smoked up the money she made getting high last night and tried to convince me she got robbed! I tried to break that bitch's neck this morning when she told me that shit," he said angrily to his brother. "I told you to stop messing with those smoking ass hoes. They ain't nothing but trouble, and they ain't gonna do nothing but get you busted. You wait and see," the other twin replied. "I know that Jacob, but the bitch makes good money when she wants to, and she's loyal," twin said, sitting back in the booth. His name was James Spears, better known on the streets as killer, and his brother was Jacob. They both were notorious drug dealers and pimps, but you could see James was the meaner of the two evils. Regina later found out he was the one driving the big, black hog. They ran the south, and everybody knew it. They were both nice-looking men in their early 30s, and you could tell underneath their frowns they were actually quite handsome.

They had light brown eyes and stark, strong cheekbones. They were well built and had skin that was the color of strong black coffee with a hit of cream. "Hey honey, can I get another cup of tea?" James called out to the waitress, "And make sure it's in a to-go container," he replied. "Sure thing, baby," the waitress answered, grinning at them with crooked teeth. She made sure she catered to their every need because they were regulars and always left big tips. As Jacob looked around the restaurant, he noticed Regina staring at them. He smiled at her, and she quickly began to blush. She wasn't much to look at back then, but she had a wholesome aura about her. She was skinny, had thick, medium-length hair, and needed a straightening comb. She had pretty straight white teeth and an oval-shaped face with deep-set dimples. She didn't wear makeup much, but when she came to visit Val, she would straighten her hair and make up my face with stuff she stole from her Auntie's dresser.

The best thing Regina had going for her was her long, athletic legs because she ran track in school every day. She had big breasts she inherited from her mom's side of the family, but other than that, she considered herself a plain Jane. "Why is you looking so nervous?" Val asked as she tried to occupy herself with the menu. "I'm not nervous," she replied, trying to play it cool. "Excuse me, honey," Val called out to the waitress who was leaning over the twin's table so they could look down at her top and see her big stretch-marked breasts. "Can we order today, please?" Val said, annoyed that they had been waiting to be served for over 10 minutes. "Just a second, sweetie," the waitress replied back in a southern drawl. "Is there anything else I can get you, boys?" She asked the twins as they looked at her, amused by her flirting. "Yeah," James said, "Your phone number so I can call you later," knowing in his mind he was spinning this bitch already. He had a way about him; he knew he could make a woman fall for him in an instant when he wanted them to. "You ever been to California, darling?" He asked, knowing she was falling for the bait. "No," she said shyly, thinking he was really feeling her. "Well, you should let me take you there one day and make you a star," he said, making a mental note that he could use a bitch like her in his stable. She wasn't much to look at in the face, but she had a body he knew could make money. He already had five girls working for him on the streets, but he was always out recruiting. They made him plenty of money, and adding another one was worth the extra cash flow. The waitress hurried and wrote down her number and slid it across the table to him.

She knew he was a pimp, but she didn't care. She saw the way he took care of his girls when they came into the diner and figured anything was better than working in this greasy spoon for pennies an hour. While she stood there grinning and talking, Val got pissed. "Yo, chick, are you gonna take our orders or what!?" She said, now yelling at the top of her voice. She knew what the twins were over there doing, and she never interrupted their business, but she didn't care. She was hungry and wanted to order. "Don't get your panties in a bunch," the waitress said as she walked over to their table. "How can I help you, little girls, tonight?" the waitress said spitefully. "Well, it's about damn time," Val said as she looked over the menu.

"I'd like the all-star breakfast platter with a pecan waffle and a sweet tea with extra ice," Val said. "And you?" The lady looked at Regina like she was the one giving her the attitude. "Oh, I'll have the same," Regina said in a hushed voice. "OK," she said as she took the menus off the table and walked away. "Hey Val, what you doing out this time of night?" Jacob yelled over at their table. He had been watching them the whole time. "Minding my business, Mr. Jacob, and staying out of trouble," Val said playfully. "Yeah, right; you better take your behind home and get off these streets," he said, knowing how likely she was to get into trouble. He had known Val and her mom for years and, at one time, even dated her mom until he found out she was a crackhead. She would steal his product and money from him whenever he'd come to their house to visit. He allowed it to continue for a while because he really liked her, but after he found out she was tricking in the streets, he cut her off.

Val liked him being with her mom even though she knew what he did for a living, but he always made sure they had food in the house, and he took care of them and treated Val like a daughter when he was around. Even after he had stopped dating her mom, whenever he would see her in the streets, he'd still give her a few dollars to have in her pocket. "I will, Mr. Jacob, I promise. I'm just out having a little fun with my cousin for the holiday," Val said, sounding like a little girl. "Your cousin?" He said, sounding surprised, "Who's your cousin?" He asked, now eyeing Regina up and down. "She looks like a little boy," he and his brother chuckled. Regina felt so embarrassed. "Come on, Mr. Jacob, don't go messing with us tonight. Were just getting something to eat and going home afterward." "OK, don't get into any trouble," he responded before turning his conversation back to his brother. Regina sat there mortified. She couldn't believe this man just said she looked like a boy. She felt liking crawling under the table she was so embarrassed. She was so happy when they saw the waitress coming over to their table with their plates.

When the food arrived at their table, Val and Regina scoffed it down as if they hadn't eaten in days. They had been laughing and talking so much that they forgot they were supposed to be paying attention when the twins left so they could warn Candy. They hadn't even noticed them leaving the back exit of the restaurant, and Regina was relieved they were gone so they couldn't ridicule her any further, but then she felt bad for the lady prostitute. "Oh, my goodness Val, you didn't page that hooker to tell her that the twins left already." Val said she didn't care, that it was on Candy for messing with the twins' money, and whatever she got in return, she earned it. "Come on, girl, let's get out of here and head on back to the house before grandma sends the police out looking for us," Val said, noticing the clock on the wall marked 2:30 am. As they left the Waffle House, just up the street, they saw the twin James pulling Candy from the club and throwing her in the back seat of his hog, and all Regina could do was think if he really was gonna put her in the hospital as he had promised.

4
CLAYTON

When Clayton walked out onto Market Street, he felt higher than the tallest building in the city. He had just completed a multi-million-dollar agreement with Ethan Price, one of the best attorneys in town, and he could finally relax about his business. He put on his ray bans and walked across the street to where he parked his Cheyenne truck. He was excited to get back to the salon and share the good news with Geneva. She had been Clayton's friend and assistant for eight years now since he started out cutting and curling hair in his basement. She was a dedicated friend and a loyal companion. Geneva was a very pretty lady short and petite in stature but super thick in all the right places.

They had met one day when she came to his home in Germantown and asked him for a Tara weave. "I'm sorry, pretty lady, but I don't do ghetto girl hairstyles," he informed her. She looked offended and said, "Oh, so you are not a true gay diva hairdresser then!" "Gay? Wait a minute, baby, there is nothing gay about me," Clayton replied, feeling equally offended by her comment. "I would dick you down so good you would be cross-eyed," he told her as he grabbed his man piece, and they both fell out laughing and have been best friends ever since. They really were not each other's type, so it made it easier for them to become close, and their relationship flourished. Deva (which was his nickname for her) was like a sister to him, and she protected Taylor Enterprises as if it were her own. They both had put a lot of sweat and tears into making it the hottest place in the city, and now that they were expanding, they felt like their love child was finally growing.

Money had never been an obstacle for him as it was for Geneva, since he had a fortune hidden she knew nothing about. He did not want to open a business right away because He didn't want to cause attention to himself with the IRS or the police. That was one of the reasons why he started doing hair in his home in the beginning. As far as Deva was concerned, they had worked hard together and, over time, acquired loans, built a clientele, and put in long hours so they were able to create the salon and spa of their dreams. She had no idea of Clayton's past, and she was better off for it. He had done a lot of things he was not proud of, but he was a changed man now and was ready to be a big-time business mogul. As he sped down JFK Boulevard, he thought about the woman who made him a success: his mother. She was the reason he was so talented at making a woman look and feel beautiful. Clayton grew up poor in the back woods of the south, living in a small shack of a house with his mom and autistic uncle. He had no father, and he was told that his dad was killed in the bed of another woman when he was just six, and he really had no memories of him. His mother always worked odd jobs around town to provide for her son and brother and he recalled many nights they would go to bed hungry. It wasn't until Clayton was twelve that his mom finally landed a job that brought money into the house, and they were finally able to move into a more suitable space. She started working at the local brothel.

His mother wasn't a call girl. She was just the lady that made them beautiful. She had a cosmetology degree, and she would take him along some days to work with her, and he would watch her transform some of the ugliest women into beauty queens. Clayton's mother did their hair, nails, and makeup each day before they went out to turn tricks. The women were always nice to him, giving him quarters to run to the store to get condoms and mints to put in their purses for the night. They would let him cop a feel sometimes when his mother wasn't looking, and by the time he was fifteen, he would let them practice their blow job tricks on him. They taught him how to please a woman in every way, and he became a skilled lover at an early age because of it. He practiced what he learned on a few girls in school and had a little black book full of phone numbers of girls always wanting more. Growing up in such a place was not ideal for a young boy, but it kept food on the table and clothes on their backs. He loved watching his mother work. He used to observe how skillful she was, and he would offer to help her shampoo from time to time so that she could get more people done in the few hours that she worked and make more money.

She had a way of making women feel beautiful and special even if they were hoes, and he knew when he grew up, he wanted to do the same thing. His boys would always tease him and called him names like little baby trick and sissy boy because he knew how to apply makeup and do women's nails but what they didn't know was he was having a lot of sex with the prostitutes, and he could never reveal that secret cause if his mom's found out she'd never let me come back to work with her again. And knowing her temper she would have beat every bitch up in the spot for turning out her baby boy. And Clayton wasn't doing anything to jeopardize his mom's steady job. Clayton did a lot of fighting growing up, but he always thought of what his mama told him: "You listen here, Clay. No matter what people say, you fight for what you believe in and never let anyone stop you from following your dreams." As he thought about it today, he was always thankful his mother taught him her skills and talents cause look at him now. He was one of the top Hair designers in the country in tip-top shape and quite the heartbreaker.

When he pulled up to the salon, he sat in his truck to stare at the beautiful building that adorned his name. It was made of glass and slate grey iron, and lights glowed over the name like the monarch of a Broadway play. It was packed with beautiful ladies and a few men who considered themselves metrosexual and loved to pamper themselves with makeovers as well. As he pulled his blackberry from his suit jacket, he noticed he had five missed calls from Geneva and one from a private number. He got out of the truck and grabbed his briefcase from the back seat. When he walked inside, he smiled at the receptionist and headed toward the back of his office. As he passed the steam room and shampoo stations, he noticed every seat was filled. The salon was really buzzing today.

Entering his office, a big grin came across his face. There was a big bouquet of flowers on his desk, along with a bottle of Don Julio 1942 and a card that read, "Congratulations on your successful merger." He knew it was from Geneva because she knew how much he loved tequila. He placed his briefcase in one of the leather chairs and took a seat at his marble desk. He picked up the phone to call her just as she entered his office. "So, how did everything go?" She asked as she walked over to the bar to get two shot glasses. "Fantastic! The deal went through smoothly, just as I planned, and Mr. Price is going to handle the mergers exactly the way I want," Clayton said excitedly. "That is great, Clay," Geneva squealed as she wrapped her arms around his neck and gave him a big hug! "I knew you could do it, baby. You are the man pots and pans," she said in her B-girl voice.

"I knew we could do it," he corrected her as he poured two shots of the expensive liquor into the glasses she handed to him. He always knew none of his success would have been possible if it was not for her. "So, what's next?" she asked as she plopped down into one of the beveled chairs he had surrounding his desk. "Well, we have to start planning for the big gala next month, start thinking of the new décor for the locations and interviewing for the staff," Clayton said as he relaxed in his butter leather recliner. "Business looks really good out there today," he said as he took a sip of his drink. "Yes, we have been double booked for the last 3 weeks. We even had to turn walk-ins away today because every stylist's schedule was full," she said happily. Clayton grinned hard as he looked at her. He loved seeing her so excited and happy.

"So, how are things going with that new man of yours?" Clayton asked as he and Geneva sat back, sipping their cocktails and chatting like they were sitting on his deck on a warm summer day. He knew that she had started dating someone new and was wondering if the glow he was seeing was because of it. "All is good so far," she said, crossing her fingers and closing her eyes like she was making a wish. Clayton chuckled at her candor. "Look, as long as you are getting some, that's all that matters," he said sincerely, hoping his friend had found a good man in her life for once. Ever since he met Geneva, the only disagreements they ever had were about the men she dated. She had terrible taste in men as far as he was concerned.

The few Clayton had met in the past were assholes and were only dating her because they knew she had some money. They used her and lied to get what they wanted, whether it was sex or materialistic things, and then they would bounce once they were done, leaving her hurt and broken. She was too trusting when it came to men, and he really wished she weren't so much. "Ray and I are going away to Atlantic City this weekend for the old-school party at the Borgata, so it should be very romantic," she said as she winked at him. "Well, make sure you keep me updated and call me if that nigga gets out of line," Clayton said in a brotherly, protective tone. He loved Deva and worried about her like his little sister, and he would bring anyone down who tried to hurt her.

"Wait a minute now. Since we're prying into one another's private lives, what about you, mister?" She asked curiously, "Whose panties have you been sniffing lately?" she asked with a smirk. "Well," Clayton said, "I did meet a really lovely young lady today at the attorney's office. Her name's Regina and she is Price's paralegal. She really sparked my interest. I gave her my card and invited her to come by for a makeover, so hopefully she takes me up on my offer," he said, thinking back to this morning when he met her. "Hmmm, sounds like you digging her," Geneva said, watching him closely. "You know what I think? I am digging her, too," he said honestly. "I just hope the feeling's mutual," he said as they toasted their glasses.

5
EVELYN

Evelyn stepped off the treadmill in her home gym soaked in sweat. She was satisfied with the 40-minute workout she had just finished. Her body felt toned and lean, and she could not wait to soak in a nice, hot bubble bath. As she entered her bedroom, she started looking over the gowns she had in her massive walk-in closet. She really wanted to look sexy for Ethan tonight, she thought to herself. She had every intention on finishing the night with some passionate lovemaking. He deserved it she thought since they hadn't made love in months. It wasn't because they weren't attracted to one another anymore. It was just that Ethan was working so hard these days that by the time he got home, he was exhausted and not in the mood. That really didn't bother Evelyn much because she had an entourage of men at her disposal whenever she needed to get off, and her husband was none the wiser.

It would have broken his heart if he knew someone else was fucking his beloved. He just assumed she pleasured herself with various kinky toys he purchased for her entertainment. Ethan was a good lover and whenever she was with him, he showered her with passion and romance, but secretly Evelyn was a freak and every now and again she needed that rough dirty thug fucking that only her boy toys could provide. That way, she kept herself balanced giving Ethan what he needed and getting exactly what she wanted.

After going through her closet, she went and relaxed in her bath. About an hour later she stepped out of the soaker tub still covered in bubbles and stared at her image in the full-length mirror in her master suite. She loved the way she looked. Her breasts were firm and still perky for a woman in her early forties without any implants, and her stomach was as flat as a washboard. Her skin was flawless and smooth, and you could barely see the knife wound right above her left thigh anymore. She could have long since gotten it removed with plastic surgery, but she decided to keep it there as a reminder of her past. A reminder that she survived a cruel and brutal childhood.

Evelyn St. James was not always rich, glamorous or beautiful. But you would have never known it just by looking at her. It took a lot of lying, stealing and conniving to make her the woman she was today.

She was born Alisha Louise James, one of five bastard children to Monique Shantel James, better known on the streets as Candy. Her mother was a hoe and gave birth to Alisha in the back of a taxi after turning a date a few minutes before. The guy had been fucking her so hard her water broke, and when he saw the blood pouring out from between her legs, he thought he had killed her baby and took off running, leaving her in an alley contracting and in severe pain. "Come on, man, don't leave me here like this," she cried out to him, but he was already three blocks away by then. Her mother tried to pull herself together, but as she made her way through the trash-filled street, she doubled over in excruciating pain. She felt the baby coming fast, and she knew she had to get to the hospital quickly before she had her child on the cold hard cement. She didn't see a phone booth to call Smitty, her pimp at the time, and as she rounded the corner, she didn't see any one of the other working girls out on the street. She began to cry more because the pain was coming fast and hard, and she could feel the baby's head crowning between her legs. Just as she felt like she was going to faint, she saw a taxi coming down the road. "Taxi!!!!" She yelled and waved her arms frantically.

The cab came to a screeching halt, and Candy climbed into the back seat. "Please, sir, take me to the nearest hospital," she begged as the cabbie looked at her skeptical. He was a fat, white man with dirty fingernails and yellow teeth, and he smelled of whiskey. His raspy voice sounded like he smoked five packs of cigarettes a day. "Listen, lady, do you have any money? And if you just got beat up by some pimp, I'm not getting involved, so you can just get out of my cab right now," he said, not even noticing she was pregnant. "Listen, you asshole," my mother shouted, "I'm having a baby right now. I'm having contractions, and I feel the baby pushing out as we speak, so get me to a damn hospital now!" And then she blacked out.

When she finally came too, she was in a hospital bed and was told she had given birth to a baby girl in the back of the taxicab and the driver was still in the lobby waiting to get paid his fare. Candy was furious as she reached into her purse, flung a hundred-dollar bill at the nurse and then ordered her out of her room. She picked up the phone next to the bed and dialed Smitty's number. It was only three o'clock in the afternoon, so she knew he was at home getting pampered for tonight's playa's ball. It was a big deal in the south and to him because he got a chance to show off his girls, jewelry and cars and try to regain his name as playa of the year. He was still fuming he had lost last year, and he was determined to regain his title. "Hello," she heard Tex say when she answered the phone. "Hey girl, this is Candy. Can I please speak to Smitty?" she said in a rushed voice. "Daddy, it's Candy," she heard Tex say as she could hear her pass him the phone. "What the fuck does she want?" He said in an angry voice. "How the hell should I know? Take the phone and find out," she said, annoyed. Smitty took the phone and shot Tex a look to let her know he wasn't in the mood either. He placed the receiver to his ear.

"Bitch, where the hell you at and where is my money? He snarled into the phone. "Smitty, I had the baby last night. I'm at the hospital, can you come to see me?" She asked, sounding childlike. "Come see you? Why the hell would I do that? That bastard child ain't mine," he said angrily. Candy felt tears run down her face as she tried not to let him hear her crying. "OK, daddy, it's cool. The doctor said I have to be here for a few days, so can you send one of the girls over with some of my personal belongings, please?" She asked him, knowing he really didn't give a damn about her or her new baby girl." I'm sending Rachel over, all right, but not to bring you anything. She's coming to pick up my money you made last night," he said matter-of-factly and hung up the phone. Candy lay there crying silently and wishing she had never hooked up with the likes of Smitty.

Some time had passed when the nurse came in holding Candy's new baby. "Ms.St. James, would you like to see your baby now?" She asked as she placed her in Candy's arms. When Candy looked down into her baby's eyes, she noticed how beautiful she was. She was so light she almost looked white. Candy was not sure who the father was, just like her other kids, and she felt sorry for this beautiful angel she held in her arms. She had made up her mind when she found out she was pregnant this time to keep the baby and try to do right by her. She just didn't know how she was gonna do it. All her other children had been boys, and as soon as she had them, Smitty made her send them away to live with her mama. He told her that having them around would make her lose focus, and she wouldn't be able to concentrate on making him his money. But Candy was determined to keep this one with her, no matter what. She even stopped getting high to make sure her baby was healthy.

She still turned tricks every day because she needed to show Smitty that she could still be a pleasing hoe, even with a baby in her. "Hello there, precious," Candy said in her pretty little girl's ear." I'm your mama; it's very nice to finally meet the one that has been kicking me like crazy," she said softly. Her baby started to smile, and Candy's heart melted. "What are you going to name her, Ms. St.James? The nurse asked. "We must fill out the paperwork for her birth certificate." Candy thought for a minute and said, "Alisha Virginia St.James, after my great-grandmother." Grandma Virginia had meant so much to Candy. She loved her more than anything else on this earth, and she was going to shower her beautiful baby girl with the same love she had gotten from Granny Gin.

The phone rang, snapping Evelyn out of her thoughts. "Hello," she said hurriedly when she answered the phone. "Hello, Ms. Price, this is the car service. We are calling to confirm your pickup time for 7 pm." "Yes, 7 will be fine, thank you," Evelyn said as she looked at the clock on the wall. She only had an hour left. When she hung up, she made her way to her dressing room to get ready for tonight.

Ethan had left the office at around 4 and strolled down the jeweler's row feeling good. He had just closed a huge deal with one of the biggest business moguls in town, and life couldn't have been sweeter. He was finally on top, and nothing could stop him now. As he walked down the cobble-stoned streets, he looked through the windows of the expensive Jewelry stores. He was trying to figure out which one he would go into to buy Evelyn a nice piece of Jewelry. He wanted something special for her to show how much she had meant to him over the years.

He stopped in front of Steven Singer and went inside. "Hello, Mr. Price," the older gentleman said as Ethan entered the store. He was well known and liked in the diamond district and had spent quite a lot of money over the years. "Hello, Benjamin," Ethan said, happy to see his old friend. "How is your lovely wife and the kids?" Ethan asked as he shook the elderly man's hand. "Everyone is great! Diane sends her best regards to Evelyn for the lovely brunch they had two weeks ago in Delaware," he said to Ethan. "Oh, I will be sure to tell her," he replied with a smile. His wife was quite the socialite around town, and he knew she always entertained with the elite.

"So, how can I help you today, Mr. Price?" "Well, I am here looking for a stunning gift for Evelyn. I just closed an especially important deal today, and we are going to Ruth Chris tonight to celebrate." "Oh, how wonderful, sir. And what exactly did you have in mind?" Benjamin asked, delighted. "I was thinking of the lovely piece Evelyn was eyeing at our last visit. I just know it needs to be something spectacular," Ethan replied as he looked at the showcases full of diamonds. "Oh, well, Mr. Price, please come this way, and I will show you the new collection pieces that just arrived," the man said, leading Ethan to the back showroom.

When they entered, Ethan noticed the armed guard standing in the corner and knew this was where the store kept its most rare and expensive pieces. "May I offer you a glass of champagne?" Benjamin asked as Ethan took a seat in one of the lovely crafted wooden chairs. "Yes, that would be great," he replied as he relaxed and waited. Ethan couldn't believe he was finally on top. It still felt like a dream, but he knew it was all real now. He had worked his ass off to get here and was finally getting what he deserved.

He had come a long way from the streets of West Philly, where he was a lookout kid for the local drug dealers. They would pay him 50 dollars a night to stand on the corner and alert them when he saw the po-po coming. He jumped at the offer when Snake, the lieutenant who ran 52nd Street, stepped to him one day. "Hey, slim, come here," he yelled out to Ethan when he saw him playing ball in the schoolyard. "What's up, Snake?" Ethan said to him as he approached him at the bleachers. "How would you like to make some extra cash and come work for me?" he asked as he puffed on a black and mild. "Hell, yeah," Ethan exclaimed excitedly. He was finally gonna come up. He had watched Snake for years running West Philly and wished he could get in on the action. "Aight, kid, I need a lookout, and I'm willing to pay you good money, and if you do a decent job, I'll even raise your pay and make you one of my soldiers," he said, knowing he could use a guy like him on his team. Ethan had a reputation in the West for being a good fighter. He was a top contender in his division at the local boxing gym, and Snake knew he could whoop some ass if necessary. "Cool, man. Thanks," Ethan said as they gave one another a pound. "When can I start? He asked Snake, anxious to work. He was ready to make some money. He got a few dollars here and there from his aunt and uncle, who he lived with, but he wanted to know what it felt like to have money of his own in his pocket. He had tried getting summer jobs around the city, but nothing was ever available. "You can start tonight, young boul," Snake said to him.

That's what's up. I'll be there early," Ethan said and gave Snake a brother man hug. He was so excited he went straight home after meeting with Snake. He wanted to take a shower, grab a bite to eat and take a nap so that he could be alert for his first night on the job. When Ethan walked into the apartment, he heard his aunt in the kitchen singing her gospel music while she fried fish for dinner. "E, is that you?" She called out when she heard the door closed. "Yes, auntie, it's me," Ethan said as he entered the kitchen. "It sure is smelling good up in here," he said as he planted a kiss on her cheek. His Aunt smiled at her handsome nephew.

"What are you cooking for dinner, auntie? He asked as he started lifting the lids of the pots on the stove. "Get away from here," and she flagged him away from the food. "You will see when I'm finished." Ethan loved his auntie Mae and Uncle Frank.

They had been raising him since he was three years old after his parents died in a fire. His dad had been smoking a cigarette and fell asleep on the sofa, and the whole house was set ablaze within five minutes. A neighbor had managed to get inside and pull Ethan from his bedroom, but his mother and father weren't so lucky. The firefighters had found his mom in the hallway. Ethan had always known she died trying to make it to his bedroom to save him. His father was still on the couch. He had died from smoke inhalation in his sleep and never woke up during the fire.

Ethan was an only child, and when he lost both his parents, he thought he was going to be placed in foster care. But his father's brother and his wife volunteered to take him in. They didn't have children and were happy to raise Ethan as their own. His uncle Frank worked for Septa as a train conductor, and his aunt was a cashier at the local Walmart. Their income was far from that of the upper class, but they made a modest living and took care of Ethan the best they could. It broke his heart often to see them struggle, and he always knew that when he made it big, he would take care of their every need just as they did for him.

He would never tell them about his new job with Snake because it would break their hearts, but he was determined to make his own money and try to relieve some of the pressures they had trying to provide for him. He didn't ask them for much, but there were things he would have liked to buy for himself. And because he was always broke, he never really had a chance to keep a girlfriend. The girls he dated were not gold diggers, but they did want a man who could take them out for a Big Mac every now and again.

"OK, auntie. I'm going to take a shower; call me when it's ready," he said as he walked out of the kitchen. He knew that he could have dinner with them, watch a little TV with his uncle and then when they went to sleep for the night, he would sneak out and go to work for Snake. He had his whole plan together and hoped everything would go smoothly, that he would finally be making some money, and that life would be a lot sweeter.

Ethan looked up when he heard Benjamin enter the room with two champagne flutes filled with crystal. "Here you go, sir," he said as he handed Ethan his glass. "Now, are we ready to pick a piece of Jewelry that will set your wife's heart on fire?" "Absolutely," he answered and then took a sip of the fine golden liquid.

Clayton lay back on his plush cream color sectional in his massive living room right off the deck and sipped on his Grand Mainer. He had just come in from having dinner with Geneva and her new boyfriend, Ray. He usually didn't like being a third wheel, but Deva had convinced him to come along. He decided to say yes so that he could size Ray up and see if he was really all she said he was. He was a decent guy. He ran a car detail shop in North Philly, and he owned his own home in the Mt. Airy section of the city. He was well-educated, and he seemed to be head over heels in love with her. That was the most important thing to Clayton: seeing her happy. They dined at Foo De Go Chow, one of Deva's favorite restaurants in the city, and the evening flowed with ease. They talked about business and the stock market, and Clayton was extremely impressed with his knowledge of finance. "So, Ray, how long have you been investing?" Clayton asked over desserts and coffee. "Well, my father was a trader back in the day, and he taught me a thing or two about researching and investing in the right companies," Ray said between bits of his cheesecake.

"Oh, so have you put any money into TAYLOR industries yet?" Clayton asked, curious to know if he was trying to capitalize on his relationship with Geneva. He knew that Ray was aware that she was the COO of his company and was wondering if he was another nigga trying to go for her checkbook. "Actually, no, Clayton, I don't mix my business ventures with my personal ones," he quickly stated, looking insulted that Clayton had even considered that of him. Clayton eyed Ray for a moment and realized that he was being sincere about what he said. After that, he backed off and just enjoyed the evening with them.

When they finished dinner, Ray suggested they go into Old City and hit the night scene for some dancing, but Clayton declined and thought it best to head home. "Come on, Clay, hang out for a while; you'll have fun," Geneva pleaded in a childlike voice as they stood at the Valet waiting for their cars. "No, you two go ahead. Be with your man, girl. He's a good catch, and he really makes you happy," Clayton said to her as he climbed into his Porsche truck. "I'm tired anyway and need to head home for some rest. Call me tomorrow and fill me in on the details," he said as he kissed her gently on the forehead. "OK, be safe. Love you, baby, and thanks," she said as she stepped back from the curb. She watched him speed down Chestnut Street and smiled. She loved him so much and hoped that one day, he would find happiness, too.

Clayton reached for the remote control that lay at his feet and turned on the stereo. The room was filled with the beautiful voice of Phyllis Hyman, one of his favorite female singers. He listened as she sang about living her life all alone, and Clayton wondered if he would be dealt that same fate. He had a cell phone full of phone numbers of beautiful women he could have at any time, but he was longing for something more. He wanted a woman with a mind as well as a banging body. He dated off and on, but none of the women he was seeing seemed to satisfy him. He got off sexually, and they were always willing to do anything he asked of them, but he still yearned for that woman that could stimulate his brain as well as his dick. His latest quest, Naomi, was nice, and she was drop-dead gorgeous. He met her one day when she came into the spa for a massage. She was a former model at the Robert Powers agency, and now she is a dancer for the Exclusively Yours entertainment theater.

She was tall and thin, and she had long, graceful, muscular legs. She spoke with a soft, sexy voice, and she carried herself with class and elegance. When she entered a room, you noticed her immediately. "Excuse me," she said to the receptionist at the desk, "I'm looking for a Clayton Taylor," she said removing her designer shades. Clayton was standing in the hall and heard her say his name. "Yes, how can I help you?" He asked as he walked closer to her. "Mr. Taylor, my name is Naomi Franklin. I was referred by a friend of mine to get a massage here."

"I heard you were the best, so I decided to give you a chance," she said as she looked around the room and took in its entire marvelous ambiance. "Well, we are here to please, and you have come to the right place. May I ask who referred you?" Clayton asked, taken aback by her beauty. "Yes, my girlfriend Monica is a massage therapist as well, but she said I had too many knots and tension and needed to be worked over by a true professional," she said, visibly impressed by what she saw.

"That's no problem. May I take your coat?" Clayton asked as he reached out for the blue mink jacket she wore. "We have several packages available for you to choose from, and I will be sure to set you up with the best massage therapist we have here," he said, making sure she got well taken care of. "Oh, won't that be you?" she asked, sounding almost disappointed he hadn't offered to massage her himself. "Well, Mrs. Franklin," he said, "Oh no, it's Miss," she interrupted. She wanted to make sure he knew she was single and available. "Miss Franklin, I would love to service you, but at this time, my schedule is booked. I have a wonderful staff here, and I will make sure you are treated like royalty," Clayton said, flashing his million-dollar smile." OK, I'm going to trust you, Mr. Taylor," she said as she relaxed a little and took a seat in one of the lounge chairs in the lobby. "Please, call me Clayton."

After a few more visits to the spa, he decided to ask her out. He knew she had been expecting it. She could feel the chemistry between them just as he did. Their first date was a nice lunch at the Marathon Grill, and then it became dinner once a week at the restaurants of her choice. He always aimed to please her by showering her with gifts and romantic getaways, and Naomi was always willing to show her gratitude each and every time he asked. It only took him two dates to get her into bed, but he could say it was well worth it.

She was a beast between the sheets. She would fuck him for hours, and she gave the best head he had ever had. He liked being with her, but she just didn't give him what he was missing. He wasn't quite sure exactly what that was yet, but he knew she wasn't giving it to him. They didn't really have many conversations. Their dating consisted of him taking her to fancy restaurants and long weekends at the shore or shopping sprees in Manhattan and then going back to her place for some hot sex and then Clayton going home. He had never brought her to his place, and she never seemed to care. She was ok with the arrangement they had, and it suited him simply fine as well for the time being. Whenever she came to the spa, all the employees treated her with respect because they knew she was dating the boss, and she had a sense of power whenever she stopped by. Deva, on the other hand, was not a huge fan of hers, but she tolerated her for his sake.

"When are you going to stop fucking the tramp with the big tits? She said to him one night while they were closing. "Oh, come on, Deva Naomi is not a tramp. She is fun and sexy, and I like her," he said, trying to convince her to be nice. "Fun, sexy and dumb as a doorknob," Geneva said laughingly. "I know she's not the sharpest knife in the drawer, but she takes care of my needs, and you're the one that said I needed to get laid so I could stop being such a hard ass," he replied. "Yeah, I told you to go get some ass, not attach yourself to one," Geneva replied sarcastically. "Oh, am I sensing someone is jealous?" Clayton said in a playful tone. "Jealous? Are you kidding me?" She said, surprised he had even made that comment.

There was nothing romantic about his relationship with Geneva. They had tried to fuck once a few months after they had met years ago, but they both realized neither had what the other was looking for sexually, so they got out of bed, got dressed and went out drinking. They had a good laugh about the situation and from then on had been like brother and sister. "Come on, bro, there is nothing to be jealous of. I just want you to date a smarter girl and not some dumb airhead, is all I'm saying," Geneva replied.

She was just as protective of him as he was of her. "I will meet that special someone one day, but in the meantime, I'm sticking with the airhead that gives good head," he said, and they both busted out in laughter.

When Clayton got up to change the playlist, his cell phone rang. It was 1:00 in the morning, he thought, and was wondering who could be calling him at this time of night. Naomi was out of town with her dance theater, and she knew he was going out with friends tonight, so he wasn't expecting her to call. Then he got nervous. Maybe it was Deva calling to tell him that her prince charming had turned into a troll, and she needed him to come whoop his ass. Clayton answered the phone quickly. "Hello," he said sternly. "Mr. Taylor, this is Gloria. Down at the Center we have been trying to contact you all day regarding your uncle's care," the woman on the other end said in heavy southern drawl. "Yes, ok, what seems to be the problem?" Clayton asked, aggravated they had called him so late at night.

"Well, it seems Michael is not responding well to his new medications, and he is starting to act out again. Dr. Bronson needs you to sign and fax another authorization form so that we can start him on something new. Would that be ok? She asked. "Yes, sure, no problem," Clayton responded, trying to hurry her off the phone. "I'll have the form sent back first thing tomorrow morning, and listen, do not ever call me at this time of the night again," he said, and then the line went dead.

Clayton was fuming when he got off the phone. He went into the kitchen to pour himself another drink. He didn't have a problem with the clinic calling him if it was an emergency; he just wasn't in the mood to fill his thoughts with his uncle right now. Michael was his mother's only younger brother, and he had suffered from a severe mental illness since he was a child. When his grandmother died, his mother took him in to care for him. She could barely take care of Clayton, being a single mother, but she always told him to look after his family son no matter what, so Uncle Mike moved in. He was 23 at the time, a lot older than Clayton, but because of his childlike mind, they appeared to be the same age. To Clayton, it was great because he had a playmate, someone he could relate to and talk to. He reminded him of a fictional character he had seen on TV, and Clayton liked hanging out with him. Uncle Mike had no recollection of any of the heartache and pain his family had suffered, and Clayton was determined to keep it that way. When Clayton's mom passed away ten years ago, he remembered telling him she went on a trip and maybe someday he would see her again. He knew his uncle didn't fully understand the concept of death, and Clayton felt that it was better that way so he wouldn't suffer from the loss. He never forgot the promise he had made to his mama to always look after his family. He had placed his uncle in the best mental facility North Carolina could offer, and he paid a hefty price to fulfill his mother's wishes.

62

8

REGINA

For the life of her Regina could not fall asleep. It was almost 2 am, and she had been lying in bed for over an hour wide awake. She tried watching TV, but there was nothing that she wanted to see, so she turned it off. She had put on some soft music to try and relax, but that didn't help either, so she got up and went into the kitchen to make herself some tea. Regina's apartment was small, but it was tasteful. It was a two-bedroom, one-and-a-half-bath condominium in the up-and-coming Brewery town district of the city. It had beautiful charm and character, and as soon as Regina saw it, she knew she had to have it. It was conveniently located near public transportation, and the neighborhood was remarkably diverse. She had moved there about a year after she got to Philly. Even though she loved her cousin dearly, she knew she had to hurry and move out because she couldn't take the loud music and company she entertained. Besides, she didn't really like living with anyone; she had grown accustomed to being with just her daughter for the last ten years in her own space.

"I found an apartment in Mo," she remembered telling her cousin the day she signed the lease. "Oh, that's wonderful," Monica said as she sat on her futon in the living room. "Yes, girl, it's near the zoo and a lovely park. It's perfect for me and Nyla," Regina said as she wrapped her pictures from the walls. She decorated Monica's apartment with some of the things she had returned with from down south to give it a more homelike feel for her daughter. "The Zoo? Why the hell would you want to live near there? Didn't you get enough of that shit living down south around all those smelly animals?" Mo asked, amused. "Shut up," Regina said as she tossed a pillow at her. "I want to live around culture and a place I can take Nyla on nice sunny days."

"Suit yourself, honey. I am simply fine right here among the rich white folks and preppy socialites," she said, reclining back on the sofa. "I love this neighborhood too and would have loved to be this close to South Street and Penn's Landing. It's just that I need more room, and your private activity is not exactly what I want to expose Nyla to," Regina added with a frown. "It's cool," Monica responded, a little hurt at Regina's comment. She knew she liked to party, and the men she dated were not exactly saints, so she understood where Regina was coming from. "It's just I'm going to miss you guys being here," Monica added. "You always kept the place so nice, and I loved coming home to your great leftovers you would leave in the microwave for me," Monica said, pouting. "Well, you know you're always welcome at my place if you ever need to just get away," Regina said, knowing her ill cousin really would miss her.

Regina had even felt a little guilty about leaving her cousin now. Monica was in a really bad space at the time. Her latest boyfriend, Kadeem, had been going at it with her nonstop, and she could tell Mo was getting fed up with his nonsense.

He was living with her while he waited for his sentencing. The law office Regina had gotten hired with was representing him on his multiple outstanding cases. She looked at Mo, feeling sorry for her. "Girl, why don't you just put his ass out?" She asked as she continued packing. He had been staying at the apartment for the last few months since his court appearance and release from the county jail, and he had been arguing with her cousin constantly every day. Regina hated him being there, and the moment he arrived, she decided it was time for her to start looking for a place and move on. She really did not want to leave her cousin like that, but this living situation was not good for her and her daughter. "Well, you know he stressed," Monica said in his defense. "Girl, he is about to go to jail for life, and he just doesn't know how to handle it. He knows your boss has done all he could to help him, but he's still scared," she said, feeling sorry for her man. "Chile is lucky he's not getting the death penalty," Regina said matter-of-factly. "Mr. Price got him the best deal he could have given his circumstances. He should be glad to know all he will be doing is sitting in Grater Ford prison instead of dying by lethal injection." "I know you're right, but I promised him I'd stick with him till he goes in, but when that day comes, he knows I'm out like the wind," Mo replied. "I'm a rider till I'm not, she added. Besides, he is still paying the bills, and he's set up a bank account in my name so that I can send him some money to put on his books. I told him I could do that for him since he doesn't have anybody else out here on these streets," she said, trying to convince Regina why she was still with him. "I know," Regina said in a motherly tone. "Just be careful. You know that's drug money you dealing with, so make sure you have all your bases covered. If not, you gonna end up in a cell next to his." Regina knew from experience. "But know, I will be here if you need me, OK? She leaned over and gave her cousin a big hug.

The whistle from the teapot got Regina's attention. She walked over to the stove and removed it from the fire. She was hoping the tea would relax her and she could finally go to bed and rest. For some reason, she was feeling anxious tonight, a feeling she hadn't had in quite some time. She decided to walk down the hall to Nyla's room to check on her. When she entered, she saw her fast asleep with her cell phone stuck to her face. She knew she had been on FaceTime with Asia, her best friend. When she reached down to move the phone, she saw Asia fast asleep on the other end. She smiled as she hung up the phone and placed it on the charger. She sometimes wished she had another baby at some point so that Nyla didn't have to grow up alone, but she was thankful for her just the same. Another child would have complicated her life even more, and she did not want to be responsible for protecting three lives instead of two.

As she walked back to the kitchen, she heard a noise coming from the hall closet. Her heart started beating fast, and a sudden fear washed over her entire body. Even though she was comfortable here, she was always on guard and ready to escape at a moment's notice. Regina eased over to the closet door as she reached for the baseball bat lying next to it. Whoever was in that closet was about to get their head bashed in. She grabbed the knob slowly and took a deep breath. When she yanked open the door, she started swinging the bat furiously as her cat Honey jumped out and ran down the hall. Regina sank down to the floor, feeling terrified yet relieved. She was happy it was just the cat, but she was shaken just the same. She knew the Twins were out there looking for her. She just hoped they wouldn't find her too soon.

9
EVELYN

Evelyn gave herself a once over in the mirror before she walked out the door. She looked and felt beautiful. The car had arrived at 7 on the dot, and she was ready for a splendid night with Ethan. She had chosen to wear her red satin Dior gown that hugged her hips perfectly. She wore matching red stilettos that made her 3 inches taller than her original height. She had her hair down the way the husband liked it, and she had put on the black Victoria's Secret thong Ethan had delivered to the house for her a few hours ago. She was absolutely stunning as she made her way down the driveway to the waiting Bentley he had sent for her. She wore her black sable fur tonight since there was a slight chill in the air. "Good evening, Mrs. Price," the driver said as he opened the door for her. Hello Randolph, she said to the familiar face. You look lovely as usual he said as he helped her inside the car. "Thank you, dear," she said seductively. Randolph was one of the many conquests she had from time to time, but he always remained professional and never gave Ethan a clue he was banging his wife. As they got onto I 95 heading south from Bensalem, Evelyn checked her makeup in the mirror. She made sure no hair was out of place, and her lipstick was applied perfectly when she arrived at the Center City restaurant. She wanted to make sure she looked perfect for her darling husband. He sounded so happy on the phone when she called to let him know she was on her way. She couldn't wait to see him. Evelyn felt like tonight was going to be a game-changer. She was actually excited to spend the evening out with him.

As the car cruised down the highway, Evelyn thought about the surprise Ethan had said he had for her. She was happy with anything he gave her, especially the sweet, thoughtful gifts he surprised her with when they first started dating. He could not afford much back then; he would pick up little trinkets at the tacky jewelry stores up and down Chestnut Street. But now that he was a big-time attorney, the gifts became more lavish and expensive. The last big account he landed was when he bought her a beautiful diamond tennis bracelet from Tiffany's in New York. And the deal before that, he bought her the sable coat she was wearing that night. She could not imagine what the gift would be this time. Evelyn looked down at her diamond-encrusted Michele watch and saw that it was 7:45. They were almost there, and she was pleased that she was right on time.

When the car pulled up to the curb in front of the restaurant, she saw her husband standing at the door chatting with a group of men. He looked so handsome in his black tuxedo. She assumed they were his golf friends from the club and paid no mind to the men standing there. When Ethan turned around, he saw the car and headed toward it to open the door for her. As he got closer, she got a look at the men he was speaking to. Evelyn almost fainted. It was Jacob and James Spears, the pimps from North Carolina. She was as white as a sheet as she exited the Bentley. "Oh, baby, you made it safely," Ethan said as he helped her from the car. When Evelyn stepped out, she felt her legs tremble under her gown. "Don't you look amazing," Ethan stated as he looked at her and kissed her lightly on the cheek. Evelyn was speechless as she watched the Twins look in her direction. They had a surprised look on their faces as well. Ethan took her hand and led her over to the men standing there talking. "Jacob and James Spears, I would like you to meet my lovely wife, Evelyn," he said to them.

She didn't know what to say. She felt like she had just been punched in the gut. From Ethan's expression, she knew he had no idea what was happening. She had no clue how Ethan had known them, and there was no way he was aware she had a connection with these men. A connection that would tear her world apart. "Gentlemen," Evelyn said in a shaky voice. "Are you ok, honey?" Ethan looked at her with concern on his face. He could feel her shaking underneath her fur. "It's just I am suddenly not feeling too well, sweetheart," she said as she felt herself about to vomit. "Oh, wow, you should have told me, darling, and we could have gone out another time," he said, feeling pity for his wife. "Guys, I'm sorry, but I'm going to have to take a rain check for dinner tonight," Ethan said to the twins. "It's cool, my man. Take your woman home and put her to bed; she looks like she just saw a ghost," Jacob said with a sinister laugh. Ethan hadn't noticed the cold, hard stares they were giving Evelyn as they stood in front of the restaurant. "You're right. She does appear to be terribly ill," he said as he wrapped his arm around her waist. She was glad he did because she felt herself about to fall to the ground. "Listen, I'll call you tomorrow, and we can finish our business then." "Ok," Ethan said as he shook their hands. "No problem, man, we got all the time in the world," James said as he grinned at Evelyn. "It was a pleasure meeting you, beautiful," he said to her as he watched her turn back towards the Bentley. She didn't say a word as she reached the car door. Ethan helped her back inside of the car and climbed in beside her.

He had never seen her look so sick like this before, and he silently hoped she was pregnant. She laid her head in his lap and began to cry. #What's the matter, sweetheart?" Ethan said to her as he stroked the back of her head. "Everything, babe," she said through her tears, "Just take me home," she sobbed as she closed her eyes and said a silent prayer. Jacob and James stood there in front of the restaurant as the Bentley pulled away. "Can you believe this shit?" Jacob said to his brother. "We have been looking for that bitch for over ten years, and just like that, she's delivered to us front and center," he said as he patted his brother on the back. "Yeah, we got real lucky with this one, but we still gotta be careful. Who would have thought that conniving ass bitch could land a square dude like Ethan Price. He can't know what happened with that slut back in the day," James said suspiciously. "We got to play him real close if we are going to get that bitch." "You're right, James, but if he gives us any problems, we're just gonna have to dig his grave next to hers," Jacob said to his twin. "Brother, you were reading my mind. I guess it's true what they say: great minds do think alike," James said as he flagged for the valet to bring him his Cadillac.

Evelyn's head was spinning when they arrived home. She could not believe she had just seen the twins. She felt like she was in a nightmare, and she knew all hell was about to break loose. When they entered the house, Evelyn ran straight for the powder room downstairs. She felt so nauseous she could feel the room spinning. "Babies, are you ok? What's wrong with you?" Ethan yelled out as he ran after her. "Come on, E, talk to me," he begged outside the bathroom door. She hadn't said a word since they had gotten into the car. She was in shock. She just couldn't understand why her husband was associated with those thugs. She had been in the bathroom for almost 10 minutes, and Ethan was really starting to worry. She didn't seem to be ill when he spoke to her earlier in the day. She had been acting a little distant lately, but he just assumed she was preoccupied with one of the charities she was always working with. He wasn't sure when her last period was, and he was silently praying she was having his child. He knew Evelyn was dead set against having kids, but he hoped maybe she had a change of heart over the years. He started to feel good despite her actions. Just imagine how lucky their lives would be if she were carrying his seed, he thought. They could be the happy family he always wanted. But he couldn't have been farther from the truth. Not only was Evelyn not bringing a life into the world, but little did he know theirs may soon be taken.

10

ETHAN

Ethan continued to bang on the bathroom door. Evelyn had been in there for a long time now, and he was starting to worry. He needed to know if she was ok. He couldn't understand what had happened to what was supposed to be the best night of his life. He had purchased his wife the most spectacular diamond and emerald necklace, and he was on cloud nine as he headed back to his office. He had decided to stay in the city and get dressed there since it was already after six, and he was sending a car service to pick her up. As he headed back to his midnight blue BMW, his cell phone rang. It was Jacob Spears, one of the twins he had done business with a few years ago when he started his own law firm.

They had come to his previous firm, where he was a junior partner and asked if he could represent them on the murder rap charge they were facing in Virginia at the time. Ethan was skeptical of them at their first meeting because he had never met them, and he wondered why they had come all the way to Philly to retain a lawyer, especially him. "Gentlemen,

Davis and Shultz is a brokerage law firm. We don't do criminal law here," Ethan informed them. "Man, we know that, but your name was given to us by someone you represented on a drug case a few years ago. You did some pro bono work for a dude out in West Philly. He said you won the case at the preliminary hearing," one of the twins said to Ethan. He thought back to the trail he helped Snake out with.

His old boss from the streets had been locked up for transporting five keys of cocaine across state lines, and he came to Ethan for help. "Hey man, I know this ain't the kind of law you into, but I really need your help." He remembered Snake pleading to him one night at a bar on Woodland Avenue. He had just been released on bail and asked Ethan to meet him there. "Snake, come on, brother, I don't know about representing you, man. I used to work for you back in the day hustling drugs, and now you want me to represent you in court?" Ethan had said as he sipped on his Heineken. Ethan had gotten out of the game when he received a full scholarship to Penn State University to study law. Snake had been really proud of him to see a young man finally getting out of the ghetto and making something of himself. "Yo, man, just don't forget about us niggas down here in the trenches when you become a big-time attorney," he remembered Snake saying to him as they smoked a blunt in Snake's Chevy Malibu the night of his graduation. Ethan was leaving in a few weeks, and he wanted to hang with his friend before he left.

"Come on, man, you always gonna be my squad," Ethan replied. "Besides, you niggas are gonna need somebody to represent yall's black asses one day," he said, feeling a buzz from the weed. Ethan had worked for Snake for three and half years but knew him all of his life. He had finally made it up in the ranks as one of Snake's bodyguards from lookout boy when he first started hanging with him. Snake really liked Ethan, and he knew he was gonna make something of himself one day. Snake was 15 years older than he was and always treated him like his little brother. He never let Ethan handle any drug transactions when he was around because he never wanted to tarnish the young brother's future. "Never get your hands dirty, young blood, unless you have to," he would say to him when he went along with him to drop off the product to the neighborhood kids who were slinging." He saw something different in Ethan, not like the other knuckle-heads he had working for him. "Yeah, look here, man, you go finish school and make the money the right way," Snake had told him, "and keep your nose clean, you hear? One day, people are gonna be knocking down your door to represent them. Mark my words," he said as the weed started to take over his thoughts.

Ethan appreciated what Snake had said to him, and he would never forget his kindness. Years had gone by, and Snake was still in the game. Ethan had wished he would have retired, but Snake told him the streets were all he knew, and that's where he was gonna die.

Ethan had graduated and landed a job at a law firm in Bucks County straight out of college. He had assumed the job would be challenging, and he'd be defending the city's most notorious gangsters, but he wasn't so lucky. Davis and Shultz was a small firm that handled business mergers and corporate law. Ethan was not thrilled about his new gig, but it paid the bills, and he was learning a lot. In his spare time, he studied criminal law and went down to the criminal justice center to watch different cases and see how the big-time attorneys handled things. He knew deep down he wanted to be the next Johnnie Corcoran of Philadelphia.

"Look, E, I know you into that bullshit law with those white folks out there in the County, but man, I really need you." Snake pleaded his case. "These crackers are trying to put me in jail for 50 years over this shit, and I can't go down like that," he said as he nursed his rum and coke the barmaid sat in front of him. "I need your help, man, and remember you owe me," he said, hoping he would recall all the favors he did for him when he was one of his soldiers. When Ethan had gone away to college, Snake gave him 5000.00 to get him a whip and a new wardrobe for college, and he would also go by and check on his aunt and uncle. He would give them money every month and told them it was what he owed him for helping him in his car garage, which he used as a front for his drug house. They were none the wiser that Ethan was involved in the drug game, and he made sure they never did till the day they left this earth. They thought he had gotten a job working with Snake fixing old cars for a living, and they were always proud of him for making his own money. Snake looked out for him better than any friend he'd ever had. "Aight, man, I'll do it. I'll go to court for you and help you out," Ethan reluctantly agreed. He just hoped he learned enough from those criminal law books to help his friend and wouldn't land him behind bars.

"Um, yes, you are referring to Vincent Shaw," Ethan replied, calling Snake by his government name. "Yeah, Vincent," the twin said. "He told us you were like a bother to him, and you looked out when no one else would when he needed you the most," Jacob said to him knowingly. "Listen here," James said, tired of wasting time, "we got a lot of money to spend for this case and we need you to help secure our freedom. If you make this happen, you can kiss this bullshit place good-bye, and we will make sure you have all you need to start your own business," James said as he looked Ethan dead in his eyes. They knew he was desperate to leave Davis and Shultz, and they knew they had just the right amount of money to make that happen for him. Believing he could do it, Ethan made a deal with the devil and signed the deal. By the end of the week, he had turned in his resignation, and the twins retained him as their attorney. Ethan knew he had his work cut out for him, but he was determined to win this case. Because of Evelyn and the law firm, he had made a lot of good connections with politicians and businesspeople in other states over time, and he used them to gain leverage over the assistant DA assigned to the case. In the end, he got both twins off free with a not guilty verdict.

He worked that trial so well he was offered a job in the State of Virginia. Ethan graciously declined. With a murder and drug case win under his belt, he knew he was about to rise to the top. The Twins had paid him 100 grand to represent them and made a deal to front him: 10 million dollars to establish Price and associates. They gave him three years to pay them back with 10% interest, and he jumped at the opportunity. Besides, they were sending him half their employees to represent. Ethan handled cases from armed robbery to child support for the twins, as well as mergers from big companies and the money never stopped rolling in. He was truly making a name for himself and was making enough money to spoil his wonderful new wife, as well as to pay the twins back with ease.

"My man, Jacob, how are you today, sir?" Ethan said into his iPhone when he answered. "What's happening, brother," Jacob said back into the receiver. "I am doing great," Ethan replied. "Did you get the check I sent over to you?" Ethan asked, hoping there wasn't a problem with his last payment to them. "Oh yeah, we received it. Thanks, man. It has truly been a pleasure doing business with you, and James and I really respect your work as a lawyer," he said to him. "Awe, man, I'm the one that should be thanking you guys. I am doing better than I ever could have imagined, and it is all because of you," Ethan said, sincere in his words. "Look, we are glad we could help. You are one hell of a lawyer and it's nice to know if ever we are in trouble, we can call on you." "Yes, indeed," Ethan said proudly. "So, the reason we called was because we wanted to sign the final paperwork with you and get the hell out of this bullshit city," Jacob said. Ethan wanted to get this final business over with as well and was glad he didn't have to call them suggesting it.

As friendly as they both appeared to be with Ethan, he knew they were ruthless killers, and he knew never to piss them off or get on their bad side. That murder case was not the only court appearance he had to make for them over the last three years. They stayed in some crooked shit, but Ethan never complained. He just kept representing them and prayed he kept winning their cases. "Maybe we could meet tonight if that's okay with you," Jacob asked. "Sure, that would be no problem. I'm still in the city, actually. I'm meeting my wife for dinner at Ruth Chris at eight, so maybe we could meet beforehand and have drinks when we finalize the deal." "That sounds like a plan, brother," Jacob said and told him he would see him later that night.

Everything was going perfectly, and that's why Ethan was so confused when the whole fiasco happened with Evelyn. They had just finished signing the papers and toasting the end of their deal. He had walked the twins to the door of the restaurant and was waiting with them while the valet went to retrieve their car. He was so excited when he saw Evelyn pull up in the Bentley. He wanted to introduce her to the men who had made him a tremendous success, but instead, the introduction turned into a total disaster and the beginning of the end.

11
REGINA

The next day, Regina woke up with a splitting headache. She was hoping that her anxiety attacks weren't starting again. She had not slept well the night before, and she was still shaken from the cat startling her. She stood at the kitchen sink filling up her tea kettle when the phone rang. It was 7:00 on a Saturday morning, and she knew it was Mo who wanted to know what time they were meeting to go to the gym. She hadn't taken her medication yet and really was not in the mood for her raunchiness this early, but she didn't want Monica to know she was having her anxiety spells again.

"Good morning, Miss hoochie mama," Regina said into the receiver, trying to sound cheerful. "Good morning, Ms. Allen; this is Nancy from work," the woman said shyly on the other end. "I'm sorry to bother you at home on a Saturday, but you received a message from a Mr. Taylor asking that you return his call right away. I was told by Mr. Price that if this client calls to contact you immediately." "Yes, Nancy," Regina replied, embarrassed by her telephone greeting. "That's fine;

I will return his call right away. Thank you for calling," Regina said, then hung up the phone, feeling flustered. She was surprised and wondered why Clayton had called the office on a Saturday morning, but she was getting excited to talk to him again. She did not think anything went wrong in the meeting yesterday, and she was praying he wasn't calling with unwelcome news that she would have to give to Mr. Price. She reached for her purse to retrieve his business card from it when the phone rang again. This time, she knew it was Mo.

"Hello," Regina said cautiously in case it was another office call. "Girl, why you sounding all business like this early in the morning?" Monica asked in her usual loud, cheerful voice. "Girl, I thought it was the job again," Regina said, relaxing her tone. "A business call?" She replied, "You get business calls on the weekends now?" Mo asked, sounding surprised. "I thought u was strictly Monday- Friday, and the weekends were your own." "That's usually the case, but we got this new client that Mr. Price decided to tell that I would be available 24 hours, and he's taken advantage of the situation and left a message on a Saturday morning," Regina said, half annoyed that she was even getting calls before her first cup of tea. "What's up, girl," Regina asked as she searched her bag for the card. "Just calling to see if we are hitting the gym this morning," Mo asked happily. "Well, I'm not quite sure at this point, Mo," Regina said, eyeing the card as she removed it from her bag. "I need to find out what's so urgent that Mr. Taylor couldn't wait till Monday." "Mr. Taylor?" Mo exclaimed excitedly. "The Mr. Taylor of Tailored To You hair and spa studios?" Monica said loudly.

"Yes, girl, calm down. He's Mr. Price's new client, and we are representing him for his new salons opening in New York, DC and Atlanta," Regina said calmly. "OMG, girl, why didn't you call and tell me he was your new client?" she yelled excitedly. "I have been trying to meet him forever; I have even tried to get a job in his place for over a year! I sent some high-class chicks from my gym there to put in a good word for me, hoping he would be impressed by my referrals, but it didn't work. Those hoes were probably jealous and didn't even say anything. Oh, Gina, you have got to introduce me to him, honey." "Calm down," Regina said, laughing. "Give me a chance to get to know him, and of course, I'll hook you up with an interview or something. You my lil cuz, and you know one hand washes the other," Regina said sincerely, knowing she would do anything to help her as much as she had been there for her and her daughter. "Well, Suga, forget the gym; you go ahead and do your thing with Mr. Man and call me later," Mo replied, excited and happy for her cousin. "You charm the pants off him, and maybe you might get a piece in the process," she laughed. "Shut up, crazy. Sex is all you think about. I'll call you after my conference call and let you know what's up, ok?" Regina was starting to feel some excitement herself. "And you know it," Monica said, laughing. "OK, I'll be waiting by the phone. Love you, cousin." "Love you, too, big head," Regina said, then hung up the phone.

She walked back over to the counter, got her cup of hot tea and pulled her laptop out of her briefcase. She figured she'd get all the paperwork out and be ready if Clayton needed some new numbers or information regarding his mergers. She took out her reading glasses and set herself up at her kitchen table already for the call. She was hoping it wouldn't be too long because she wanted to take Nyla out bike riding through Fairmount Park later that morning.

She picked up her cordless phone and dialed the number on the business card. It rang three times, and then she heard soft music playing in the background, then his voice on the other end. "Well, good morning, Miss Allen," she heard Clayton say in a rich husky voice. "Good morning, Mr. Taylor," Regina responded, a little stunned he answered the line and knew it was her. "It's Clayton, remember?" "Oh, yes, good morning, Clayton," Regina replied, blushing on the other end of the line. "And it's Regina, sir." She tried staying professional, but his voice was so alluring she kept getting distracted. "Sir Clayton," he replied and then chuckled. "Just kidding, how are you this lovely morning?" he asked in a soft, subtle voice. He was trying to sound casual. "I understand there's a problem, and you needed my assistance right away"? Regina said, trying not to get lulled in by the sexy tone of his voice. "All business, huh, so early in the morning," he replied playfully. "Yes, I assumed something was wrong with you calling on a Saturday morning and all," Regina said, not sure where this call was headed.

"Well, actually, Regina, I was calling on a personal and business note to find out if you would come by the studio today to take a look around and see what my place had to offer. You could assess the value and report back to Mr. Price that his services will be well utilized," he said, hoping that would give him the opportunity to see her again. "Well, Mr. Ta... I mean, Clayton, I did make other plans, but if you insist this be done today, I will just have to make it happen," Regina replied flatly as her heart skipped a beat. She was so excited, but she had to contain herself. She didn't want him to know how happy she was. "Excellent!" Clayton exclaimed. He felt just as good that she accepted his offer on such short notice to come by the salon today. "How does noon sound?" he asked. "That sounds great," Regina said. "I will see then." She was feeling nervous but elated at the same time. "Great, see you then, Ms. Allen," Clayton replied softly and seductively. "Regina," she said, whispering as she heard him hang up the receiver. Regina lay back in her chair and closed her eyes as she smiled widely. Her headache was suddenly gone. She was going to see her dream man at his place of business, and she was thrilled. She thought back to yesterday and imagined him kissing her hand, and she began to tingle all over. She jumped up from the counter and ran to her bedroom. She had to go decide what to wear, and she felt so good she forgot to take her medication, and her anxiety felt miles away!

As Regina looked through her closet, she started to feel depressed again. She realized her wardrobe was filled with not-so-attractive clothing, and to be honest, Clayton was far out of her league. She felt silly to think that he was really interested in her in the first place and just chalked up the attention as being a ploy to get closer to Mr. Price. Either way, she knew she had a job to do, so she cleared her mind of the fairytales she was creating and pulled out her outfit for the meeting.

She picked a lovely cream mock neck sweater that complemented the sandy curls of her hair and a pair of Carmel riding pants that hugged her hips and the curves of her backside. She paired the outfit with a pair of stilettos that added to her 5'7 frame. She thought the outfit was a little too casual for a business meeting, but she rationalized that it was Saturday and her day off, so she could wear what she damn well pleased.

She laid her outfit on the bed and went into the bathroom to turn on the shower. When she re-entered her bedroom, she saw her daughter Nyla going through her jewelry on her vanity. "What are you doing, missy?" Regina asked her as she gently swatted her with the towel she was holding. "Good morning, mama. I was just checking to see if you had any diamond studs I could borrow," Nyla said in a childlike voice. "Really? Borrow? When have you ever borrowed my jewelry and returned it?" Regina replied, looking at Nyla with a slight grin. She knew anything she let her borrow was never returned. "Oh, mom, come on, you know I lost mine at my last recital and have needed some ever since," she said, whining. Ok, ok, I'll go through what I have and see if I have an extra pair to let you borrow," Regina said, dragging her words. "Now get outta here and go get dressed for our bike ride," she said, shoving her daughter out of her bedroom.

Little did she know, but Regina had already bought her beautiful sapphire studs from Macy's and was going to surprise her tomorrow for getting such an awesome report card last week. She loved spoiling her daughter when she could, and because of the bonus Mr. Price had given her for helping to secure the Taylor account, she had some extra cash to splurge a little, and she was all too happy to do so on Nyla. She had been such a good kid transitioning each time they had to run, and she never asked questions. She looked at Regina one day and said, "Mommy, I don't really know what's wrong, but I know something is, and I wanted you to know it's ok cause I know you will always protect me." That brought tears to her eyes hearing that from her then 7-year-old baby, but she made sure to keep that promise and never let any harm come to her at any cost. Regina looked over at the clock and saw that it was 8:15. She knew she had better get a move on if she planned on bike riding with Nyla, taking her to I Hop for breakfast and then coming back home to re-shower and changing to be at Taylor enterprises by noon. She hated rushing her time with her daughter, but this was a once-in-a-lifetime opportunity, and Regina wasn't gonna miss out on it. Clayton was indeed a client, but to Regina, she was hoping it would turn out to be something more. If ever there was a chance to finally connect with the man of her dreams, she was not gonna pass on it, and she thought now was the time to shoot her shot.

12

CLAYTON

As Clayton entered the main house from his weight room, the sun was shining brightly, and his skin glistened in the light. It was a beautiful day, and he wanted to make the most of it. He looked down and realized he was dripping sweat on his bamboo wood floors, but he didn't mind because his vigorous workout had made him feel great. His body was tight, toned and chiseled. He admired himself in the full-length mirror in the living room and saw his workouts were definitely doing him justice. He was proud of the body he was creating. He walked into his kitchen and headed to the subzero refrigerator to get a protein drink. He felt dehydrated from all the exercise he had just done. The whole time he was pumping iron, his thoughts were on Regina. He thought of her smile and her pretty face and how she was checking him out, thinking he hadn't noticed. A smile came across his face as he thought about how shy and timid she seemed. He liked her and was sure she was digging him, too. He knew he wanted to see her again, but he just didn't know how he would. He thought about waiting till Monday to call the office but decided today would be better. He was contemplating how he would get in touch with her. She had been on his mind all night. He didn't have her personal phone number, so he knew he would have to call her office and pretend it was business so they would contact her on a Saturday. He was confident they would reach out to her because Ethan had told him she would be available to him day or night.

"Good morning, this is Clayton Taylor from…" he started to say before he was interrupted. "Oh, Good morning, Mr. Taylor; I know very well who you are," the young lady said on the other end of the phone. "How may I be of service to you today?" she said in a flirtatious voice. Clayton couldn't help but smile. He loved how women toyed with him, even over the telephone. "I'm trying to contact Regina Allen. It's an important business matter," he said, making sure the call seemed urgent even though, by the tone of the young lady's voice, he knew he could get her to do anything he wanted.

"Sure thing, Mr. Taylor. I will reach out to her right away. Oh, and would you like to give me your personal number just in case she doesn't call you back?" she asked seductively, hoping he would say yes and she would have a way to contact him privately. Clayton chuckled. "No, that won't be necessary. She has my card, so she knows how to reach me." "Ok, no problem, sir," the operator said, sounding defeated. "I will be sure to get her the message," she said and hung up. Clayton knew she was flirting with him, but he wasn't interested. He pictured the woman as a Girl 6 type. She had a beautiful voice, but he had his sights set on Regina. He was confident she would get her the message right away.

Everyone at the office was now aware that Mr. Price had landed one of the most successful eligible bachelors in town, and every woman that worked there, single or married, was quite smitten with him. Clayton was glad it worked. He was actually nervous when he heard the telephone ring 20 minutes later after calling her office. He knew it was Regina on the other end because he had given Her his private line on the business card. No one had that number except for Lisa and the hospital his uncle was in, and he had already spoken to them both that morning, so no one else would be calling. He let the phone ring about three times because he didn't want to appear too anxious.

When he answered, he prayed the conversation would go smoothly. "Well, good morning, Ms. Allen," he said happily. They spoke for about 10 minutes, and he was glad he had convinced her to come by the spa. He knew once there, he would surprise her with a makeover and, hopefully, dinner. He couldn't stop thinking about her since they had met the day before, and he really wanted to get to know more about her. She seemed different from all the other chicken heads and gold diggers he had met, and there was something intriguing about her that he couldn't seem to resist. He was surprised that he was feeling a little nervous since he had never had a problem with women before, but there was something about her that felt different. It was like he saw something in her eyes that made him sense pain in her soul, which sparked something within him, but he also felt a calmness that made you feel safe around her. He wanted to know more about her, and he was destined to find out. He walked into his massive bedroom and lay across his king-sized bed. It was only 7:20, and he had already done his morning workout, so he decided to take a nap before getting dressed to head to work. He wanted to be well-rested and refreshed when he saw her. He lay there, closed his eyes, and allowed the sound of his waterfall in the pool to lull him to sleep. "Come on, Clay, please help me," he heard the sweet female voice say in his ear. "I don't know if I can do something like that, Lou. I love you and all, but what you are asking me to do is dangerous."

"I know, baby, but you said you would do anything for me, so why you acting funny now?" the teenager said, pouting. "Cause I'm scared if we get caught, we going to jail or worse." "Nothing's gonna happen, baby," she said seductively, "I got the plan all worked out; they will never know what hit em." "That's what you keep telling me, Lou, but I don't know if I could risk it," he said, feeling panicked and scared.

Suddenly, her sweetness turned to anger. "Look, stop being a bitch and man up. You want this just as much as I do! They owe us, damn it, and we need to take what's finally ours," the girl said, pulling the gun out of her bag and handing it to him. As he tried to take it from her hand, it went off, shooting her in the face. Clayton jumped up, wet with sweat and shivering. He realized he was having a bad dream again. Lately, his dreams had been turning into nightmares. He couldn't understand why he was now dreaming about her dying. He was disoriented and confused. He glanced over at the clock and realized he had slept for more than 3 hours. It was almost 11:00, and he was meeting Regina in an hour.

He got up off the bed, still a little dazed, and went into his master suite to turn on the shower. He was wondering why he started having those damn dreams again and why all of a sudden, she ended up dead. All that shit had happened so long ago. He was just a kid, and it took him a long time and lots of counseling sessions to forget that awful night. He hated thinking about what had happened. He reached into his medicine cabinet and took out a bottle of pills. He took 2 of the yellow oval-shaped pills dry as he looked at himself in the mirror. He had not taken these drugs in quite some time, but he felt like it was time to call in his prescription and make an appointment with his shrink asap.

13
EVELYN

Evelyn finally exited the bathroom, looking pale and disheveled. She had been in there for almost an hour, and Ethan had threatened to call an ambulance if she didn't come out soon. He had been sitting on the floor in front of the door when she opened it. "Oh my God, honey, are you all right?" he said as he jumped to his feet when she came out. "Yes, darling, I'm fine. I just got lightheaded, is all," Evelyn said, lying but trying to stay calm for him. "I think I might have exhausted myself working out today," she said as he helped her over to the sofa. "Oh, baby, if you were that tired, you shouldn't have agreed to dinner out. We could have stayed home and celebrated here," Ethan said, genuinely concerned about his wife. "Here, lie down, and I'll make you some tea and then take you upstairs to bed," Ethan said as he propped up some pillows for her. "No, sweetheart, that won't be necessary," Evelyn said as she stood up from the couch. "I'm going to go up now and get ready for bed. I suddenly feel worse and think I need to lie down upstairs." She leaned in and gently kissed him on the cheek. As she slowly walked over to the staircase, Ethan watched her to make sure she did not lose her balance. He was convinced she was pregnant and was concerned she might hurt the baby.

Evelyn cautiously walked up the steps to her bedroom. As she entered the room, she started to cry again. How could this be happening? She thought. How in the hell did Ethan know those gangsters, and what else did he possibly know? As she tried to undress, she replayed how twenty years early she had gotten even with those bastards and thought that ten years ago, she had made sure they were put away for life. How the fuck did they resurface? How were they here in Philadelphia, and how the hell did they know her husband? She had been incredibly careful when she started dating Ethan and made sure she knew everything there was to know about him, his background, his family and his friends. She paid a lot of money to find out everything there was to know about Ethan Price, and she was convinced he was a square that could in no way find out about her past or associate with anyone from it. Besides, he was so in love with her that he didn't even ask any personal questions or seem interested in her life except for him being in it. From the beginning, he was content believing that she grew up in Long Island, New York, with her grandparents and that her parents had died in a plane crash when she was nine. He never pried into her private life, and she liked it that way. She knew he could never under-stand or respect her real life. How could he ever understand that her mother was a whore and that her father was a drug addict in the South?

Evelyn laid on the bed, closed her eyes, and envisioned the life she had worked so hard to forget. "Get your ass in this house before I skin your tail," she heard Mavis yell to her from the porch of the battered shack they lived in. Mavis was the mama of the whorehouse, and she kept everybody in line, from the tricks to the prostitutes down to their children. She was a nice woman and she treated us kids real good, like her own. "Yes, ma'am," Alisha said as she scurried into the house from the yard. "Miss Mavis, can I please have a piece of chocolate cake, please?" she begged as she came inside. "Yes, you can just as soon as you wash your hands and face," she said as she patted Alisha on her behind and hurried along toward the kitchen. Miss Mavis was the big mama of the whorehouse and the only stability Alisha had. She had two children of her own, two boys, one that Alisha later found out was actually her brother. She would bring them over to the house with her when she came to work, and they would play together. When Miss Mavis was there, her life almost felt normal.

Her mother was named Monique, well, Candy, to the tricks she turned every night. She was the best prostitute Smitty had in his stable. She made him the most money, and she worked 24/7. That's why when her mama had her, he let her bring Alisha home with her because she told him, "If my baby girl don't come with me, I ain't coming back!" Smitty didn't want to lose her because he knew she was the best, so he allowed her to bring the baby to the whorehouse to live. Alisha's other siblings were not so lucky. Because mama had two other children that were boys, Smitty said they weren't allowed to live there. Mama used to tell her, "There could only be one dick in the house getting money from a bitch!" She didn't under-stand what that meant until she was older, and she knew

Candy never had any intentions of telling her the truth. As Alisha entered the kitchen, she saw Mavis' children, Clay and Mike, at the table eating cake. "Hey, big head," Clay said to her as she sat down. "Whatever, punk," she laughingly teased back at him. Clayton was her friend, and she loved him like a brother until they got old enough to see each other differently. He was always nice to Alisha and would do her hair and paint her nails when they were alone. She thought he was a fruit, you know, funny until she realized he was learning a skill from his mama.

Miss Mavis was the best hairdresser in town, and she kept every one of Smitty's girls looking beautiful. She especially liked doing Candy's hair. She said she must have had Indian in her family cause her hair was so naturally tamed. Clayton used to tease Alisha as well and say she was a little Cherokee cause her hair was just as straight and fine. As he and Alisha grew older, their brotherly and sisterly feelings started to change, and they began to like each other in other ways. Clayton was growing up to be so handsome, and he had a mustache and goatee by the time he was 15. He used to tell her that going down on a girl made the hair on his face grow. She thought he was kidding until one day, he asked if he could do it to her, and she swore a week later that he was growing a beard. They didn't let anyone know they were having sex. They kept that little secret because Clayton knew his mama wouldn't let him come back if she knew he was getting freaky with a prostitute's daughter. So, they would sneak out into the woods to do it and come back like nothing ever happened and pretend to everyone that they were just kids being kids playing. For many years, they were one big happy family. By the time Alisha was 16, though, things started to get bad. Smitty started pressuring mama to make her daughter a whore. He kept saying men would pay a lot for a sweet young thing like Alisha and that Candy wouldn't have to work so much cause her daughter could take up the slack. But mama wasn't having it; she told him if he laid a hand on her baby, she would kill him, but that only made Smitty more determined. He would flirt with Alisha and offer her money to sit on his lap, but she would always refuse. When Clayton found out, he wanted to kill Smitty too, but she told him no cause if he did something like that, then they wouldn't be together anymore. She told him she could handle herself and not to worry. He was gonna get him soon enough.

As time went on, drugs became more popular in the South, and Alisha's mama started doing drugs to ease the pain of all she was going through. Alisha knew that she loved her and wanted to protect her, but the crack she was smoking started to take over her life. She had started getting high so much that she would sneak and buy her drugs from the twins so Smitty wouldn't know. She had gotten so far in debt with them that she had to trick all night most days just to have money to support her habit, leaving Alisha to fend for herself most of the time. Alisha never forgot the day the twins came to Smitty's house to talk to him about her mama's debt. "Hey man, your bitch is really out there," they told him. "She into us for five stacks, and we want our money, so what you gonna do?" they asked. Smitty, being the son of a bitch he was, told them she wasn't worth the money to pay back anymore and said they could have her. Knowing that Candy was a great money maker when she was clean, they accepted the deal. Smitty really didn't wanna let her go but realized five grand was too much to pay out for a used-up whore. "But you gotta take her smart-ass mouth teenage daughter with you too," he said, knowing that even in her worst state, Candy's threat of killing him was valid. She kept close tabs on Alisha even though she was a friend. If Smitty tried to keep her there and pimp her, Candy would come back and kill him dead for sure. He decided to let that fate fall on the twins. She loved her baby and made sure that none of these pimping-ass thugs got a hold of her. "Whatever, man, as long as the bitch works and pays off her debt," they told him, happy they were getting Candy. They knew even in her worst state, she was a great money-maker. So, Candy and Alisha packed the little clothing they had and went with the twins. They were going away from the only home, as fucked up as it was, that Alisha ever knew, her family, Miss Mavis, Michael, and especially Clayton. Her life was never gonna be the same, and things were gonna get worse before they would ever get better.

Arriving at the twins' house, surprisingly, wasn't as bad as Aisha had thought. It seemed way better than living with Smitty, but it was still rough. The twins owned two three-story houses downtown that had eight bedrooms, three baths, and two kitchens. There were five girls living there at the time, which meant Candy and Alisha could each have their own bedroom and room left for one more. On the outside, the houses were meticulously kept with flower boxes on the edge of each step and a welcome mat in front of the door. The neighborhood seemed family-friendly enough during the day, with kids playing outside and a fire hydrant spraying water to keep them cool under the hot southern sun. There was a fruit stand down the road that sold watermelon, cotton candy, and cold soda pop, and it was run by a man named Lulu. Lulu was an older Hispanic man who had lived in North Carolina for most of his adult life, migrating from Cuba. He had two children and a wife who was hooked on drugs, and he worked for the twins selling fruit and drinks to support her habits. One of his daughters had supposedly run away from home at the age of ten, never to be heard from again, and the other was a prostitute for the twins, and her name was Kim. She was only 19, but looking at her, you could see that the street life was not kind. She looked to be in her 30s, which was sad because you could tell she was really beautiful. Her bedroom was across from Alisha's, and eventually, they would become fast friends. The day they arrived at the twin's domain, everyone was at home; the ladies were all gathered in the kitchen, and the twins were sitting on the stoop eating crab legs. It was a rare early Sunday afternoon, and they had given the girls a few hours of downtime.

"Well, well, look who finally decided to join the winning team," Jacob said in a joking tone as Candy and Alisha walked up to the step. "Hey, Jacob, James," Candy spoke to them in a childlike voice. "This is my daughter, Alisha," she said as she pulled her closer to her side. "Hey girl, you hungry?" Jacob said in a friendly tone, looking her up and down. "No, I'm fine," she responded in a firm voice, trying to make it clear she didn't want anything they were offering. "She got a funky little attitude, don't she?" James said in a harsh voice in response to her response. "No, she good, James, she only tired, is all," Candy quickly said to calm

James down. "We had a rough day, you know," she said, defending her daughter's tone. "Well, take y'all tired asses on in the house, and Candy, get ready for work tonight, you got a lot of money to work off, sister," James said, chuckling. "Yes, Daddy," mama responded, hanging her head low in shame.

"Girl, just because you won't be selling ass, you still gonna have to earn your keep around here," Jacob yelled out as they walked up the front steps. "Get your behind in there and wash some clothes, clean the kitchen or something. Nobody lives here for free," he added in a menacing tone. As they walked in the front door, they heard lots of chatter and music coming from the kitchen. There was a strong stench in the air that filled the hall with weed and sweat, and there were used condoms in the corners of the doorways. As they made their way up to the second floor, they could hear moaning and cursing coming from a few of the bedroom doors. "Fuck me, sugar, come on, suck it," Alisha heard a man's voice say to one of the whores he was tricking with. "You gotta come up with more money, honey if you want me to keep going," a female voice replied.

Next thing you know, they heard a loud crash, and the bedroom door flung open, and a man came stumbling out holding his head as it gushed with blood. "Daddy! Daddy!" The woman started screaming as she ran from the room, nearly knocking Alisha back down the steps. Just then, James rushed in, cursing and screaming. "What the hell is going on, Sandy?" He asked, furious! "This muthafucker kept trying to make me suck his dick, but his time was up, and he don't have no more money!" She yelled. Then, when I tried to get up, he grabbed me by my neck and tried to choke me!" She said angrily. "That's when I cracked his ass in the head with the beer bottle," she added, still holding on to the broken glass. The man was bleeding badly from the cut to his forehead as James grabbed him by the arm and rushed him down the steps. Jacob came rushing to try to figure out what happened. "Yo, what the fuck is going on, man?" He asked James. "This nigga tried to beat up Sandy and get a free blowjob, so he got to go," James said as he escorted the drunken man to the front door. No one seemed phased by the scene that just took place, and once the man was thrown out the door, everyone went back to what they were doing as if nothing happened.

Alisha had never seen anything like that before at Smitty's, but that's because no tricks were allowed inside to do their business. They had to take the whores down the road to the abandoned shack to get their sexual favors performed. Smitty's whore house was for women only, except for Clayton and Mike, and that's because they were Miss Mavis's children, and she took care of his girls and their kids. Smitty was serious about the only dick that would be in his place was his own. Alisha didn't know the twins allowed the girls to trick at home. This concerned Candy because, even though she knew her daughter was aware of what she did, she never actually saw her do it. Now, every illegal activity performed, whether it be drugs or prostitution, was front and center to her. It completely made sense why Alisha was allowed to have my own room so that her mama could work whenever the twins said she had to. This whole situation was heading for disaster, but this was the price Candy had to pay for her addiction.

14
REGINA

Regina walked along JFK Boulevard, and she couldn't help but marvel at the beautiful buildings she passed. She had never been to this stretch of the Center City, and she was amazed by the architecture and design. All the buildings were each a unique structure that set them apart from one another. They were very lovely, to say the least. Regina was on her way to meet Clayton at his spa, and she was both excited and nervous to see him. She decided to walk from her home since, according to Google Maps, she was only 20 minutes away on foot, and she could use the exercise as well as the time to get her nerves together for the meeting. She was already an hour ahead of schedule and in great shape, so this walk was gonna be a breeze for her. She had practiced in her head what she was going to say when she saw Clayton as she strolled casually down the street. "Mr. Taylor, this is a lovely place you have here," she silently rehearsed and then decided not to use those words because she felt like it made her sound like a southern belle. "Lovely? Really, Regina?" she said aloud.

"Wow, this place is off the chain," she said, then chuckled to herself. "Now you sound like you're a nineties yo MTV rap fan," she said to herself. "Oh, goodness, how am I going to greet him?" She said aloud, frustrated at herself, just as she approached 19th Street. When she looked up, she realized she was standing in front of his building. She saw the name of his Spa in beautifully gold-tone lettering amidst hand-crafted metal and stone that read Tailored To You FULL-SERVICE SALON AND SPA.

Suddenly, Regina felt clammy and sweaty and wished she had decided to take an Uber to the location instead of walking. "Get it together, Regina," she murmured to herself as she smoothed out the wrinkles in her pants. "He's just a man, not the prince of Zamunda," she smirked, referencing one of her favorite movies, "Coming to America." "Get your mind right and get in there," she rationed with herself. "This is a business meeting, not a date," she was reminded as she looked down at the slightly worn leather briefcase she carried. "You are here for business, nothing more. Now, get it together and move it," she said aloud to motivate her feet. As she pulled open one of the large glass doors that led into the massive lobby, she was hit with an intoxicating fragrance of lavender and peppermint that tingled her senses. As she looked around, she marveled at the massive exotic sculptures.

Beautiful artwork and flowers adorned the walls and the glossy marble floors that looked like glass. There were three long leather couches along the walls with glass tables in front. In one corner, there was a mini bar that had champagne fruit and bottled water as well as crystal stem glasses, and next to it, a fountain flowing water the color of the ocean. It was truly a sight to see. "Can I help you?" A beautiful woman with a thick, rich accent, seemingly of Brazilian descent, asked from behind a lovely hand-crafted wooden desk. "Oh, yes, I'm here to see Clayton Taylor," Regina stuttered as she quickly turned her attention to the lady. "He is expecting me."

The woman then smiled politely as she picked up the telephone. "Hi, this is Francisca, there is a..." she paused and looked at Regina. "May I have your name, please, Ma'am?" she said shyly, embarrassed that she didn't ask before making the call. "Oh, Miss Allen. Regina Allen," Regina replied. "Ah, yes, there's a Miss Allen here for an appointment with Mr. Taylor. Yes, ok, I'll send her back," the woman said into the receiver. "Ms. Allen, please walk straight back," she replied, gesturing toward a large wooden barn door. "Thank you," Regina replied as she walked towards the door. As she got closer, the door started to open, revealing the most beautiful sight Regina had ever seen.

It looked like a room straight off a page of the lifestyles of the rich and famous. Through the door revealed a room full of leather recliners and Hair stations, all occupied by clients. There were beautiful people everywhere, from the shampoo bowls that were against the stucco walls to the hair dryers that lined the center of the floor. There were people comfortably lounging at a fully stocked bar and women on the other end of the room receiving foot massages while they leafed through glamour magazines. It was high society at its finest. As Regina walked through the door, she was approached by a stunning lady wearing a Gucci Romper and sandals that fit her silhouette to a tee. She stood about 5'5 with cocoa-brown skin. Her hair was perfectly done in a tight bun that sat on top of her silky mane, and her nails were long and sparkling with Swarovski crystals.

"Hello, Ms. Allen," the woman said as she came closer to Regina. "I'm Geneva, Clayton's partner," she said as she took Regina's hand to shake it. "Hello, nice to meet you. It's Regina," she said as she shook the beautiful woman's hand. "Great," Geneva said as she looked Regina over. "Clayton is expecting you; unfortunately, he hasn't gotten here yet, stuck in traffic," she said, knowing that she was lying per her instruction from Clayton. He had called Geneva that morning and told her Regina was coming in and asked if she would stall her and convince her to get a makeover in the meantime. He wanted to give Regina a preview of his salon and allow her to experience everything his business had to offer. Afterward, he wanted to invite her to dinner and get to know her better. There was something mysterious and sexy about her, but it seemed as if she had a shield up protecting her from something, and Clayton was determined to find out exactly what it was

"Please, follow me, Miss Regina," Geneva said, taking Regina by the arm and leading her down a corridor. As they walked down the hall, they passed by several rooms. Each one had a distinctive sign on it stating what services were being offered. Regina saw signs that said full body massage, steam room, private manicure, facials, and the list went on. She realized this place had it all everything you could wish for, a truly full-service papering at its best. "Wow, this place is amazing," Regina said as they walked along the corridor. "Yes, it is," Lisa said as she glanced back at Regina. "I am walking you through the heart of our business so that you can get a full sense of what we offer here. This is a place of tranquil serenity and peace, and we make sure that every client who books a day here has the ultimate experience," she said as she stopped in front of a door marked VIP services.

"Right this way, Miss Regina," she said as she entered the room. When they walked in, she noticed it resembled a suite from a 5-star hotel. The furnishings were contemporary and classic. Inside was a sitting area that had a pair of chaise lounge chairs with white mink throws on the backs, a beautiful linen sofa against the wall, a round, sleek metal and glass coffee table between the two chairs and a fully stocked bar over in the corner. There was a large 75-inch flat screen on the wall as well as a surround sound Bose stereo system on the bookshelf. It made you feel like you were in a penthouse in Manhattan, NY. "Welcome to the paradise room, ma'am. This will be your retreat while you wait for Clayton," she said as she spun around like Vanna White, showing off a display of prizes. "Um, what do you mean?" Regina asked, puzzled at the offering. "I mean, please enjoy a complimentary day of pampering and relaxation. Tailored To You," Geneva said, smirking at her reference to the business name.

"I don't understand. I'm only here for a business meeting with Mr. Taylor, not a spa day," Regina said, confused. "Oh, I'm sorry, honey. I know you're here for a meeting, but I thought you would like the opportunity to relax and see what we're all about," she said, knowing this was all Clayton's plan. "Clayton is probably going to be a while, so instead of just sitting around and waiting, please partake in our services, complimentary of course," Geneva said with a smile. "This is very generous of you both, but I just don't think it would be professional to accept a gift like this, you know," Regina said, knowing she could never afford even a nail polish change here. "Don't be silly. We just want you to experience our business. Besides, you can convince your boss he made the right decision taking us on as clients," she said, winking at her. "Come on, relax, sit back, and enjoy your day here. Clayton will be here soon, and then the two of you can go over your business plan or whatever it is you need to do," she added, waving her hand around in the air. "Clayton handles the work; I handle the peace," she said, taking Regina's briefcase from her hand. "You will be fine, and if there's anything you need, just press nine on the phone, and I'll be here. Regina, try to relax and take advantage of this opportunity," Geneva said, trying to ease her nervousness. "Ok, ok, you convinced me to stay, but please make sure to add this to the law firm's fee." She would just find a way to include it in the company finance report without Mr. Price's knowledge. "Whatever you say," Geneva said, smiling as she exited the room. Regina was in awe of the beautiful scene. She had never seen a room so exquisite except on her favorite shows on HGTV. She walked around, touching the lovely fabrics and admiring the delicate pieces all around. She noticed there was another door and walked towards it. She listened intently to make sure it wasn't occupied, then tapped softly and waited for someone to answer. When no one responded, she carefully opened the door, not knowing what to expect. What she saw was amazing. Inside was a huge king-size bed with lush pearl white linens and tons of pillows. The white plush carpet was on the floor, and a beautiful gold vanity sat next to the glass sliding doors. Through the doors was an infinity pool filled with glistening blue water surrounded by marble. Through another door in the bedroom was the bathroom, which was equally stunning.

It had double sinks made of glass as well as a glass shower and steam room, and through another door was the toilet. It was crazy! The bathroom alone was more beautiful and more expensive than her condominium. She went back into the bedroom and noticed a folded note on the vanity. She wasn't going to touch it until she saw her name written in gold letters on the front. She picked it up and read what was inside. "Hello, Ms. Allen. Welcome to Tailored To You exclusive salon and spa. We are pleased that you took time from your busy schedule to join us today. May your time here be enjoyable and your experience beyond your expectations. Sincerely, Clayton Taylor." As Regina read the note, tears welled in her eyes. No one had ever been this kind and sweet to her in her life, and she could never afford a place like this, not even in her wildest dreams. When she entered the bathroom again to get some tissues to wipe her tears, she noticed a scroll sitting on one of the sinks.

She pulled it apart and saw that it was instructions and an itinerary of the day's services for her. She first had to go to the closet in the bedroom, disrobe and put on the beautiful soft robe that was inside, along with the matching slippers. Then she was supposed to go into the bathroom, take a 15 min steam, shower, afterward go out to the bar in the sitting area, pour herself a glass of Moet, gather fresh fruit from the fridge and change into one of the bathing suits that was provided to her and then make her way to the infinity pool to relax before her full body massage. Right before her massage, she was to order lunch from her private chef so that it would be prepared by the time her massage was complete.

Regina could not believe any of what was happening. She felt like she had died and gone to heaven. As she sat in the pool, she wondered if this was how Beyonce and Jay Z lived or maybe the royals Meagan Marple and Prince Harry. She felt like royalty herself as she sipped the delicious fragrant champagne and chomped on the wonderful fresh strawberries and pineapples that were in the fridge. She couldn't believe this was really happening to her. She felt like Julia Roberts in the movie Pretty Woman and was anxious and excited to see what was next. As she leaned back in the pool, she thought to herself, if only James could see her now! She smiled. Her daughter's father always told her that she would never amount to anything without him. He would constantly kill her self-esteem and confidence she had and would make her feel so bad about herself. She was so happy when she finally realized enough was enough and got herself and her daughter away from him.

She knew leaving him was the best thing she could have ever done, but she also knew that it would come with a price. He told her the only way she would ever leave him was in a body bag. She had been on the run for several years, going to different cities where she had hoped he wouldn't find her. But he was crafty, and he always managed to locate her, and she would have to run again. She could never be comfortable anywhere she went. Deciding to come back to Philly was risky, but she figured he would think this would be the last place she would return to because of such bad memories. It had been hard on her when she lived here many years ago as a child, but she knew at the end of the day Philly was home.

After what only felt like a few minutes, Regina was jolted from her thoughts when she heard a male voice come over the intercom. "Hello, Ms. Allen; this is Maurice, your concierge. I am ready to take your lunch order to be prepared by Dominic if you are ready, Madam." Regina was startled at first. She hadn't even known there was an intercom out on the terrace by the pool. "Oh, wow, hello Maurice, um, I haven't even thought about what I would like for lunch. I'm still trying to get used to all this," she said, waving her hand around the pool and towards the bedroom as if he could see her. "Oh, Madam, I am sorry to interrupt you. Would you like a few more moments to decide?" he asked, sounding apologetic. "Oh no, that won't be necessary," Regina said. She felt like she was being ungrateful to the kind man on the speaker.

"I'll just take whatever is on the menu, Maurice." "No, ma'am, this is made to order. Whatever you would like to have, the chef will prepare," Maurice said, making sure she understood she had her own personal chef. "Wow, ok, so I guess I would like some salmon and vegetables and a fresh green salad as well," she said as she started to feel more relaxed. She knew she was starting to feel the champagne she was sipping on, and she had to admit she liked the tingle it was giving her. "Yes, Madam, your lunch will be arriving right after your massage. Would you like a cocktail or more champagne or reading material while you wait?" he asked, making sure she had everything she could possibly want. "Oh goodness no, I'm fine, Maurice, and thank you for asking."

"You are quite welcome, Miss Allen, and if there is anything I can do for you in the meantime, please don't hesitate to ask," he responded in a soothing, friendly tone. "Your massage therapist, Brandon, will be arriving shortly, ma'am. Enjoy," he said and then disconnected from the intercom. Regina took another sip of her champagne and then realized she needed to get out of the pool and dry off for her massage.

As she stood up in the pool, she felt like she was floating. This whole scene and moments were like something right out of a fairy tale. She couldn't wait to tell Monica about this day. She stepped out of the pool onto the marble slat, reached for a towel that was lying on one of the lounge chairs and made her way to the bedroom. As she dried her skin with the supple towel, she looked inside the closet. There, she saw an array of designer dresses. Damn, these are gorgeous, she said aloud as she ran her hands across the expensive fabrics. I wonder who these belong to, she thought.

Just then, she heard a soft knock at the door. She opened it to see a handsome man standing there holding some towels and a bottle of oil. "Good afternoon, Ms. Allen. My name is Brandon, and I'm here to perform your massage, ma'am," he said, smiling at her. "Oh yes, please come in," she said as she stepped aside to let him enter. "Thank you. It will take me a few minutes to set up. If you would like to take a moment to freshen up, have a drink, and change," Brandon said as he went to a closet in the sitting room Regina hadn't even noticed was there. "Uh, yeah, change... change into what?" she asked, confused.

She had never had a full body massage before; actually, she had never had any type of massage at all, for that matter, which was strange since her cousin was a licensed therapist and massage therapist. "Well, ma'am, you can fully disrobe, or you can wear your underwear or bathing suit; it is really your choice," he said in a professional tone. "Ok, I'll just go into the other room and disrobe," Regina said, walking towards the bedroom door. As she started to remove her clothes, she thought there was no reason why she couldn't be naked in front of Brandon. Besides, he looked young enough to be her son, and she knew she would never see him again because there was no way in hell she could afford to come back here on her salary. So, she decided to throw caution to the wind and be totally butt naked for her full-body massage. When she re-entered the sitting area, it had been transformed into a totally different-looking space. The chaises and the coffee table had been removed. A long massage table had been put in its place; the room was dimly lit except for candles placed in every corner. There was the smell of jasmine and mint in the air, along with the sounds of the ocean hitting the rocks on a secluded beach. You could also hear Sade playing in the background, soft and low, "The Sweetest Taboo," she wailed beautifully in perfect melody.

The complete setup was enchanting. Regina stood for a moment, taking everything in, and the only word that could come out of her mouth was, "Wow." "I hope everything is to your liking," Brandon asked as he folded down the sheets on the table. "Everything is perfect," she replied as she looked around the room. "Great, so we can get started whenever you're ready," Brandon said as he gestured for her to get on the table. "I will step out of the room so that you can take off your robe and get under the sheets," he said politely and stepped out into the hallway. Regina walked over to the table and removed her robe. She carefully got onto the table and laid down, raising the cool sheets up onto her skin, and closed her eyes. She had never experienced something like this before, but she was ready, and a few seconds later, she heard Brandon's voice as he gently placed his strong, warm hands on her shoulders, "Ms. Allen, we will now begin."

15

CLAYTON

Clayton pulled into the garage of his building downtown, and he felt great. Geneva had called to let him know that Regina had arrived, and she was getting the full experience pamper package he requested. He was extremely excited to see her reaction when she was done, and he was looking forward to taking her out on the town later that evening. He noticed how pretty she was at her office, but he knew after a makeover at his studio, she would be a showstopper. As he stepped out of his truck, he admired himself from the reflection of his Beemer. "Damn, you look good, bro," he said to himself as he smiled. He was glad he chose a casual look today. He wore a pair of Armani jeans with a white strip on the sides, a Givenchy button-down and a belt, and his footwear was a pair of low-cut Air Force 1's new out of the box. He had his barber stop by that morning to give him a fresh cut and detail his beard to perfection. As he glanced once more in the side view mirror, he put on his aviators and walked towards the elevator. He was in a terrific mood and was glad that his weekend projector report had exceeded all expectations.

Yeah, Tailored To You was a success, and he was well on his way to being the next African American billionaire along with Jay Z and Kanye.

As he waited for the elevator, he thought back to when he first knew he wanted to make women beautiful. He was only eight years old, and his mama used to make him shampoo his hair and shave woman legs. "Boy, get in here and wash this ho's head before Smitty starts fussing about her not being ready." "Yes, ma'am," he would say as he climbed up on the wooden box at the sink to reach the woman who bent over it. At the time, he hated doing it because as he reached over them, all he could smell was stale cigarettes and liquor seeping from their skin. It used to make him feel nauseous, but after he lathered their scalp with the berry shampoo Mama used, they would smell as fresh as clean laundry dried by the sunshine. "Mama Taylor's son sure does know how to use of them hands," the women would say to Mama. "My head feels cleaner than a baby's bottom," they would shout with laughter. "Thank you, honey. I'm grooming him for success," Mama would say.

At the end of the day, she would tell me there's no shame in being a man and making a woman beautiful. "I know it seems like a woman's work right now, but baby, let me tell you, the future is bright. Beauty is gonna be all a woman wants and desires. You take my word for it, Ya hear?, and you are gonna already have the know-how to make it happen." Clayton smiled as he thought of his mother's words and wished she could see him now. He was one of the top hair stylists and makeup artists in the Game, and he knew she would be immensely proud of him. When the elevator doors opened, he stepped inside and rode up the two floors to his private office. He had the architect design the building that way so that he would have his own private entrance and exit just in case he needed a quick getaway. Even though it had been many years since that awful night in North Carolina, and Clayton hadn't had any issues, he was still cautious.

When the doors opened, he grinned as he walked into the room. There was a bottle of 1800 chilling in a bucket next to his desk, as always, and a bouquet of summer flowers that made the room smell like a garden in the vineyard. Laying on the sofa was a demo of the new uniforms he ordered for all the employees. He knew they had arrived, and Geneva put one in his office so that he could see the finished product. As he walked over to the sofa, she came into the room. "Well, hello there, handsome," she said, eyeing him up and down, admiring the lay he chose. "Don't you look like a page straight out of GQ magazine," she commented. "Thank you, bae," he responded, knowing he definitely picked the right outfit.

"Your Cinderella is in stage 3 of her session, Prince Charming," she said sarcastically as she went over to the bar to pour herself a drink. She knew Clay's first question was gonna be about Regina. "Thank you, smart ass, but I wasn't gonna ask about her just yet. I was actually about to comment on how great these uniforms looked," he said as he held up the nice smock that was lying there. "Oh yeah, they are pretty dope," she said, looking at it in his hand. Darin, his best friend and up-and-coming designer, had done a fantastic job with the engraving and artwork. "They sure are. He captured every design I asked him about, and then some," Clay said as he examined each article of clothing. Darin owned PARADUX, an exclusive apparel company to the stars, and he happened to be Clayton's right-hand man. "The staff is gonna look great in these. I can't wait to present them at the Gala next month," Clayton said, thinking about the big party he was hosting to launch the openings of his three new spas in New York, California, and Atlanta. It had been a long and stressful process, but Clayton Alexander Taylor was finally on top. "Deva, baby, this Gala is gonna be outta this world," he said as he walked over to her and twirled her around. "I made the final arrangements this morning, and I couldn't be happier. We've got the ballroom at the Ritz Carlton, and the catering will be done by none other than Chef Gordon Ramsey. Isn't that fantastic?" he said as he lifted her in the air. "That's amazing!" She screamed as he lifted her.

"How'd you ever pull that off?" she asked, curious about how he got one of the most famous chefs in America to host his event. "Girl, it ain't about how you know but who you know," he said as he poured himself a shot of Tequila. "Remember a few months ago when I went to Atlantic City to see Dominic do a cooking battle at Chef Ramsay's restaurant in Caesars Hotel and Casino? Well, Chef Ramsay was there, and I got a chance to meet him. He actually said he remembered seeing me in the Forbes Top Businessmen issue, and he was impressed. I explained that I was expanding and that I was throwing one of the biggest galas Philadelphia had ever seen to launch the new studios, and he said he would be honored to cater the event. How do you like that, woman?" Clay exclaimed as he sipped on the strong libations. "That is wonderful, shug. I knew you would succeed," Geneva said, proud of her partner and friend. "I am super excited about this party, baby. I have to go shopping for the right outfit," she said, contemplating her wardrobe choices for the extravagant event. "I might have Darin hook me up with a bomb-ass gown," she replied with a twirl as she headed for the door. "Well, you know I'm gonna be drippy," Clay said, admiring himself in the huge full-length mirror on the wall. "You are such an arrogant asshole," Geneva kidded, fondly teasing Clayton. She loved him dearly and couldn't be more excited for his success. "Arrogant, confident, and fine as hell," he responded with a grin.

16

REGINA

After her massage, Regina ate her delicious lunch by the pool. She sat back in one of the lounge chairs and looked over the terrace at the magnificent view of the city. The sun was shining brightly in the sky, and she felt like she was on top of the world. She was anticipating her next session on her itinerary, which was a mani Pedi and fresh cucumber facial. She had never had a full-service treatment like that before, and she was beyond thrilled. She was still wearing the robe she'd put on after Brandon worked her body over in ways she had never felt before. It seemed as if he rubbed away all of her anxiety, fears and tension, if only for that moment, and she felt amazing. As she sipped her 4th cocktail, she thought that the champagne tasted like liquid gold as it went down her throat, and she felt warm and safe inside as she listened to Roberta Flack and Donny Hathaway sing out where is the love in the background. It made her start to wonder where her love was. She had been lonely for the last few years since fleeing from North Carolina. She never stayed any place long enough to have a real relationship with any man, and all she relied on for any sexual pleasure was her vibrating rose and pictures of Idris Alba on her laptop. She longed to be desired again, to feel the soft embrace of a man, but frankly, she could have just used a passionate, hard fuck to make her orgasm straight to the moon. She chuckled aloud at her thoughts.

What a difference a dick makes, she hummed. When she got up to reach for the remote to change songs, she heard a knock on the door. "Come in, I'm on the terrace," she yelled into the other room, assuming it was the young lady coming in to do her nails, feet and facial. She was totally taken by surprise when Clayton entered in all his fine glory. "Oh, hello, Clayton," Regina responded nervously, not expecting him. "Hello, beautiful," Clayton said in his deep sultry voice. "Are you enjoying yourself?" He asked, amused by the way she was lounging in the chair. "Oh, my goodness, yes, this is gorgeous," she stuttered, looking around as she sat upright and pulled her robe tighter against her so as not to expose any unnecessary skin. "Well, I'm glad you are enjoying yourself, my dear. There's much more ahead," Clayton said, delighted as he turned to leave the suite. "Clayton, wait," Regina called out.

"Um, aren't I supposed to be here for a business meeting?" She asked, wondering why he was about to leave her suite. "Yes, you are, pretty lady, and this is the first half of the meeting," he said as he gently kissed her hands. Regina felt her whole body quiver from his lips. "Now, go back to relaxing. Get your facial, and I'll be back to see how everything is going," he said, leaving the room. Regina was stuck in the spot; she was in a trance from his Tom Ford cologne. "That man smells amazing, and he has got me all the way turned out," she thought to herself. She went back over to the stereo and played the Prince track If I Were Your Girlfriend. Every lyric of that song was how she felt about Clayton right in that moment. She sang each word as if she were serenading him with poetry. While she listened, she closed her eyes and imagined him walking up close to her. She could feel his breath softly on her skin. He was untying her robe and sliding it slowly to the floor.

Then he would start kissing her lightly on her neck, working his way down to her shoulders. Next, his hands would gently rub up her body from her hips until he reached her full, firm breasts, and he caressed them. He reached down and started to suck on each nipple, pulling and tugging while she moaned in ecstasy. He would then lift her and take her over to the bed, where he would lay her down and start to lick her body. His tongue is moist and soft. Around her sides on her stomach, softly licking her hips and thighs, reaching every crevice of her frame until he made it to her moist, pillowy, soft center. He grabbed her knees and pushed them back, exposing her dripping wet womanhood. He devoured her, savoring every drop. Regina moaned softly as her hands wandered across her body like they were Clayton's lips, and just as she was near climax, she heard the door again. She jumped up from the bed and quickly put her robe back on. She was flushed from her exotic reenactment. "Uh, just a min," she shouted as she got herself together. This time, she went to the door and opened it. It was Natasha, the technician who was there to do her mani and Pedi. "Hello, Ms. Allen. Are you ready for your treatment?" She asked in a cheerful tone. "Yes," Regina responded, sheepish and embarrassed. She was ready in more ways than anyone could have imagined, but not for the treatment Natasha was there to perform.

17
EVELYN

When Evelyn finally opened her eyes, she saw that it was morning. The curtains had been opened, and the sun was shining brightly in her bedroom. She had never gotten back up out of bed after getting home with Ethan the night before. She was still in her gown, and her makeup was smeared on her pillow. When she sat up, she felt her head pounding. She realized she hadn't eaten anything since the following day, and her mouth felt like cotton. When she reached over to the nightstand for her aspirin, she saw a note from Ethan along with a long black velvet box. Ignoring the gift, she grabbed the pill bottle and popped two ibuprofen dry. As she stood to her feet, she felt lightheaded. She made her way to the bathroom. When she passed the full-length mirror, she stopped and stared at the disheveled figure she saw. "What is happening to your life?" She said to her image in the mirror. "How is everything going so wrong?" She whimpered as tears started to flow from her eyes, slowly bringing her black mascara down her cheeks. She turned and walked slowly into the bathroom. There, she took off her gown and turned on the shower. As she walked back over to the sink to remove the remainder of her makeup, Henrietta's voice came over the intercom.

Good morning, Mrs. Price. I see from the motion sensors that you are up. Would you like some coffee, Madam?" She asked with concern in her voice. Mr. Price had informed her that Evelyn wasn't feeling well and asked her to prepare some soup for lunch. "Thank you, Henrietta. Coffee would be great right now, and some dry toast, place it on the terrace in my bedroom. I will get it when I'm done with my shower," Evelyn responded, thankful she had such a caring house-keeper. "Right away, Mrs. Price," Henrietta responded. As Evelyn stepped into the shower, she felt her heart begin to race, and her body started to tremble. She was having an anxiety attack. She quickly got out of the shower, went to the medicine cabinet, took the last two yellow pills in an unmarked bottle and sat on the side of her claw foot tub. "No, dammit, you will not crumble, Alisha," she said aloud. "This is not the end," she kept repeating as Henrietta entered the bedroom. "Mrs. Price, are you ok?" She asked toward the door. Evelyn quickly rose to her feet, "Uh, yes, Henrietta, I'm fine. Just leave the coffee and go," she said as she closed the bathroom door. Henrietta was concerned for her. She had seen her on several occasions talking to herself and recalled her saying the name Alisha.

For a woman who, on the outside, appeared to have it all together, Henrietta had seen her break down on many occa-sions. She was informed when she was hired a few years ago by Mr. Price that his wife had suffered from post-traumatic stress disorder since the loss of her grandparents and that she was on medication to control her symptoms but that her condition was managed and not to worry. However, Henrietta had noticed Evelyn's condition worsening. Lately, she was asked to refill her prescription for her medication more often, and Evelyn seemed more jittery and on edge. "No problem, Mrs. Price. Your coffee is on the terrace, and your medication refill is in the safe, as requested. If you need anything else, I'll be downstairs, ma'am," Henrietta stated as she exited the room. Evelyn sat at her vanity in the bathroom and waited for the pills to kick in. She gazed at herself in the mirror, trying to make sense of all that was going on. Her life had been great up until 24 hours ago, but now it was all spiraling out of control.

"Look, if you say you love me, then you will help me do this," Alisha said to Clayton in the back seat of his mama's 1961 Desoto. They had just finished having sex, something they had been doing for over a year now, and Alisha was again trying to convince him that if he helped her, they could have all the money they could ever need and be together forever. "I don't know, Lee-lee," Clayton said. "I'm scared we could get caught. I cannot afford to put my mama through no more drama; she already got enough, don't you understand that?" he pleaded as he pulled up his ball shorts. "Really, Clay, you're scared of getting caught? Well, I'm scared of what's gonna happen to me now that Candy is dead at the hands of those bastards!" she screamed, tears rolling down her face. "I watched them pump her with drugs all because they had to keep making money off her. She tricked and sold her body for those assholes and made them tons of money, and all they ever did was abuse her, treat her like shit, and damn it, they are gonna pay!" Her voice dripped with hatred and revenge. "Baby, I know, and I'm so sorry about your mom," Clayton said, thinking about the hooker Candy his mama used to make beautiful. He hadn't seen her since Smitty had made her and Alisha move in with the twins for a debt, but he knew from Alisha that she had gotten strung out pretty bad on drugs and that she had all but given up on life.

"I know you wanna hurt them and have them locked up for what they did to her, but babe, you gotta know they are ruthless and don't care about shit," he stated, trying to sound as sincere as possible. "Have them locked up? No, I wanna see them dead just like my mama," she whispered in a low evil voice. Alisha was devastated when Candy died a few weeks prior. She had come home from a movie with Clayton and saw her mama's clothes had been in a pile on the floor in the living room. "What's going on?" she had asked Kim, who was sitting on the sofa smoking a Newport. "It's not good," Lee said as she nodded toward the stairs. When Alisha walked into the hallway, she saw Jacob standing in the stairwell. "Hey, little bits, something happened to your mama," he said sympathetically. "What? What happened to her?" Alisha asked as her heart started to race. "Well, she was smoking that shit with one of her tricks, and he said she just stopped breathing. I don't know, you're gonna have to talk to James; he can tell you more," he said as he walked down the steps and out the front door.

"Mr. Jacob, wait, where is my mama, and where is Mr. James?" Alisha cried. He took her down to the hospital. He had to get her out of there before someone called the cops. "Look, just wait for him to get back, and he'll tell you every-thing that's going on," he said and climbed into his silver Maserati that was parked in front of the house. Alisha was in a state of shock. She ran upstairs to her mama's room.

After they had moved into the twin's house, mama seemed to have gone into a deep depression once they started living there, and Alisha could tell her spirit had been broken. Her once beautiful brown eyes were dull and lifeless. She had changed from being the fast-talking, feisty call girl who could scam and charm anyone to becoming a hollowed shell of a woman who had nothing left to live for, not even Alisha, whom she loved very much and would have killed for. Alisha remembered that just a few days ago, she noticed she was acting strange.

As they sat on the front stoop, Candy stared at her daughter. "What's wrong, mama?" Alisha asked, concerned about her. "There's some things I wanted to tell you, baby," she said, sounding tired. "I wanted you to know how much I love you and that bringing you into this world was the best decision I ever made," she said as tears welled in her eyes. "Aww, mama, I love you too, but why all the seriousness today?" Alisha asked jokingly but was slightly afraid because she had never seen Candy sympathetic or emotional. "Oh, I just wanted you to know that no matter what this world brings to you, I pray it's a life way better than what I gave you or at least better than mine, that you live it to the fullest and that you always be grateful to God because without him you'd be dead and in the ground," Candy replied.

"Ok, mama, you starting to freak me out. Why you talking all Spiritual and shit?" Alisha asked, really frightened now because Candy hardly ever spoke about God or even uttered a religious word in all of Alisha's 16 years.

She knew her mama believed in God and that she was raised in the church all the way up till she ran away from home at the age of 13, but she had never really spoken about God before or had she ever taken Alisha to church. The closest she had ever gotten to religion was when Candy would let her go to Sunday services with Clayton and his mama when they lived with Smitty, so this was coming as a surprise to her by the words her mama spoke. Candy knew she was spiraling out of control now that she was using heroin and felt her life slipping by. She was closer to death than she had ever been when she started shooting up, and her life was closer to the end every day. The drug had taken hold of her, and it was impossible to let go, and her desire for it grew stronger each and every day. She really wasn't concerned about her life ending at this point since it had been crushed when she took her first taste of the deadly poison in her veins, but her heart broke every time she thought about leaving Alisha out on these streets. Unfortunately, at this point, Candy knew her death was inevitable. There was nothing left for her to do to save her only baby girl. She knew she was too far gone. She just hoped and prayed that Alisha would see what these streets had done to her and do better. "I'm trying to get you to understand that there is more out there for you, baby. A life that has promise and goodness regardless of what you've seen here," Candy said as tears rolled down her cheeks. "I want you to leave this awful place and seek something more fulfilling," she continued. "No, mama, I'm not leaving you. Why are you saying things like that?" Alisha cried. "Because I know things are only gonna get worse," Candy responded. She knew she didn't have the strength anymore to fight for her daughter and knew that it was only a matter of time before the twins would try to put Alisha to work.

They had been eyeing her a lot lately and making comments about how Candy had been strung out on drugs and their money had suffered. They noticed how beautiful their daughter was becoming. Now that she was 16, she had developed into a stunning young lady. She was the spitting image of Candy in her young days. She was tall and curvy with full lips and a size DD cup. She had grown up and out. Her skin was smooth and golden like honey, and she had the sass to match. Candy was afraid that they would make her get on the strip sooner rather than later. She had put fear in Smitty some years back, but the twins were different, and Alisha was older now. Besides, back then, Candy wasn't doing the hard drugs. She would have gutted Smitty without hesitation if she ever laid a finger on her daughter, but she wasn't addicted to heroin, and the twins were a different kind of fearless. Candy had witnessed things the twins did that would put the fear in even the strongest man, and she knew she wasn't a match for them. They could manipulate people to do whatever they wanted, and they enjoyed bringing pain both physically and emotionally to people.

They made sure Candy had her supply of drugs to keep her weak and obedient, and even though they were mad she wasn't pulling in the cash and clientele like she used to, they knew she had a new sweet piece of meat staying just across the hall waiting to be groomed given the chance. They figured, eventually, she would be so strung out she wouldn't notice or care that they got a hold of Alisha. James had told Kim to hang out with her more because they figured they could get her to turn Alisha out. Kim was the best money maker in the house at that point because she was young and only smoked weed. All the money she made went to the twins, and she never stashed any away for drugs.

She wasn't the best thing to look at, but she had a body that turned men on. She stood about 5'4 and had short, curly reddish-brown hair. Her brown eyes were big and round and set deep into her face, and she was missing a front tooth. It was rumored that her old pimp knocked it out for coming up short with his money. She had long, thin legs that were bruised, but she had a humongous behind that could barely fit on a fold-up chair. It was hard to tell she was part Dominican by looking at her because her striking, attractive looks had vanished and been replaced by hard cold features that now showed, except when she spoke, she had a strong Spanish accent, and tricks loved when she yelled poppy while they were fucking her.

Her father ran the fruit stand a mile away, and you could see the hurt in his eyes every time she passed in a car or on foot on her way to the house or the alley to give a trick a blowjob. Her mother had gotten strung out on crack a few years before and had given a local Jon her daughter as payment to get high when she was only 14 years old, and she had been a prostitute since. She was only 19, but Kim had aged badly in those five years. You could see the abuse, the beatings and the torment she suffered in her eyes. Her mama had been killed a few years back for trying to rob a trick. He had choked and suffocated her in an alley after realizing she had taken his wallet while she was giving him head. Her body lay there for days before she was discovered by her daughter. But Kim really didn't have any emotion about her mother's death because she had sold her for drugs years prior, and to Kim, her mother was already dead. It made Kim emotionless and bitter, and she never forgave her for ruining her life. Kim wasn't close to her father either; she felt like he should have saved her and her mama from such a horrible life, and he did nothing to protect his little girl.

"Girl, get outta that room before twin gets back here and whips yo ass," Kim yelled up the steps to Alisha. She liked the young girl and didn't want the fate that she had to be bestowed on her. Alisha knew Kim was looking out for her because when James returned, they both knew he was gonna be furious. This wasn't the first time a ho had died in here, and he knew the heat was gonna be on the house for sure.

Alisha came down the stairs, walked into the living room, and sat next to Kim. "What happened to my mama?" Alisha asked in a trembling voice. Kim hung her head, feeling sorry for this young soul. "Girl, yo mama was a ho. She was on that shit, and, honestly, she lost her fight." Tears rolled down Alisha's face as she listened to the fate that fell on her mama. "At about 4 o'clock, she came downstairs amped up, looking for a hit. James told her he wasn't gonna give her no more horse, seeing as though she had been getting high all day. Well, she got dressed and went out on the stroll, and about 10 minutes later, she came back with a trick. It was dirty-ass Sunny from in town, and you know all he does is smoke dope and fuck hard," Kim explained. "Well, he must have caught a Vic earlier in the day because he had a pocket full of money. Anyway, he bought about 100 dollars worth of crack from James and told ya mama that once they were done, he'd give her 100 dollars for herself."

"They went upstairs, and about 20 mins later, we heard Candy screaming. Instead of James going to see what was happening, he figured Sunny was just fucking her real hard, and he paid it no mind. He knew when Sunny took a hit of that shit, he turned into a beast. That's why a lot of the hos never liked dating him because he was rough with them. Eventually, the screaming stopped, and Sunny came out of the room looking real zombie-like. He bought 100 dollars more crack and left. When James went up to get his cut from the date, yo mama lay trembling and foaming at the mouth on the floor. She was naked and had the syringe still in her arm. Her eyes were open, and she had a bag of dope in her hand." Alisha trembled as she listened to this horrific story. "So, wait, Sunny killed my mama?" Alisha asked, becoming angry. "No, Suga, that shit killed yo mama. She must have tried to shoot up the crack instead of waiting to get some horse afterward," Kim said. "She wanted to get high so bad she would have put comet in her veins." Kim noticed her shaking and put her arm around her shoulder. "Listen, little bits, there was nothing nobody could do. Candy was too far gone, baby; she's at peace now, you gotta believe that. Don't you go worrying yourself sick," Kim said, trying to comfort her. "You just got to figure out your next move before the twins get back. They ain't gonna let you stay here without putting yo ass on those streets," Kim said, afraid for the teenager. "If I were you, I'd get outta here as fast as you can, 'cause who knows what they gonna do," Kim cautioned. "I ain't got nowhere to go, Kim. What am I gonna do? I ain't got no money, no family, nothing," Alisha said, scared for her life.

"Just then, Kim reached into her bosom and pulled out a wad of cash. 'You take this, and you leave. Go find somewhere, anywhere better than here, you hear me?' she said. 'This life ain't for you,' she told her. 'I done seen more than I should have, and I know this is the only thing my life is gonna be,' Kim said sadly. 'Why don't you come with me, Kim? We could leave together,' Alisha pleaded, not wanting to leave the only female friend she ever had. 'Kim was like a sister to her and taught her a lot about the streets and the con game. 'We could go to Philly or New York, make our own money there. You told me you had friends in Philly; maybe we could go and stay with them; what do you say?' Alisha asked, pleading with her friend to leave that awful place with her. 'I can't, little bits, my daddy needs me,' Kim said, as tears welled in her eyes. Even though Kim barely spoke to her father, she still watched out for him. He was the only family she had left, and she knew he only ran that fruit stand down the road to be near her. 'There was nothing he could do to take her away from that life now, but he stayed around to protect her the best he could regardless. 'No, you take this money, and you get outta here. I'll be fine. Make a good life for yourself if you can, and don't turn into no ho or fiend like your mama, you hear?' Kim said. 'She was really gonna miss Alisha; she was the only loyal friend she ever had, and when they spent time together, she felt happy."'

She had lost her sister when she ran away from home, and Alisha was the closest thing she would ever get to another one. She put the money in her hands and looked her in the eyes. "Look, go get some of your things and go, please. I couldn't live with myself if anything happened to you," Kim said, now crying herself. "The twins are evil, and they are not gonna let money slip through their fingers. They been examining you for a long time, and they were gonna make their move real soon on you; that's why yo mama was so depressed. She knew there was nothing she could do, and that's why she started getting high so much. She felt lost, disconnected from life, Sugg, there was nothing left for her here except you, and she felt like she failed you too," she told Alisha. "She used to tell me how she wanted a better life for you; she just couldn't give it to you, but you've got a chance. Do you hear me? A chance to be somebody, so you go and make your mama proud. I love you, little bits, now go," Kim said as she gently nudged her to stand.

Alisha ran up the flight of steps back to Candy's room. She grabbed a bag and put in it all the things that meant something to her and her mama. She found the picture of the two of them the day she bought her home. One of the nurses had taken it for her at the hospital. It was tattered and worn, but Candy kept it in a frame on her nightstand every day. When she looked in her dresser, she found a chain and locket that Candy kept safely under her belongings. In it, there was a picture of Candy's Grandmom, the woman Alisha was named after. She grabbed the locket and placed it carefully in the bag. She grabbed a couple of articles of clothing and shoes that she liked, and that were still in good condition from her closet, and right before she exited the room, she noticed a wooden box under the bed. Knowing she didn't have much time to look at it, she threw it in the bag and headed back down the steps.

There was nothing in her room she needed or wanted, for that matter, so she had had all she needed and was ready to go. She had put the money Kim had given her down in her underwear, a trick Candy had shown her so she wouldn't lose it. Kim had given her fifteen hundred dollars, and Alisha wondered where she had gotten all that money. Kim wasn't a thief or addict, and she always turned all her money over to the twins because she didn't want no trouble out of them for not pulling her weight, so Alisha wondered where she got all that loot. When she got back downstairs, Kim was cooking in the kitchen.

"What you doing, Kim?" Alisha asked, watching her peel potatoes. "I figured I'd make James something to eat and have it ready when he gets back. He's gonna be in a bad mood, but I figure if he has a meal prepared, it'll lessen his anger," Kim responded. "You got everything you need, little bits?" she asked as she rose from the kitchen table. "Yeah, I guess. I just wish I wasn't leaving you like this, you know?" Alisha said, feeling sad. "Aww, me too, Suga," Kim said as she hugged the young girl. "But this is how it gotta be. Your time here has run its course, and now it's time for you to get out there and see what this world has in store for you. Don't you settle for less in life, ya hear?" Kim said as she took Alisha's face in her hands. "I love you, little bits. You take care," Kim said as she kissed her on the forehead. Alisha grabbed her bag and walked slowly to the front door. She looked back, closed her eyes, and thought of Candy. "I'm leaving, mama, and I'm gonna miss you, but I promise I'm gonna get even with those bastards if it's the last thing I do," she said aloud and then walked out into the dark of night.

18

ETHAN

Ethan had a headache by the time he went up to his bedroom. He had been worrying about his wife half the night. Their perfect evening had turned into a disaster in a matter of moments, and for his life, he couldn't understand what happened. His day had been perfect. He had acquired a new client that would make his law firm the top in the country. He had bought his wife the most stunning gift he had ever purchased, and he had finally made his last payments to the twins, which, for him, was his biggest accomplishment of all. He was finally freed from those bastards, and they no longer had a hold on his life. He felt the weight lifted off his back. He had been indebted to them for three years, and today, he had cut the ties. He owed them 10 million dollars plus interest, which he thought was an insane amount, but he knew if he wanted to succeed, he'd have to take the deal. He made a lot of money off cases their crew retained him for, but it never seemed to be enough; thank goodness he had other clients to help him foot the bill. His wife had known he had a large loan to repay, but she never knew to whom. She had offered him the money on many occasions, but he always declined because he knew that would strip him of his manhood and get her involved in his seedy business, and he never would allow that to happen. Evelyn was always there for him, showing support any way she could, helping him get clients and doing fundraisers for the firm, but Ethan would only let her get so much involved. He never told her about him being friends with Snake when he was a teen, and he definitely would never tell her about his involvement with the twins and their illegal history. No, that was something he felt he would take to his grave. He loved his wife and vowed never to keep anything from her, but certain elements of his past were taboo even to the woman he loved.

When he entered the bedroom, Evelyn was asleep. She had been locked in the bathroom for what felt like hours before she went upstairs to lie down. She was still in her gown from earlier, but Ethen was too mentally exhausted to wake her and have her take it off. He was hoping they could finally make love tonight since it had been so long since he felt her skin next to his. He had been so busy with work and taking trips out of town for business that whenever he was at home, he was too tired to perform his husbandly duties. He was glad that Evelyn had a trusty rabbit and an extensive porn collection to keep her satisfied when he wasn't there. He was so looking forward to making love to her. He had even had his secretary go to Victoria's Secret and pick up a sexy thong to wear under her dress. He was hoping they could start their lovemaking in the car and then fuck all over the house like they used to when they first got married. His wife was a freak, and he loved that about her. When they first started dating, she would come by the office and give him a quick blowjob during his lunch break, and sometimes she would even let him screw her in the executive washroom if she was in the mood. She always took care of him and made sure he was happy. But tonight had been ruined. She had met him downtown for dinner, and as soon as she stepped out of the car, she became deathly pale.

He just couldn't wrap his mind around why, though. She had seemed okay earlier on the phone, and even when she called to let him know she was on her way, everything seemed to be wonderful. Ethan was positive she was pregnant, and she didn't know how to tell him. Man, it would be great to finally have a child, he thought. He absolutely loved children. He thought how great it would be to pass on his legacy. He remembered telling his aunt Mae when he was a boy that he was gonna be rich and famous and have lots of kids, but so far, only half of that was true because Evelyn was dead set against it. She said her childhood was filled with too many bad memories and that she wasn't capable of giving a child the love and nurturing they deserved. Ethan could never understand why she felt that way. She was such a loving and kind soul, and he knew she would have made a terrific mom. So, he never pressed the issue, and he saw that she always kept a supply of birth control and condoms handy whenever they did have sex. But maybe, just maybe, the last time they were together, the condom had broken. There was the possibility. They had both been drinking heavily that night, and Evelyn was filled with uncontrollable passion. She let him put her in positions they had never done before, and he had busted a nut so hard he felt it down in his toes.

"Damn baby, what you trying to do to me?" Ethan remembered asking her while they were sprawled out on the dining room floor. "What do you mean?" She asked playfully while she traced the sweat that was on his brow. "I'm just trying to keep my man satisfied so that he won't go out in the streets and find some hooches mama to do it," she said as she worked her hand down to his genitals. "Whoa baby, what you doing?" Ethan said as he grabbed her hand, "Little papa's not ready for round 3 yet," he said playfully as he placed her fingers into his mouth. They had been screwing for over 2 hours, and he was surprised she was still so hungry for more. He was sure she had climaxed at least four times already. "Come on, baby, I can't get enough of daddy's long, big stuff," she said in a seductive tone. "Daddy?" Ethan raised his brow, "Since when did you start calling me daddy?" He asked. "Since now," Evelyn responded. "That's a trick term," he said, remembering how the hookers down Girard Ave would try to pick up dates by calling the unsuspecting vics daddy. "What the hell is that supposed to mean?" She asked, offended, as she sat up off the floor. "I didn't mean anything by it, babe. I was just saying that's a word hookers would use, that's all," Ethan replied, not sure why Evelyn all of a sudden got up from his embrace. "Are you ok, babe?" he asked. She seemed to have lost the heat that was generating from her skin. "Yeah, I'm fine. I just don't like it when you start talking about prostitution, that's all," she said, thinking back about Candy. Ethan had no idea about her past, so he was puzzled by her reaction.

"I think it's funny, that's all," he said, amused. "You think what's funny?" she asked defensively. "I was just thinking maybe you wanted to roll play, that's all. I could be the Jon and you the ho," he said jokingly. "Well, that shit ain't funny, ok? And I would never wanna play that type of game with you, ever. You understand?" she said angrily.

Evelyn pulled away from Ethan's grasp and went to stand up. "Wait, baby, where are you going? I was just playing around, that's all. Don't be so serious; I was just joking around," he said, feeling bad he had said something so stupid. "Ok," she replied hesitantly and laid back in the cuff of his arm. "Listen, I don't know why I said such a dumb thing like that. I would never think of you that way, and I'm sorry," he said, hoping to ease the tension that had suddenly cast over their mood. "It's ok, babe. I just don't like talking about things like that, ok?" She said as she thought about her friend Kim. "No problem, I will never bring it up again. So, with that being said, how about we start warming up for round 3?" He asked as his hand traveled down to her soft middle. "That sounds just fine to me," she whispered as she climbed on top of him and inserted his now rock-hard penis into her moistness. They had fucked continuously for an hour longer, and he knew he had come inside her at least twice during that time, and secretly he was hoping at least one or two of those little soldiers would penetrate and produce a seed. He smiled, thinking back to that night.

While he lay next to his lovely wife in bed, he noticed his penis starting to swell. "Dammit," he said out loud. He wished she didn't have a meltdown tonight because he realized he was horny as a teenage virgin and needed to release some tension now. He quietly climbed out of bed and went into the bathroom. He turned on the shower and figured the cold water would calm his horniness and maybe allow him to get some sleep. When he got into the shower, the cool water felt exhilarating on his skin. He stood there as the water flowed from the multi-jetted shower head. It felt comforting to him as the jets massaged his tight muscles. He reached for his body wash and started to lather up. As his hands moved across his tightly defined body, he felt the blood flowing down to his manhood. "What the hell?" he said out loud and took his pipe into hand. He started imagining Evelyn in the red thong he bought for her, and it didn't take long before he exploded with pure delight and pleasure. When he was done pleasing himself, he grabbed his loofa and washed his body clean. When he got out of the shower, he wrapped a soft, oversized towel around his waist and went back into the bedroom. Evelyn was still asleep, snoring lightly. He took out the black velvet box from his suit jacket that held the eight-caret platinum diamond bracelet he had bought for her. When he opened the box, he smiled proudly. He had made it, he thought to himself.

He was finally able to afford the finer things for his beautiful wife, and he knew she was gonna absolutely love this gift. He noticed her eyeing it on a woman's arm at a dinner party they attended last spring in New York, and she had even inquired about it to their jeweler one day when they went to have her wedding ring cleaned. They were told that the estimated cost of a gem that unique was close to a million dollars. Well, even though they were both well off, it was way too expensive for them at the time. But Ethan knew Evelyn really wanted it, so when he closed the deal with Clayton earlier that day, he knew that was the gift he had to give to his wife. He felt like

George Jefferson because he was definitely moving on upward. He sat the box on her nightstand for her to see it in the morning when she woke up and then kissed her softly on the forehead. He climbed into bed and spooned up close to her to take in her sweet scent. As he held her, he silently said a prayer for how lucky his life was. Little did he know his happy ending was about to become a terrifying nightmare.

19

REGINA AND CLAYTON

Regina had been at Tailored To You for over 4 hours now, and she had never felt more beautiful in her life. She had gotten a complete beauty makeover, and she felt like Cinderella in a fairy tale. Clayton had come in from time to time to check on her and make sure she was being taken care of, but she couldn't thank him enough for his generosity. He had even asked her out to dinner once her transformation was done, and after heavy prodding, she had finally agreed. She felt and looked so beautiful she didn't want this day to end. She had called her cousin and asked her to check in on Nyla, so there was nothing stopping her from going out and having a great time with this handsome man. She put on the gorgeous black and white Valentino dress and stunning Christian Louboutin stilettos that were in the closet, and she felt like she was floating in the air. She had never seen herself look so beautiful.

Her hair was done impeccably, and it wasn't out of place. The stylist suggested an updo to show the lovely features of her face, and the makeup artist chose soft, natural colors to bring out her glowing skin tone. Her fingers down to her toes were tingling with excitement.

She took several pics of herself in the full-length mirror to remind her she wasn't dreaming. As she was posing, she heard Clayton enter the suite. "My, my, my, don't you look lovely," he said as he eyed Regina lustfully. "Thank you," she said as she quickly stuffed her phone into her coach bag. "Are you ready to go?" He asked, anxiously anticipating their evening out on the town. "Yes, I am," Regina smiled. Clayton looked amazing in a dark blue Italian suit he had changed into for their date. He had made dinner reservations at Morton's steak house and wanted to look his best for Regina. He knew she was going to look wonderful after her makeover, and he was not disappointed at the results. "Damn, we are a fine-ass couple," he said as he escorted her into the salon lobby.

Regina was all smiles as they made their way down the hall. Geneva was at the reception desk when they walked up. "Wow, you too look fly as hell," she said as she admired her friend and his lovely date. "Thank you, baby," Clayton said as he smiled and winked at her. "Regina, you are truly a show stopper, honey," Geneva boasted loudly. "I do clean up well," Regina responded to the compliment. "You were beautiful, to begin with, honey; all we did was add to your package," Geneva said, trying to give the shy woman more confidence. "You even make this man look better," she added, pointing to Clayton. "Indeed, she does. Thanks, Deva," he replied, glad to see his partner happy for him. Geneva felt so proud of Clayton. He seemed really happy, and she felt like, this time, he had truly found the one he had been searching for.

"Hey, so we are gonna head on out to the Restaurant. We have reservations at seven," Clayton informed Geneva, even though she already knew their plans because she had made them. "Close up for me, and I'll call you tomorrow," he said as he gave Geneva a quick peck on the cheek. "Sure thing, boss. Have a wonderful night, you two", she shouted to them as they exited into the beautiful night air. "It feels great out here tonight," Regina replied as a light breeze swept across her skin. "Yeah, it is a lovely night," Clayton said as he opened the passenger door of his Beemer. He had his valet bring it around to the front of the building after he had it detailed. He wanted everything to be perfect for his first date with her.

Regina slid into the seat of his BMW X6 and looked around in awe. She had never been in such a luxurious car, and she was quite impressed with Clayton's style. When he got in, she commented on how lovely it was. "Thank you," he said as he adjusted the mirrors and started the truck on the keyless ignition. He wasn't trying to impress her with his luxuries, but it didn't hurt that she was. "So where are we headed?" she asked as she settled comfortably into the plush leather. "It's a surprise," he responded mischievously. "A special night for a special lady," he added. Regina was very excited. All her life, she had dreamt of meeting Prince Charming, and it looked like tonight her dream was coming true. He pulled out into the light traffic with ease and headed toward the restaurant. Clayton was close friends with the owner and had him close the VIP room, especially for him and Regina.

He had a private chef come in and prepare different delicacies for their tasting, and he ordered several bottles of champagne for them to sip while they ate. It felt good to know people in high places to pull off such an extravagant evening. He felt something wonderful about Regina, and even though he hadn't known a lot about her, he knew she was something special. He felt like he needed to take care of her and show her the finer things in life, and he was very fortunate to have the money and clout to do just that. As they rode down Market Street, he opened the sunroof, exposing the city's beautiful skyline. It was only 6 o'clock, but the sky was black. The stars were shining brightly through, and the air was crisp. He was glad that the September weather was cooperating.

"Would you like to listen to some music?" he asked as he glanced over at her. "Sure," she replied, enjoying the smooth, comfortable ride his truck provided. "Any requests?" he asked as he started pushing buttons on the steering wheel. Just then, the car was filled with Anita Baker's strong, soulful voice. "Oh, I love this song," Regina said as she started swaying to the lovely sounds of "Sweet Love." "Yeah, this is a banger," he responded and then turned up the volume. As they drove along, they both joined in with Anita. "Hear me calling out your name; I feel no shame; I'm in love." They were both singing way off-key and when the song got to the high part, they both busted out in laughter because neither of them could hit the notes. "We both made wise career choices," Regina said, still laughing.

"Hey, you bussing on my soulful voice?" Clayton said jokingly. "Of course not, you sound great," Regina said, knowing full well she was kidding. Their chemistry was undeniable, and for the first time in years, Regina felt relaxed and happy. They continued to kid each other as they drove to the restaurant. And by the time they arrived, they felt like they had been friends for a lifetime. They felt totally at ease with each other, and Clayton was thrilled he followed his instincts to ask her out and get to know her better.

The valets walked up to the truck to open their doors when they pulled in front of the restaurant. "Good evening, Mr. Taylor." They both greeted him with a smile. "It's a pleasure to see you again, Sir," Marcus said. He was the youngest of the two men, and he knew Clayton well. He had met him a few years back in front of his studio when he was out there hustling bottles of water, and Clayton felt sorry for the young teen and gave him a job. He could see he was struggling and just needed an opportunity. Marcus had told him he had a two-year-old daughter to support, and he didn't wanna be on the streets hustling drugs and risk going to jail. Clayton admired that about him and wanted to help in any way he could.

He had also gotten him a second job at the restaurant a few months ago when he told him his girlfriend was pregnant with their second child. "Youngblood, you gotta learn to wrap up your piece," Clayton had warned him, but Marcus expressed how he was in love and planned on marrying his girl. They both wanted a big family, and he was overjoyed each time she got knocked up. After hearing about the arrival of his second child, Clayton reached out to his friend to get the young man more help. "How's Samantha?" Clayton asked as they shook hands. "She's doing great, sir. Her due date is fast approaching. We're hoping for a boy this time around," he said excitedly. "That's really great," Clayton said and handed him a hundred-dollar bill. "Here, put that towards the kid's college fund," Clayton said as he placed the money in his hand. "Yes, sir, Mr. Taylor, and thank you," Marcus responded, thrilled with his boss's generosity.

Regina walked over and took Clayton by the arm. "You have such a positive effect on people," she said, noticing the friendly exchange between the two men. "Yeah, he works for me in the mornings at the shop," he stated, telling her about Marcus's situation. "Wow, you're really a saint," Regina said, liking him even more. "No, I'm far from sainthood. I just care about our younger generation, and if there is anything I can do to help them stay on the straight and narrow, I will," he replied. Regina hadn't told him she had a 15-year-old daughter, but seeing his caring sensitivity, she was sure he wouldn't have a problem with it at all. "Shall we?" he said as they walked toward the restaurant doors. She beamed, looking up into his beautiful brown eyes. When they walked in, they were greeted by Miguel, the owner of the establishment. "Ahh, Clayton, you have arrived," the man said as he walked over, hugged him, and kissed both of his cheeks. "Miguel, my friend, how are you?" Clayton said, happy to see him. "I am good but not as well off as you. Who is this magnificent angel?" he asked, taking Regina's hand and kissing it. She blushed at the comment and gesture. "Hello," she replied. "I'm—oh, excuse my rudeness," Clayton chimed in. "This is Regina Allen," he said proudly. "Oh, Ms. Allen, what an honor and pleasure to meet you," Miguel said pleasantly. "I have your room ready, right this way," he said and walked toward the inside elevator in the back of the room. "Our room?" Regina whispered to Clayton. He grinned, pleased with the evening he had in store for her. As they walked through the restaurant, all eyes were on them. They were a stunning couple, and everyone was taking notice. Regina felt like royalty on Clayton's arm. He was super fine, and every woman in the room eyed her with envy.

When they got on the elevator, they rode up to the top floor. The doors opened, and Regina almost fainted. The room was filled with red and white roses and candles. The ambiance was spectacular. "Omg, Clayton, is this all for me?" She asked as tears filled her eyes. She had never seen something so beautiful. "Yes, baby, and this is just the beginning," he said as he escorted her off the elevator. "So, everything is to your liking?" Miguel asked, pleased with Regina's expression. "You've gone above and beyond, my friend," Clayton said, patting him on the back. "Everything is absolutely splendid."

"Wonderful. Well, I shall leave you now. Enjoy your evening," he said, and then he got back into the elevator. Regina was frozen still as she looked around. There was a man in a tuxedo in the corner playing a lovely harp, and in the center of the room was a round table covered with beautiful crisp white linens, an array of fresh fruits and delectable appetizers. There was a sterling silver bucket placed next to one of the chairs, which had a magnum-sized bottle of champagne and two crystal flutes. And standing next to the table was the chef.

"Good evening, Mr. Taylor. Madam," he nodded. "Welcome to your Morton's experience," he said, greeting them as they walked over to the table. "Everything looks delightful," Clayton said, smiling at the man. "I'm glad it is to your liking," he responded, proud of the arrangement he set up for them. "Yes, Francis, everything is perfect." Clayton pulled out one of the chairs for Regina. She was still in awe of her surroundings and couldn't believe he had done all this for her. She felt like a queen. "Thank you," she said as she took her seat. "Clayton, this is incredible," she tried hard to contain her joy.

"This experience was straight out of a romance novel for her, and she could have never imagined a day so perfect. Clayton took a seat across from her and grinned. 'Are you enjoying yourself?' he asked her. 'I am having the time of my life,' she responded bashfully. 'You are treating me so good, and although extremely appreciative I'm wondering why,' she said cautiously. What did he want from her, she wondered. He had already gotten Mr. Price to agree to all his terms, and their business deal was already in progress, so she was starting to get a little apprehensive about his motives. It couldn't have been pussy he was after cause, as fine and rich as he was, he could get any woman he wanted in the tri-state area and beyond. Clayton raised an eyebrow at her question."

"'What do you mean, why?' he asked, not sure of what she meant. Usually, women were impressed by the royal treatment. 'I just mean I haven't done anything to deserve all this,' she said, waving her hand around the room. 'Yes, you did, Regina. Just being yourself is all you need to do. You are a beautiful woman, and you deserve the finer things in life,' he said, taking her hand. She had never felt more special in all her life. This was a moment she had always prayed about.

She asked God daily to bring a man into her life who would love and protect her, and her prayers were suddenly being answered. 'But you don't even know me,' she said in a low voice, hanging her head. 'That's why I asked you out tonight because I want to get to know you. I wanna get to know your likes and dislikes, what makes you happy and what pisses you off,' he said playfully."

"'I want to get to know the extraordinary woman Regina Allen is, inside and out,' he smiled at her softly. No man had ever been that genuine and kind to her. She had been in abusive relationships for most of her life, and she wasn't used to a man showing her kindness like this. 'That is the sweetest thing anyone has ever said to me before.' He softly laughed at her answer. 'What do you mean?' he asked, shocked once again at her response. 'I mean, no man has ever cared about my likes or dislikes, what makes me happy and what makes me sad. My ex was only concerned about himself,' she said sadly. 'Well, I'm glad he's now your ex,' Clayton stated, happy to know she was single and available."

She hadn't mentioned someone special in her life when she accepted his invitation to dinner, so he had just assumed she wasn't with anyone right now. Not that it would have both-ered him because he was confident that whatever or whomever he pursued, he always walked away with the prize. Arrogance was a part of his personality, and he was proud of it. "Look, we are here to relax, have a good time and enjoy a lovely meal, ok? I want to learn more about you and have fun if that's ok with you," he said, hoping to lighten the mood a little. "Fine, ok. What is it that you wanna know?" She said, taking then a sip from the fragrant champagne Francis poured before going to get their salads.

"Well, ok, let's start with how you became a paralegal," he asked, genuinely interested. She laughed, thinking back to the day she actually got the job. She was putting together the short version in her mind as she spoke because as much as she liked this guy, she wasn't ready to give him all the details of her sordid past.

"I had only been back in Philly for a short time, and I was living with family and trying to get back on my feet when my cousin asked me to go with her to pay her boyfriend's lawyer retainer fee. Well, while we were there, I noticed Mr. Price didn't have someone doing the grunt work for his cases at the time, so I asked if he could use a part-time assistant, and surprisingly, he said yes. I came back a few days later and interviewed for the position, and he hired me on the spot. I told him how much I was interested in law, and since I had a business degree, I could really be of good service to his financial accounts. I was really lucky to get that job because I had my twelve-year-old daughter to care for at the time." Regina paused and waited for Clayton's reaction to her having a child, but surprisingly, he said nothing and just kept sipping his drink. When she noticed he wasn't going to say anything, she kept going, "So, as time went along, Mr. Price eventually paid for me to take some law classes at community college, you know, to get a better understanding of the law. He was very kind and said he wanted to see me succeed in life, and before you knew it, I was a certified paralegal." "That's great," Clayton said, briefly wondering if she had had an affair with her boss in the past. "What about you, Clayton?

What made you decide to have a career in women's beauty?" She asked, changing the subject from herself and taking a bite of a colossal shrimp from her cocktail. "Well, it was something I was destined to do."

"My mother was a hairdresser in the south and she showed me the tricks of the trade, so to speak," he said in between bites of his salad. "Oh, so you're from the south?" She asked, curious about where. Regina had lived in North Carolina for most of her teenage life and still had relatives there. "Where exactly were you from?" She asked. "Oh, it was a little town outside of Durham called Hillsborough. You probably never heard of it," he said, knowing she wouldn't have a clue. Suddenly, the hairs on her arms rose. "Oh, wow, really?" She said, feeling her stomach tighten. "Was this just a weird coincidence they were from the same place near Durham?" She thought.

"How long did you live there and when did you come to Philadelphia?" she asked nervously. "Oh, I left there when I was a boy. My mom had gotten sick, and she had family here in the city, so we moved here," he said, embellishing his story slightly. He liked Regina and hoped to one day be totally honest with her about his past, but not tonight; it was too soon for that. "Oh," Regina sighed. She thought if he had been in Philly for the majority of his life, there was no way he could or would know or be associated with anyone from her past. "So, your mother taught you all about women's beauty secrets, huh?" Regina asked, starting to relax again. "Yeah, she taught me everything I needed to know about a woman's inner beauty," he smiled, thinking of how many of the prostitutes mama made beautiful and how they gave him the best lessons on how to please a woman's outer beauty. "My mother was a very special lady, and I'm eternally grateful for all the gifts she gave me," Clayton said, thinking of her. "She must be very proud of you," Regina said. "I'm sure she was," he responded. "Oh, I'm sorry, Clayton," she said sadly, not knowing his mother was deceased.

His mother had died two weeks after his eighteenth birthday from pneumonia, leaving him and uncle Mike alone in the world. His uncle had autism and couldn't support himself physically or financially, so Clayton had to do it alone. He tried for months to support the both of them by doing odd jobs around town, but he didn't have any real skill except for doing hair, and sadly, in the south, in the late '80s, there was no way he was gonna try to get a job as a hairstylist.

People would think he was a sissy or weak, and he wasn't having that. So, when Alisha kept pressuring him to rob someone with her, he decided to do it so that he would have enough money to support him and his uncle. Little did he know someone was gonna end up dead, and he would be on the run for the rest of his life. They thought the sting would work out perfectly. He and Alisha would get enough money to live lavishly and spend the rest of their lives together, but everything had gone horribly wrong. Lives had been taken, and he knew he couldn't stay in that hick old town any longer. They feared for their life and knew they would never be safe there, so he made the decision to put his uncle in a temporary facility and leave town. He wanted to take Mike with him, but he knew because of his mental health and issues, he couldn't keep him safe, and he would never endanger his life any more than he already had. Besides, he knew it would only be temporary till he found a good place to live in the city, and then he would send for him. He had promised his mama he would take care of him and protect him, and that was a promise he always tried to keep.

"Hey, where'd you go to?" Regina asked, snapping him out of his thoughts. "Oh, nowhere. I'm here with you," Clayton said, focusing back on her. "So, tell me a little more about yourself," he said while sipping a glass of champagne. Regina smiled; she knew now was time to tell him about Nyla. "Well, I have a daughter who I'm sure you heard me mention. She's fifteen, and she is amazing. She attends the high school for performing arts, where she's a vocal major, and she's very talented," Regina added. Clayton listened intently as she told him about her little girl. "Where's her father?" He asked, hoping she didn't have a relationship with him.

"He died when she was eleven," Regina said, lying to him. There was no way she would ever tell him that he was somewhere out there looking for her and her child to possibly harm them. "Oh, I'm so sorry," Clayton said, taking her hand to comfort her. "There's no need to be sorry. He was an awful man, so I'm glad he's gone," she said, wishing the words she spoke were true. He was a terrible man; that part was true, but he was very much alive and well. "If you don't mind, can we talk about something else?" She said, not wanting to think about that depressing part of her life. She wanted to have a lovely dinner with a wonderful man and just be happy for once, if only for a short time.

20

CLAYTON

Clayton felt energized when he got home from his date with Regina. He really liked her and thought the evening had turned out great. They had dinner at one of his favorite restaurants, and their conversation, although awkward at first, went smoothly. He had found out she had a teenage daughter and that she loved art and music. She was easy to get along with, and he really enjoyed pampering her with the luxuries of his life. When he pulled into his driveway, he noticed he had left the lights on by the pool earlier that morning. He wasn't tired from his evening, and it was only 10:30, so he decided to go for a swim. He entered his home, turned on the lights in his massive living room, and threw his suit jacket on the tan Italian leather sofa. He removed his Versace Loafers at the front door so he wouldn't scarp his beautiful bamboo wood floors. He picked up the remote to his stereo system from the glass and wooden console table and pressed play. John Legend's voice filled the surround speakers throughout the house. He continued to remove his clothing as he walked toward his master bedroom suite.

When he entered, he placed his keys and wallet on his night-stand. He noticed his home answering machine blinking. It showed he had five new messages. He ignored it, knowing it was messages from the mental facility, and he wasn't in the mood to hear from them now; his day was going too well, and he didn't want to ruin it. It seemed his uncle was having a lot of problems lately, and he made a mental note to go for a visit soon. After fully disrobing, he put the remainder of his clothing in a pile in the corner. He knew his housekeeper Tracy would get them and take them to be cleaned. He decided to swim naked since the weather was warm and his home was in a secluded area; he knew no one would see him. He liked to skinny dip and did it as often as he could. It made him feel free and connected to nature.

When he walked out onto his deck from the bedroom, a warm breeze swept across his body. He was pleased with his muscle tone and pecks. He had made a point to work out for at least an hour each day in his home gym, and the results paid off. He stared at the beautiful crystal blue water and noticed how calm it was. He dipped his toe in, and the temperature was perfect. He lifted his arms and dove in, making a loud splash. His form was that of an Olympic swimmer, thanks to the lessons he took a few years ago. He swam around the water like a shark, looking for prey. Doing laps from one end to the other. He felt the tension and stress from the day melt from his body. He stayed in the pool for 20 minutes longer before deciding to sit in the attached jacuzzi. His body felt exhilarated as he transferred to the much hotter temperature. He was on top of the world, he thought. Every-thing was lining up perfectly. Who would have thought a skinny, poor kid from the South would end up being a millionaire with one of the most successful hair and beauty salons in the country? The thought made him grin hard. The journey had been long, and although he had done unspeakable things in his past, in the end, he had come out on top. He lay back in the jetted tub and closed his eyes.

"Bitch, I'm not gonna ask you again to put the money in the goddamn bag and get on the ground," Clayton yelled at the frightened woman as he pointed the pistol at her head. "Ok. Ok. Please don't shoot me," she cried as she took the money out from under the floorboard. It had been stashed there under the carpet and boards for safekeeping. "Where's the drugs?" He asked in a grimacing tone. "I don't know, but…" the woman continued to cry as she filled the duffle bag. "Look, whore, I ain't got time for yo shit. Now tell me where the drugs are before I put a bullet in Ya head," he said as he grabbed her by the hair and shoved her hard against the wall. "Twin keeps it in the kitchen under the sink," she said, scared for her life. He knocked her to the side and headed for the back of the house. They were being timed, and they had to get in and out before the twins made it back. While Clayton searched the cabinets, his accomplice held the hookers at bay in the next room. They both wore masks so as not to be recognized and so far, everything has been going as planned. The drugs were under the sink in a bucket covered with newspaper. There were eight bricks of cocaine and five bricks of heroine, raw and uncut. Clayton had never seen so many drugs in his life. His hands trembled as he put each brick into a trash bag. They had a buyer for all of it, and they were looking to collect a cool million dollars from the drugs alone.

Clayton knew there was at least another 2 million in cash in the duffle bag being filled by one of the prostitutes, and he knew he and his girl would be set for life with that kind of money. He had never robbed anyone before, but he made sure he went over the plan several times so that there wouldn't be any mistakes.

He had watched the house and the twins intently for weeks, calculating their every move and knowing what they did like clockwork by now. He saw what time they left the house, what time they returned and what they did when they were gone. He knew every night at about 9:30; they would go into town to collect their money from the corner boys who sold their product and the hoes who worked the morning and after-noon shifts on the stroll. He saw when they ree'd up on the drugs and when they bought in their largest profits. He had the whole plan figured out. He knew there were only gonna be a few girls home that night, the ones whom the twins trusted the most. They were their seasoned bitches that handled most of their business. So, just in case someone came to cop some rock or turn a trick, they wouldn't lose any money. Clayton had decided they would enter the house a little before 10 when the twins left. They would get the money from the floor, grab the drugs they had stashed and leave without anyone getting hurt. If only that were the case. If only the night had gone that smoothly.

He remembered a woman screaming and crying at the top of her lungs, "Oh my god, she's dead." Clayton ran back into the living room and saw one of the hookers lying on the floor and Alisha trembling, holding the smoking gun. "What the fuck happened?" he asked everyone in the room. "She tried to reach for it, she moved, and I didn't have a choice. She fucking moved," Alisha said crying. "Shut up, shut up, give me a min," he said, pacing back and forth in the hallway. "Look, we gotta get outta here," he said as he grabbed her by her trembling shoulders. "Get the money and let's go," he shouted as he grabbed the large trash bag of drugs. "What about her?" Alisha said, terrified, pointing to the still body that was on the floor. The other girls had fled to the second floor immediately when the young girl fired the fatal shot. "Fuck her, we gotta go, Lee Lee, come on," the frightened boy said as he grabbed her by the hand. "Them bitches could be calling the twins right now. We gotta get the fuck outta here," he said, terrified about what Alisha had done. He had trusted her with the gun because he never thought she would use it. She had known every girl in the house, and he thought she would just scare them. Never did he think she would actually commit murder.

"Everything is all messed up now. We gotta go," he said as they ran from the house to his mama's waiting car. When they got inside, he saw that Alisha had blood on her face and clothing. She was still holding the gun as if it were glued to her hand as she placed the bag with the money in the back seat. "Come on, babe, let it go," he said, trying to take the gun from her grasp. She sat there staring forward. He knew she was in shock. "Lee, give me the gun, baby," he said again, hoping she'd release her grip. Just then, she screamed at the top of her lungs in anguish. "Clay, what have I done!" She cried. "It's gonna be alright, Lee. I promise everything is gonna be alright," he said and sped away from the curb.

Clayton jumped up from the hot tub; he must have dosed off while relaxing. He glanced into his bedroom at the clock on the dresser. It read 2:15 am. "Damn it," he said aloud as he got out of the water. He felt chilly now that the air was crisp. He grabbed a towel from the warming rack he kept by the pool, wrapped it around his waist and went inside. He felt his heart racing from the dream he just had. He sat on the edge of the bed to collect his thoughts. What the hell is going on, he thought to himself.

"Why the fuck do I keep thinking about that night?" he wondered. Just then, he reached over to listen to his messages on the machine. "You have five new messages. First message: Hello, Mr. Taylor. This is Veronica from the center. I am just calling to let you know we received the forms and have now started Michael on a new prescription, so all is well. If you have any questions, please give us a call at your earliest convenience. Have a great day!" He knew the calls were from the hospital. As he continued to listen, he went into the bathroom to turn on the shower. "Second message: Hey, sug, it's Deva. Just calling to see how your date went. Didn't wanna call your cell and interrupt in case you went back to her place. Call me tomorrow and tell me all the details. Love Ya." He smiled, thinking about his friend. "Third message: Hey man, it's Darrin. I just wanted to hit you up to make sure you liked the smocks I made for you. Give me a call when you get time, bro, peace." Clayton knew he had to call Darrin back to thank him. He stepped in the shower just as the next message played. "Fourth message: Um, hi, this is… Well, you know who. I need to speak to you immediately. Please call me back when you get this message." Clayton's heart stopped. It was

Alisha. He hadn't heard her voice in years, but as soon as he heard it, it sent a chill up his spine.

He suddenly turned off the water and stepped out of the shower. "Fifth message: I'm sorry to keep calling. I know we said we would never contact one another again, but I had to tell you our problem had risen from the dead, and we gotta handle it asap. Please call me back as soon as you can, Clayton." Then, the machine went silent. Clayton stood in the middle of his bathroom floor, dripping wet. He was in shock. He knew something bad had happened, and that was the only reason why she had called. He grabbed his bathrobe and went back into the bedroom. He replayed her messages over and over, listening to the fear in her voice. He grabbed his phone and was about to call her right then but decided to wait because it was now 3 in the morning. "Fuck, now is not the time," he said out loud, angry that his past had crept back into his present. He walked over to the bar he had in his bedroom and grabbed a bottle of 1800. He removed the top and took a long gulp of the bitter liquid.

He then went inside his walk-in closet and pressed the button that was located behind his many designer suits. Suddenly, a wooden panel door slides open. He walked inside the makeshift room. There was an array of guns and ammunition and three large safes. He went over to the larger one and entered the combination. It clicked open. He reached inside and pulled out a silver semi-automatic pistol. This was the gun that killed that poor girl that awful night and put a bullet between the eyes of that dirty scumbag Smitty. Clayton now wondered which soul would be taken next. He said a silent prayer that it wouldn't be his own.

21
REGINA

Regina was floating on air when she walked into her apartment. Her entire day had been like a fairytale. She had gotten the most incredible makeover and some glamorous new outfits, and she went out with a man who was not only super fine but had stolen her heart. Clayton Taylor was everything she had ever dreamt of. He was smart, ambitious, kind and filthy rich. Never in her wildest dreams had she ever thought she would meet a man like him. He treated her like a queen, and for the first time in her life, she knew she deserved it. They went to dinner and talked for hours, and she shared things with him. She never thought she would be with any man, especially on their first date. But Clayton was easy to talk to. He seemed interested in her hopes and dreams, and Regina had never had a man just listen. She told him that she wanted to own her own art gallery one day, and he encouraged her to do it. He told her never to give up on her passion and to go for whatever she wanted to achieve in life. He stimulated her mind as well as her body. He constantly complimented her on her beauty, and that made her heart soar.

She felt beautiful inside and out, and it was all thanks to Clayton. "Hey, mama. How was your date?" Nyla came into the living room, eating a peach. "It was great," Regina said, smiling so hard her cheeks hurt. "Dang, mama, you look so pretty," her daughter said, eyeing her new outfit and hairdo. "Thank you, baby. This is some of the perks of my job," Regina responded, twirling around so that Nyla could see her entire makeover. "I wanna come to work with you," she said, loving seeing her mom in such a good mood. "Did you bring me something home?" she asked, looking at the bags Regina had sat on the kitchen counter. "I sure did. You know I wouldn't forget my sweet baby," Regina said as she walked into the kitchen. She had bought her home a lobster and steak, some sides, and a piece of cherry cheesecake for dessert. "Clayton had insisted when she told him her cousin was keeping an eye on her daughter while she was out. 'Take her home a meal. I'm sure she'd like it way better than take-out,' he had suggested." He was even showing concern for her child, and he hadn't even met her yet, Regina thought, caring for him even more. And he couldn't have been more right because Nyla loved to eat.

Regina was glad she had a teenager with a high metabolism because she would have been big as a house the way she loved food. Fortunately, she burned off everything she put in her mouth and taking dance classes didn't hurt either. "Girl, you greedy," Regina said as she watched her daughter start smiling when she opened the food containers. "Oh, mama, this looks good," she said, doing a happy dance. "Ima tear that Jawn up," she teased. "I bet," Regina said as she walked back into the living room. "Listen, you eat your dinner out here and then have your dessert in your room, but make sure you clean up afterward and turn off these lights before you go to bed," she said to her daughter as she gathered up her things and headed toward her bedroom. "Ok, mama, I will. Thanks again for looking out for your starving daughter," Nyla said jokingly. "I'll be in to kiss you good night later," she said and continued to devour her meal. "Ok," Regina responded, smiling, and closed her bedroom door. She wanted some time alone to think about Clayton. She wasn't sure where their relationship was headed, but she was more than willing to go along for the ride. It was already starting out differently from her past, and she was grateful.

Never again did she want to experience the heartache and pain she suffered at the hands of her ex. Her relationship with James started off so good in the beginning but eventually turned into a horrible nightmare. As much as Regina tried to forget, she had a hard time erasing those memories. She had hoped he would be her forever, her one and only true love, but that relationship turned out to be far from a fairytale. She thought back to the first time they had met face-to-face and how nervous she had been. She was walking back to her grandparents' house from the store in town one sunny after-noon while visiting her family in North Carolina for the summer. She was running errands for her Medea, which was a daily task, but she always enjoyed it. It gave her a chance to enjoy the scenery of the south and escape the hustle and bustle of Philly. "Hey, girl, what you doing out here by your-self?" She remembered him calling out to her from his long black Cadillac. At first, Regina kept walking because, in a way, she hoped he wasn't trying to get her attention. After all, to him and his brother, she wasn't much to look at. All she could remember was the first time she had seen them and the comment they made about her resembling a boy. She was so embarrassed.

"Hey, I'm talking to you," he said again as he started to follow her in his car. She eventually stopped to acknowledge him. "Are you talking to me?" Regina swung around nervously with her hand on her hip. "Yeah, I'm talking to you. What's your problem? You hard of hearing or something?" he asked jokingly. "No, I'm not. I'm just not used to talking to pimps, is all," she responded back sarcastically. "Pimps? Who told you I was Pimp?" He smirked. "My cousin Val told me, and on top of that, I saw you with that hooker last year outside the club," she added, trying to jog his memory. "Girl, that wasn't no hooker, that was my friend, and I was just giving her a ride," he said, knowing that Regina was talking about the night he dragged Candy from the speakeasy for not having his money.

He could tell Regina was young and naive, but she had spunk and a good memory, so he couldn't just tell her anything, and she'd be convinced. "She sure didn't seem like a friend," Regina said, noticing the many gold rings on his fingers. He knew she wasn't from the South, and he could tell she hadn't been exposed to much of her life yet, but she was a fast observer. He laughed and quickly changed the subject. "Hey, so you related to Big Val?" he asked from the car window, remembering her from that night. "I know her from my brother," he added, trying to get her mind off his shady dealings. "Yeah, she's my cousin," Regina responded, feeling a little more at ease talking to him. She knew he was familiar with Val and that his brother had dated her mom some time ago. "Yeah, that girl is crazy," he said, laughing.

He knew that Val had a little con game going on with the local young boys in town and how she got them to give her money. He wasn't sure what Regina's deal was or if she was the same way, but he wanted to find out. "I hope you don't be doing the shit she do sometimes," he said. "Like what?" she asked, curious about what he knew about her cousin. You know… She be in town fucking with them little boys, taking they money and shit," he laughed. "No, I didn't know that," Regina said, defending her favorite cousin. She knew Val would let them rub on her breasts sometimes, but she didn't think she was actually having sex with any of them. "Yeah, well, you'd better be careful with her before you know it; she'll have you on the ho stroll," he said, amusing himself with his words. "Whatever," Regina said and turned to walk away from his car. Come on, wait, I was just kidding," he turned off the ignition and got out of the car. "I wanna talk to you for a minute. Where you going?" He asked as he gently grabbed her arm. "I gotta get home. My grandmother is waiting for me to come back," Regina said, starting to feel nervous again in his presence. When he got closer to her, she could see he was a handsome guy, but she knew he was much older than she was and into illegal activity, and the last thing she wanted was for someone to see her talking to him and tell her grandparents. She would surely be in for an ass whopping and probably wouldn't be able to come back to visit again for a long time.

"Look, I know you in a rush. I was just hoping I could see you again, maybe take you out for a bite to eat or something," he said, easing the grip he had on her arm and sounding sincere. Regina's heart started to beat fast. "Really? You wanna take me out?" She asked, surprised by the offer. "Yeah, what's wrong with that? I'm sure you ain't never been to a fancy restaurant down here before, and I'd like to show you around if you wanna go," he said, trying to convince her to go out with him.

Truth be told, Regina had never been out on a real date, more or less to a fancy restaurant, but she was scared to death to go out with him because of his reputation. Besides, he was almost old enough to be her father. "Well, I don't know. I'll have to see," she said halfheartedly, trying to hide the nervous excitement in her voice. "Here, take my number, and if you decide, give me a call." He reached inside his car for a pen and piece of paper, wrote down the number and handed it to her. "Ok, I'll think about it and maybe give you a call," she said, anxious to leave. She really wanted to get home before her grandparents started to worry and get away from him before he saw the sweat starting to stain her shirt. "I hope you call. And I promise to show you a good time," he said as he climbed back into his hog and watched her walk away. Ok, she said over her shoulder as she folded the piece of paper with his number on it and put it in her pocket. He turned on the stereo in his car and pulled off. As he sped down the dirt road, you could hear Chuck Berry and the bass thumping from inside. Everyone on the street turned to look. The elderly folks shook their heads in disgust while the younger ones laughed at his antics. He was the man around town, and people definitely took notice.

"Where in the hell have you been?" Val asked Regina as she entered the house, out of breath. She had run the rest of the way, hoping to get there fast. "Medea was starting to worry," she said, annoyed. "You know if she gets mad, she ain't gonna let us go to the movies tonight," she said, pissed that Regina almost got them in trouble. "I'm sorry, V, but guess who I was just talking to outside of the store," Regina said, anxious about telling her about James. "Who, girl?" Val said as she fixed her hair in the mirror. "One of the twins, that's who," she said as she placed the bag on the floor and removed his number from her jeans pocket.

"Gee Gee, are you insane?" Val asked in a whisper, snatching the paper from her hand. "Girl, you'd better stay away from him. They are bad news," she added. "Why you say that, Val? You always told me Jacob treated you and your mama real nice and that he was always looking out for you," Regina said, disappointed by her reaction. "Yeah, Jacob was always real nice, but not James, though, he is the mean twin. I heard he beat women for fun and made them prostitute for him after he was done using them for his own pleasure," Val told her. "Girl, no, he didn't seem like that at all," Regina said, taking the paper back from Val with his number on it. "He actually seemed nice," she said, thinking about the conversation they had and him asking to take her out on a date. "Well, just don't say I didn't warn you. Now get in there and give Medea her groceries and change your clothes. The movie starts in an hour, and I don't wanna be late," she said, hurrying her into the kitchen.

Thinking back, Regina wished she had listened to her cousin because as nice and innocent as he appeared in the beginning, she was headed for the next 12 years of disaster. Regina turned on the TV to distract her thoughts. She didn't want to think about James anymore and how he almost destroyed her life. She wanted to keep the sweet memories of her date with Clayton while they were still fresh in her mind. When she climbed into bed, she instructed Alexa to turn off the lights, and she grabbed the remote and settled in for some drama-filled reality TV. She loved watching those types of programs because it took her mind off of what was happening in her own reality. Little did she know what was in store for her life would be far more dramatic than any show could produce.

22

EVELYN

Evelyn still had a terrible headache after she took her shower and had a cup of coffee. She had taken 2 Xanax to calm her nerves and put her mind at ease from the terrible events that happened the night before, but She was still upset and wondering how the twins knew her husband. She sat on the terrace in her bedroom, trying to think of any clues from Ethan's past business deals or clients that could have led him to get involved with them. She knew he defended some middle-class drug dealers in the past and that he represented a few murder suspects, but they were all national news types, and their cases drew lots of attention from the media. So, she was certain none of those trials could have been associated with the twins because that type of attention was definitely the last thing they wanted or needed due to their violent past and history. Her stomach started to knot as she thought about the danger her husband could be facing. Now that Jacob and James knew she was with Ethan, they could possibly do harm to him to get even with her.

Fear and worry washed over her like a title wave. "What was she going to do? What was her next move," she thought. She picked up her phone from the table next to her and scrolled through her contacts. She had phone numbers of people from her past that she hadn't contacted in years because there was no need. But desperate times called for desperate measures. She stopped at a name she remembered well: Kendall. She smiled, thinking of him. Evelyn had been in Philadelphia for well over 20 years, and nearly half the people that knew about her life as Alisha were either dead in prison or living a different life as well. It took some time to erase the girl she used to be, and it cost her plenty, but to her, it was well worth it. Before coming to Philly, Alisha went to New York to hide out. She hadn't known anyone there, but she figured with such a large population, she could easily blend in and not be noticed. She had gotten a modest little one-bedroom apartment in Queens, figuring that it was a safe place and that she'd be harder to find.

The landlord of the building was skeptical at first about renting to her, saying she looked way too young, but when she produced first and last month's rent plus security deposit in cash, he instantly reconsidered. She spent most of her days alone in her apartment in fear because, for one, she was in a strange city, she had a suitcase full of stolen money, and she was really just a child. But one of the main reasons she was so scared was because the twins could find her at any time and kill her. She was lonely most days, and she missed her friends down south, Kim, Marie, and especially Clayton, but after what she had done, she knew there was no way of returning ever. After being in New York for a few months, Alisha decided to venture out and see what the bustling city had to offer. She really wasn't thinking of a job because she didn't have any skills, so she wasn't sure what type of work, if any, she would get.

Money wasn't an issue for her because she and Clayton had scored big before leaving Hillsborough, but she knew her funds wouldn't last forever, and she needed something to do with herself if she was gonna live there. Her whole life, the only thing she was ever surrounded by were junkies and prostitutes, but she didn't want any of those things in her future, so it left her limited to the realities of real life. Besides, she was only sixteen, even though she looked older. She knew how to hustle and con but only on old country bumpkins from the south, and she knew that could only get her so far in a fast city like New York. She wasn't ready for the stripper pole yet, and she wasn't sure she could handle the fast, slick-talking city dudes she encountered when she went out to the store or local stop-and-go beer distributors near where she lived. She really needed to do something with her life to have a fresh start. Alisha had been cooped up in her apartment for nearly three months, only going out for groceries, cigarettes and a drink every now and then. When she got lonely and needed to take the edge off, she would go to the liquor store and buy a bottle. She had had her fair share of libations as a child. Her first drink was when she was just five years old. Candy would give her beers or a shot of liquor to get her to fall asleep so that she could fuck guys in the next room and her daughter wouldn't hear, but as time went on, she got used to the sensations and would be up to hear the raunchy activities that took place. By the time she was thirteen, she was buying her own wine and liquor from the speakeasies up the road from their house, and the woman Miss Belle that owned the place would give her a discount half the time because she knew she was drinking to mask the pain she was feeling about having a whore for a mother. Now that Alisha was sixteen, she considered herself a pro. She could down a fifth of Hennessy effortlessly and still be on the go at any moment.

It was a particularly hot summer day in New York, but Alisha decided to get out of the house for a while. As she strolled down the pretty tree-lined streets, she was amazed. She wasn't used to the concrete sidewalks and tall buildings in the city.

Growing up, she always lived off dirt roads in plantation-style homes with swings on the porches and gravel driveways, so this was all new to her. The traffic and city lights were fascinating. She got on the subway and went into Manhattan and fell in love with the sights. She saw fancy shops, exquisite upscale restaurants, and people on street corners playing instruments. There were street vendors selling different types of merchandise, from food to art; it was quite surreal to a sixteen-year-old girl from the South. As she walked along the busy streets, she glanced inside designer store windows and shops. She eyed beautiful handbags and shoes from designers she had never heard of and shiny jewels that sparkled from the jewelry store cases. She decided to grab some lunch, so she stopped at a greasy burger joint to get a bite to eat.

It was crowded inside, but she decided to wait anyway because she realized she hadn't eaten all day and low key she was hungry.

She stood in line for what seemed like forever. "You know what you're gonna get on your burger?" She heard a man's voice say in her ear behind her. She quickly turned around to a handsome face smiling at her. "Uh, no, first time here. So, do you have any suggestions?" She asked the cute stranger. "Yeah, get some pickles, ketchup, mustard, onions and jalapeños," he suggested. "Wow, that's a lot," she said, laughing at his choices. "You have a beautiful laugh, you know that?" the guy said, looking at her lustfully. "Thanks. What's your name, by the way?" She asked as they stood in line waiting to be served. "I'm Kendall. How bout you?" He responded with NY swag. "I'm Alisha," she said, smiling at his rich B-boy accent. He had a thuggish confidence about him, and Alisha liked that he was very sexy. He was around 6'1 and looked to be in his early twenties. He had light skin like cream in steaming hot coffee, soft brown eyes, and he wore a fade. He had a diamond earring in his left ear, and his neck and arms were tatted. "Alisha, that's cute. Are you from around here?" He asked, eyeing her up and down.

"Actually, no, I'm from Philadelphia," she said, not wanting him to believe she was from a small country town down south. "Oh, for real? You from Philly? I got some peeps down there," he told her. "Yeah, Philly people good people," he added. "Really? You think so?" she said, happy she had picked that city. She knew she couldn't have passed for someone from New York, so she picked the next best place she thought of. "Yup, it's Thurl. I go there every now and again. Maybe I could slide up there and visit you sometime," he said as they inched closer to the front of the line. "That would be nice," she said. She hadn't had sex in over four months, and she needed some good dick, and just by looking at the way he stood, she knew she would fuck Kendall on their first date. "Yo, you got a number or a pager I can hit you up on?" He asked. "Oh yeah, she said happily," forgetting she didn't own either one.

Reality soon set in. "Oh my god, he wants my phone number," she thought. Just then, she remembered she never needed them because there was no one to keep in touch with or anyone to keep in touch with her till now. "Um, I forgot my beeper at the hotel I'm staying at, and I don't know the number by heart because it's new," she shuddered, knowing she was telling a lie and started to feel embarrassed. She didn't know how any of this was supposed to work. She had never dated anyone before, and the boys she had had sex with went to her school, so she would screw them in the bathroom or gym during lunchtime. She never really needed a phone or pager. But she now knew she had to purchase one to stay in the loop since she was now in a big city. "Oh, Ard bet no sweat. I'll just give you mine then, and you better call," he said in a playful tone. "I'll call for sure, honest," she said as she retrieved a pen and paper from her bag. He wrote down the number and handed it to her. "Welcome to Fat Burger. May I take your order," a young girl said loudly, clearly annoyed that they weren't paying attention and that they were holding up the line. "Yeah, let me get two impossible and two onion rings to go in separate bags," he told the girl at the register. "I got it, shorty," he said as he looked at Alisha with a grin. He reached into his pocket and pulled out a knot of money; he peeled off two twenty-dollar bills and placed them on the counter. "That'll be 27.50," the girl said, looking at Alisha, clearly jealous. Alisha quickly picked up the money and handed it to her.

Kendall went over to the window to see if his car was cool. He had parked in a no-parking lane, but he had two of his young homies inside waiting for him. Alisha took the change from the girl and moved over to wait for her food. "Hey, what you doing tonight?" Kendall asked when he walked back over to her. "Nothing really; I was thinking about going to the movies or something," she said, knowing that was also a lie. She didn't know anywhere to go in New York except the bodega at the corner and the liquor store up the block from her apartment. "Why don't you hit me up later? We could kick it for a while," he said, excited about going out with her.

He was liking her and wanted to spend more time with her. "That might be fun," she said, knowing that she was definitely gonna call him later that night. "Aight, B, I'm gonna be waiting," he said as he grabbed one of the bags off the counter and left the restaurant. Alisha watched as he climbed behind the wheel of a Chevy Impala and sped away from the curb. She liked his style, and she was happy she had found a new friend and maybe some bomb-ass dick in the big apple. When she left the restaurant, her next stop was gonna be to purchase a pager.

23
ETHAN

Ethan woke up the next morning at 5 am. He had set his alarm so that he could start his day earlier than usual. He wanted to get in a workout before leaving for the office. It was a Saturday, and he usually slept in late, but given the fact that he had just signed a new million-dollar client, he wanted to get a head start on this business deal. He sat up in the bed and looked over at his wife. He knew she must have taken a pill to help her sleep because she never moved the entire night. Ethan ran his fingers across her beautiful face and wondered again what had her so upset the night before. He slid out of the bed quietly so as not to disturb her and went into the bathroom. His body felt rested, and he was happy he satisfied himself the night before going to sleep. He would have enjoyed pleasing her more, but hey, shit happens, he thought. He brushed his teeth, washed his face and applied deodorant. He decided to wait till after his workout to take a shower before going to work.

He threw on a pair of sweats and a wife beater, then headed downstairs to the kitchen to make some coffee. He knew the house staff would be coming in at eight, but he wanted to have some quiet time alone before they arrived. He walked into the kitchen and looked around. Ethan enjoyed the peace and serenity of his home in the early morning. He rarely got the time to himself, and he wanted to savor every minute of it. He went over to the fully stocked pantry to get a bag of freshly ground coffee from inside.

He took a deep sniff of the bag and let his senses take in the rich aroma. He added the grinds to the Fancy stainless steel appliance on the counter and waited. He admired the beauty that surrounded him. The kitchen looked like a page right out of homes and gardens. The floors were made of slate tiles, while the countertops were recycled glass and cement. There were so many cabinets made of imported wood and glass he didn't know how anyone could fill them all. It was equipped with the latest high-end appliances, a subzero refrigerator dishwasher, an eight-burner gas range with a pot filler and a large stainless steel hood. The space was over 1000 square feet, with double ovens built into the wall and a 50-bottle wine rack suspended from the ceiling. There was exotic crystal stemware in the lighted cabinets and expensive hand-made China. Evelyn got flown in from different countries they had visited on vacation. In the middle of the room was a large elegant island made of marble and glass with a farm-house sink she had designed specifically for the room.

Ethan laughed to himself. She had all these shiny, beautiful things, and not once had she used any of them. He couldn't remember a time he smelled bread baking or the aroma of a home-cooked meal. Boy, did he miss the food his aunt Mae would make. He recalled going in the house on warm spring days and hearing her singing her favorite gospel tunes while she peeled potatoes and looked over collard greens before putting them in her big oversized pot. In the oven, she would have sweet potato pies and homemade biscuits she made from scratch, and sitting on the stove, she would have a big iron skillet filled with golden fried chicken.

She always used to tell him that she cooked from her heart and soul, and Ethan felt it in every delicious meal she made. He hadn't had a meal like that in years. Evelyn was great in bed, but she was not a great cook, but he loved her anyway. He knew the saying the way to a man's heart was through his stomach. Unfortunately, she did not. The French coffee press made a whistling sound, which meant it was ready. Ethan looked in the cabinet and grabbed his University of Penn mug. That was his favorite cup, and it looked out of place sitting among expensive China, but that was the only one he'd use because it always reminded him of simpler times back when he was a teen. As he poured the strong brew into the cup, he thought back to the days before he had gone off to college.

It was rough on him in the beginning. He really didn't have any money except what he had saved hustling for Snake, but that only scratched the surface of what he would need for a four-year education. He was apprehensive at first about applying to such an expensive school, but his aunt and uncle wouldn't have it any other way. They started saving for his college fund the day he moved in with them as a child, and they managed to save close to 20,000, which was huge given their modest incomes. Unfortunately, that amount would only cover one semester and wasn't even close to the cost of law school, but he was happy just the same. He remembered pleading with them to let him just go to community college, get a job, and help them save for his education, but his uncle flat-out said no.

"Listen here, boy. Mae and I have worked hard to see you succeed in life, and we both know your dream is to become a successful lawyer, and there's no way you're gonna fulfill that dream going to community college," Uncle Frank said. "Now, don't get me wrong, all education is good education; it just so happens that Penn's is a little better. That's all," Ethan remembered him saying. "Uncle Frank, I hear you, but honestly, you can't afford it, and it's already hard enough watching you and Aunt Mae struggle to provide for me now," Ethan told him as they worked on his uncle's Lincoln in the driveway. Even though Snake used the mechanic shop as a cover for his drug business, he taught Ethan a thing or two about fixing cars, which was a good thing, so whenever his uncle asked him to fix something, he could. At first, Ethan thought his uncle knew he was hustling for Snake and was spinning him about knowing how to fix cars, but after Ethan showed his mechanical skills and fixed a couple of things, he left it alone. He treasured times like this because it gave him and his uncle time to talk like father and son.

"Don't you go worrying about how we struggle and just worry about getting good grades so that you can get scholarships to pay for your remaining time there," he said as he passed Ethan a wrench. "We're proud of you, son, and know you are gonna make it in this world. My sister bore a king, and one day you are gonna sit high upon your throne, you hear me?" he said, his eyes welling up. He always gets sentimental when he talks about Ethan's parents. "Thanks, Uncle Frank. I promise you I'm gonna work hard and become so rich you and Aunt Mae will never have to worry about money again," Ethan assured him. "That's just fine, son. All we want for you is to be happy," he said as he walked back to the house from the front yard. "Hey, Unc and I'm gonna buy you a brand new Lincoln so that you can get rid of this piece of junk," Ethan yelled out. His uncle's Lincoln never seemed to run well no matter what Ethan did to it; it always broke down, but Uncle Frank refused to sell it. He turned around and looked at his nephew with a smile. "Listen, just because something is run down and needs a little work doesn't mean you should give up on it," he said. Those words always stuck in Ethan's head, and he knew he would always remember them. His uncle was always spitting knowledge that he would treasure every day. He felt like they were smiling down from heaven at him now that he was a big success, and he wished he had the opportunity to repay them for all they had done for him.

They never even got the chance to see him graduate from Penn. His uncle Frank had died in his sleep of a heart attack two years after he got his high school diploma, and the thought of not having her loving husband any longer, his aunt Mae died of a broken heart three months later. It tore Ethan up inside to lose the two people who meant the world to him, and he made a vow to finish college, go to grad school and become a successful lawyer, which was what they always wanted for him. Ethan looked up at the clock and saw that it was 6:15 he had to get a move on so he wouldn't be late for work. He still had to do his workout and take a shower. He finished his cup of java and took the elevator downstairs to his indoor gym. He had a nice setup there. It was fully equipped with the latest state-of-the-art weights and nautical machines, as well as a small boxing ring.

He used to be a pretty good fighter back in the day. He had even won a few fights at the famous Joe Frazier gym on Broad Street, but all of that was in the past. He never even got in the ring anymore and really just had it built for nostalgic purposes. He went over to his weight bench. It held two hundred and ten pounds, which was his usual pressing weight. He decided to do twenty reps of ten and then run two or three miles on the treadmill. He wanted to do some ab workouts but realized he was pressed for time. Afterward, he felt invigorated. He decided to take the stairs back up to the kitchen and grabbed a bottle of water before heading up to the bedroom. He went in, stripped off his sweaty clothes and jumped in the shower. He allowed the cool water to run on his tense muscles for ten minutes.

When he was done, he went into his walk-in closet to get dressed. He and his wife had separate closets to fit the many designer clothes they each owned. By it being Saturday, he decided on a classic polo button, a pair of khakis and some Gucci loafers. There wasn't gonna be anyone else in the office today, and besides, it was the weekend, so he could dress casually. After getting dressed, he walked back into the bedroom and heard Evelyn snoring lightly. She must have really been exhausted, he thought. He grabbed his Rolex and wallet from the nightstand, kissed her gently on the forehead and left the room.

As he made his way downstairs, he heard Henrietta and some of the other staff coming in. "Good morning, Mr. Price," she said in her always cheerful tone. "Good morning, Henrietta," Ethan responded. "Don't you look lovely as ever," he said as he greeted her with a hug. Henrietta was like family to him. She had worked for him for close to five years. She was an older woman who reminded him of his Aunt Mae, and she took great care of him and his home. She worked with a staff of five, mostly her relatives. She reassured him and Evelyn that keeping the jobs in the family would always guarantee her work, and it did. She cooked and cleaned the kitchen, polished the silver and did the laundry.

Her nephews did the landscaping and kept the grounds outside looking picture perfect. Her two nieces cleaned the windows and the other parts of the house except for Evelyn's private study and the master bedroom. Henrietta did that herself. She took care of Ethan and his wife personally and made sure they always had what they needed. "You going off to work early this morning?" she asked Ethan as he headed toward the front door. "Yeah, I have some important business to take care of, and I want to get a head start on it before Monday," he responded, looking in the hall closet for his briefcase. "Ok, you be safe out there," she yelled from the kitchen. "I will, Henrietta. By the way, the wife is not feeling well this morning. Can you please make her some soup and keep an eye on her? She's still asleep, but I'm sure she's gonna want some coffee when she wakes up," he said, knowing Henrietta would make sure she was good. "Absolutely, sir, don't you worry. I'll take care of her," she said, putting his mind at ease. He smiled, grabbed his keys, and exited out the front door.

He decided to drive his Dodge Charger to work that day. It was a sleek black convertible drop-top with silver 20-inch rims. He loved the power it possessed, and he felt like a race car driver when he sped down I95 in it. He knew all the police officers in the county, so he never worried about getting pulled over for speeding. It was a cool, crisp morning, and the smell of the morning dew tantalized his senses. He turned on the music and settled into his ride. He put on the hip-hop XM station to get him in the zone. As he pulled out of the driveway, Meek came through the speakers. He smiled, thinking of the young inspiring rapper. He was happy the young brother from his old hood was finally free. He thought to himself, one tiny step for man and a giant step for mankind.

24
EVELYN

It took Evelyn a long time to decide if she should call Clayton. They hadn't spoken in over fifteen years, and their last conversation was not on good terms. Over the years, she followed his career and knew he had a successful business as a hair and makeup designer. Whenever she read about his success, her heart skipped a beat, and she was so happy for him. She knew he had never married, but she always saw him in some magazine or on social media with some random thot on his arm. He looked happy, and that was all she ever really wanted for him. The memories of their last encounter still filled her brain with hurtful memories. She remembered that day like it was yesterday. Clayton had wanted her to drop everything, leave her new life she had taken so long to build and run off with him to live a fairytale happily ever after, but that just wasn't what she wanted anymore. So many things had changed for her since she left. She remembered they had gone their separate ways after leaving Hillsborough, NC, and they had made a promise to find each other and finally be together, but it had taken nearly a decade before they would see one another again. They both had been subpoenaed to return and give a deposition as witnesses for the murder trial of James and Jacob Spears that happened when they were kids in the South.

When the twins were first arrested, they didn't have to testify because they were minors at the time, so the DA accepted their sworn written statements, but now that they were of legal age, they had to return for their sentencing. No one ever knew about their involvement except for the twins, but Clayton and Alisha knew they would never rat on them. They had gotten away with more than five million dollars, two homicides and the twins were being charged with all the crimes. "Hey, do you think they will ever find us and get even for what we did?" She remembered asking Clayton as they stood in the stairwell of the DA's office. "Hell, no, they are getting sent up for the rest of their lives," Clayton assured her. "It will take a miracle for them to win that case, and I don't see that happening," he told her as he put his arms around her for comfort. "I hope so, Clay. I just want to put all of this behind us and move on," Alisha said, still shaken about what they had done years ago. "Listen, now that all of this is over, why don't you just leave New York, come to Philly with me and start your life over again? You're safe now, and I'll do everything in my power to protect you," he told her, hoping she was ready to be with him again.

When he left Hillsborough, he went to Philadelphia to hide out and decided that was where he wanted to stay. He and Alisha had talked a few times, but she thought it was best that they stay separated and lay low for a few months. Never did they imagine years would go by. "I don't know, Clay; things are really working out for me in New York. Kendal was able to get me a new identity, and I have a fresh, clean slate now, you know," she said awkwardly. She hadn't told him about the new man in her life. "Kendal? Who the hell is Kendal?" Clayton asked, surprised. "He's my boyfriend," she said, lowering her eyes from his, knowing she was going to have to explain. She wasn't sure how he was going to take the news, but she didn't know any other way to tell him without hurting him.

"You have a boyfriend now, Lee Lee? What the fuck?! "He said, hurt by her admission. "Yes, Clayton, I wanted to tell you a while ago. I'm sorry," she said, feeling terrible about hiding it from him. He never imagined her being with someone else. He assumed she went to New York to hide out and lay low till the twins' trial, and then they would take the money and move somewhere that no one knew them and be together. "What about us? What about our plans?" He asked, getting angry. "What about all the promises you made, huh? I did all of this shit for you," he said, remembering the awful night and what they had done. "You told me you loved me and that when this was over, we would be together, no matter how long it took," he said as tears rolled down his cheeks. "Now you telling me you with some other nigga, and I'm supposed to be ok with that?" He punched the wall, causing an echo. "Clay, calm down," she said, trying to touch his arm. "Calm down? Really, Alisha? Is that all you have to say to me? Stay the fuck away from me, ok? Just stay the fuck away. You ruined my life, Alisha. I can't even show my face in this town anymore because of you. I had to leave my uncle in a fucking loony bin and run away because of you, and all you can say is calm down?" He said, furious. "You have a great fucking life, and don't ever try to contact me again, you hear me? I am done with your manipulating ass. I hope you and dude live happily ever after," he said as he walked down the steps and left her standing there in the hallway alone. Alisha felt so bad. She never wanted to hurt Clayton, and she really loved him. She never meant for them to leave each other that way. It was just that she had been alone for so many years, and she had finally made a new life for herself in New York, and she was happy. Tears flowed from her eyes as she thought of Clayton, but in her heart, she knew he would be ok. He had three and a half million dollars, and he was talented and smart. She knew he would be successful in whatever he did in life, and she wished him well. It was best for both of them to go their separate ways. She reached into her new designer bag and pulled out a Newport. She took a long drag of the minty poison and looked out the stairwell window. She saw Clayton get into a waiting taxi out front. He looked broken. He was headed to the airport back to Philly and his new life, and now it was time for her to live hers.

As Evelyn sat on her terrace thinking of him, she relived the pain she felt the last time she saw him. Her hands trembled as she dialed his number. She had called his salon and was told he was gone for the evening. She lied to the receptionist and told her she was from the hospital his uncle was in and needed his home number because it was an emergency. The young lady quickly gave it to her without hesitation. The phone rang four times before the machine answered. "Hello, you have reached Clayton Taylor. I'm sorry I'm not available to answer your call at the moment, but please leave a detailed message at the sound of the beep, and I will return your call as soon as I'm available. Have a beautiful day, peace."

Evelyn smiled as she listened to his voice. It sounded huskier and more mature than she remembered but still sexy, just the same. She hated having to call him under these circumstances, but she knew he had a right to know what was happening, and she needed him to be careful. "Um, hi, this is…" she almost said Evelyn but knew he wouldn't know her by that name. She had shared with him that she had a new identity but never got the chance to tell him who she now was, so she asked that he call her as soon as he could, and she hung up. She waited for a couple of minutes and decided to leave another message just in case he deleted the first one. After she called Clayton, she decided to reach out to Kendal. She hadn't spoken to him in years either, but at least they were still friends. They had been in a relationship for five years, and he taught her a lot while they were together. She never told him what she had actually done in North Carolina or the horrible crimes she committed, but she did tell him that she had gotten into some trouble and needed to leave her old life in the past. Because Kendal had connections on the street, he was able to get her a new name, birth certificate, and passport. Alisha Louise James was now dead, and Evelyn Marie St. James was born. Any and all traces of her past were erased, and she was able to finally live for once, all thanks to him.

Kendal played a big part in her life, and she would forever be grateful. He was big in the drug game in New York, and he knew lots of famous basketball stars, politicians and rappers. Everyone knew him, and he carried a lot of clout in the city.

He had lots of female friends, but after meeting Alisha, he made her his main Jawn, and the streets knew it. It took her some time to get used to this newfound fame, but after some time, it became second nature to her. She knew how to handle his business, and she did it well. He would always take her out with him and introduce her as his wifey.

They would get invited to big parties and social events, and he would supply the goodies for the rich elites who attended while she mingled with ladies. At first, Evelyn would just stand around and gaze at the famous people that were there, but after a while, she started having conversations with the wives and girlfriends, and they gave her good advice about creating organizations to filter in all the money her man was making. It started off as a great cover for his drug business, but over time, Evelyn became very interested in women's rights and founding sanctuaries for the abused. "Babe, I think this is what I really wanna do." She remembered telling Kendal one night after leaving a shelter they opened for teenage girls.

It was actually a safe house. Kendal had to keep his drugs, but no one could tell from the outside. They had bunk beds and cots in the main hall, a full kitchen and even a rec room with video games and a big screen TV, but in the basement, he ran his whole drug operation. He had Evelyn go down to city hall to get the permits and put everything in her name since she was legit. "What you talking about, mommy? What do you wanna do?" He asked as they got into his C class Mercedes. "I wanna open a legit business helping runaways and teens addicted to drugs and alcohol. I wanna give young girls a chance to be something besides strippers and young mothers on welfare," she said, thinking of all the young girls that got turned out in the South by pimps. She also wanted to do something in her mother's honor since she wasn't able to help her before her death. "The city and state would be more than willing to fund a place like that since it would be helping to get young girls off the street and aid in stopping human trafficking," she said, realizing she now had a purpose for her life.

"Come on, L, you know the game we're in. We can't be drawing attention to ourselves like that," he said, hoping she'd understand his position. "I'm a drug kingpin. These shelters we're running is for show, not praise or profit. You dig me?" "I know, it's just that I had such a rough time growing up, and I see these young girls and realize that could have been me with nowhere to go or strung out on drugs," she said sadly. "I know, mommy, don't look so sad," he said, reaching for her hand to console her. "Look, if that's what you really wanna do, I'll support you, but from the sidelines," he said, knowing that they would have to stop seeing each other if she went legit. "I really love you, Kendal. I just can't spend the rest of my life in the drug game, is all I'm saying."

She hated to end their relationship, but she knew that the streets were his way of life, and he wasn't gonna stop hustling even for her. "Listen, whatever you need, I got you," he said as he pulled into the driveway of their 3000 square foot home. Their time together that night was special but sad. They made passionate love like never before, knowing it would be their last night together and by morning Kendal was gone. Evelyn lay in bed and sobbed. Her heart was broken because she was left alone again.

Another man that she loved dearly had walked out of her life for a decision she made about her future. She cried for what seemed like hours before she decided to get up. She went into the dressing room and saw that he had taken all of his clothes and jewelry from the closets and all of his guns except for the pearl handle pistol he had bought for her. She also noticed that he had left the safe behind, and her mink coats, which he had also bought for her. Kendal was always spoiling her with beautiful gifts. He told her that a beautiful woman should always have beautiful things and that whatever she wanted, he would always provide. Evelyn entered the combination to see what was inside.

He usually kept his different identification cards and birth certificates in there just in case he needed to switch up who he was to avoid the police, but Evelyn was sure he had taken those with him. When she opened the safe, she couldn't believe her eyes. Kendal had put a beautiful diamond ring and tennis bracelet on top of what looked like at least five million dollars! She was in shock. Why did he leave that there? He also left a note that she hurriedly removed and opened:

"Dear mommy, this is the hardest letter I ever had to write in my life. I know that by the time you read this, I'll be gone, but I wanted you to know that my heart is always with you. I'm so proud that you wanna make a difference in other people's lives, and I'm not gonna stand in your way. I left you a little something to get started, and if you need more, don't hesitate to hit me up. I also bought you a ring to remind you that you will always be my wifey and that I love you, B. Take care of yourself and do big things out there in the world, and always remember that the streets will forever have your back. Love, K."

Tears rolled down her face as she read the love letter. She said a silent prayer, hoping she didn't make a mistake. She put the ring on her finger and marveled at its splendor and beauty. She felt the pain all over again, the same she felt when Clayton left her in the stairwell years before. But once again, she knew in her heart that her man would be okay. He didn't need the money he had left her because he was actually a Billionaire. But every time she would ask him to get out of the drug game, he would tell her that hustling was in his DNA. He would say the streets were his beginning and his end, and for him, there was no in-between, so she knew that her wanting to go legit was something he would never do.

She couldn't believe that he had left her with so much money either. She had told him very little about the take she had stashed away, but she also never asked him for anything. She told him that she had gotten a small settlement from her mother's insurance after her death, and that's how she was able to live in a small, modest apartment in Queens, but once they started sleeping together, he told her she would never have to worry about money again, and she never did. He provided for her completely. And after just three months of dating, he bought her the house she was in. It was gorgeous. She had never seen anything like it. It had four bedrooms, five bathrooms and a large wrap-around deck. He gave her full reign to decorate it however she wanted. She never imagined she would live in a place so beautiful. "Why do we need a house so big?" she remembered asking him. "Because I plan on filling it with our seeds," he said, hoping he would one day get her pregnant. Children were definitely a subject that was taboo as far as she was concerned, but she didn't tell him that she just made sure she kept up with her depo shots every three months, and he would be none the wiser.

She never wanted to have kids because she hated the way she was raised; besides, she never felt like she would be a good mother. Candy was never a good role model, and her grandmother suffered for so long trying to raise her siblings that she decided kids weren't worth the headache. Evelyn realized that with the money Kendal had given her and her stash money, she would have more than enough to start her foundation and live comfortably. She knew she couldn't stay in her house any longer because it had been under investigation too many times by the feds because of Kendal's illegal activity, so she decided to put it on the market and finally move to Philadelphia. "She could start over," she thought. No one knew her there, not even Clayton, because of her new identity, and she could open up her shelters and start the Monique Shantel Foundation for battered and abused teens named after her mother. It was gonna be a sad time for her to be alone again, but this was something she really wanted to do. Evelyn went into the bedroom, picked up the gold antique receiver on the telephone, and dialed a number. She had made reservations for a one-way ticket to Philadelphia the next morning. She had some loose ends she needed to tie up, and she was sad that she was leaving Kendal, but she knew she was ready for the next chapter of her life. And boy, had it been an exciting ride. All of the accomplishments she achieved made her smile. Evelyn dialed the number from her iPhone and entered the five-digit code for Kendal's paging service. He was the only man she knew in the world who still had a pager.

After a few minutes, her cell phone rang from a blocked number. "Am I dreaming?" He said seductively into the receiver. "No, you're not dreaming. It's really me," Evelyn said, happy to hear his voice. "How long has it been, beautiful?" He asked her. "Oh, way too long. I've missed you," she responded. He could hear the smile in her voice. "You couldn't have missed me too much. I haven't heard from you in years," he said. "I know. My life has been busy, and, if I'm not mistaken, so is yours." She had found out through mutual connections that Kendal had gotten married and had his third child on the way. "I heard you are quite the family man now, huh?" She said. "Yeah, you know, since I couldn't marry the queen, I settled for a princess," he said with a chuckle. "Well, I'm happy for you, and congratulations," Evelyn said, slightly jealous of his life even though she was very happy with her own. She missed the street life at times but was content with being the wife of a successful attorney.

"So, I know this ain't no social call cause that ain't your style," he said, suddenly changing his tone to a more serious one. "Are you doing ok?" He asked with concern. "Actually, no," she said. Evelyn hated dragging Kendal into her past, but she knew he would be the only one who could help her deal with twins, especially if Clayton never returned her call. "I need to meet you, if possible. I have a problem that needs attention," she said, talking in code. She knew whatever it was, he would handle it. "Ok, just tell me when and where," he said. Kendal would do anything for Evelyn. He still loved her, and he remembered the promise he made to her that the streets would always have her back. "Great. I can be in New York in a day or two. Is that ok?" She asked, hoping he didn't forget his loyalty to her. "That's fine. I'll meet you at the same spot?" He asked, knowing she knew where she could always go for help. "Yes, I'll be there. And Kendal, thank you," she said sincerely. "Anything for my queen," he said and hung up.

Evelyn sat there a few minutes longer, thinking of what Kendal might do to solve her problem, but no matter what it was, she knew she could count on him. Her thoughts went to Ethan and how different the two men were. Her husband was a square and naive, and Kendal was a street dude, a killer. Ethan wasn't even aware he was involved with such deadly people and that his life was in danger, but Evelyn was determined to keep it that way. She wasn't gonna lose another man at any cost, and she would do everything in her power to protect the ones she loved.

25

CLAYTON

Clayton tossed and turned the whole night, thinking about Alisha's call. He felt like shit when he woke up and made his way to the kitchen to start his Keurig machine. He hadn't spoken to Alisha since that day back in Hillsborough when she told him she had a new guy in her life and that she didn't want to be with him anymore. He was crushed at the time and felt like he didn't have a purpose in life to go on. He had made a vow to himself to never let a woman get into his head or heart again. It took him a lot of years to get over her; he even went to therapy to help him cope with his anger and sadness. He hated Alisha, but he had finally gotten over her, and his heart had slowly begun to heal. For the life of him, he couldn't understand why she had called after all these years.

He kept replaying the messages over and over, trying to get a clue. He knew she said that their problem was back, but there was no way in hell she could have been talking about the twins. So, what problem could she possibly be referring to?

They had made sure those bastards were guaranteed to go away for life, and for them, there was no escaping that fate. So, he was puzzled about what she could be talking about. Maybe she wanted money, he thought. He didn't know what she ended up doing with her share of the take, so he thought maybe she'd lost it all, or her new man stole it from her leaving her ass flat broke.

"Yeah, that's what it probably is!" He said aloud, feeling confident he figured out why she called, as he poured himself a cup of coffee. Serves her ass right, he murmured as he sipped his brew. He couldn't believe she had the nerve to reach out to him because of her bullshit, he thought. He never got a chance to fall asleep after hearing her voice on the answering machine, and he was exhausted. He tried to jump-start his energy by drinking some coffee, but it was 7 am, and he had to get moving because he had a lot planned for the day. Clayton went into the bedroom and got his phone. He needed to call Geneva and have her set up a meeting with Darrin and the rest of the organizers for the Gala they were throwing to launch the new salons. He pressed three, and the phone immediately started to ring.

He had her number programmed in his favorites on speed dial. "This had better be an emergency, man," she said sleepily into the phone. "Rise and shine, woman. It's a new day, and we got a lotta shit to do," he said, trying to sound cheerful. "Clay, it is 7 o'clock on Sunday morning. Can't we start our day at noon?" She said, regretting that she answered the call. "No, we gotta get things cracking now. The gala is less than a week away, and we still have a lot of things to get done. Now, get your ass up and meet me at the office by nine," he said sternly. "Ok, ok, but you'd better have me a double shot venti on ice from Starbucks and a dozen fresh hot Crispy Kreme donuts waiting for me when I get there," she said with an attitude. He hated calling her this early on a Sunday morning, but he needed to get busy to get his mind off of Alisha. "You got it. I'll see you at nine, peace," he said and hung up. He noticed he still had some time to kill, so he decided to run on his Nordic track for about an hour before getting dressed.

He needed to clear his mind, and doing a distance run always seemed to do the trick. He rarely worked out on Sundays, but today was different. He had been reminded of his past, and he needed to let off some steam. He walked into the gym and turned on the eighty-five-inch flat screen that was mounted on the wall. It was tuned to ESPN. He grabbed the remote from the weight bench and flipped the channels.

He came across a TD Jakes broadcast and decided to leave it on that channel. "Man, I haven't been to church in years," he said to himself, turning on the treadmill to get ready for his run. He knew his mama would have been very disappointed in him that he hadn't been to the lord's house in so long. He remembered how she used to drag him and Michael to Sunday school in the wee hours of the morning so that she could get a front-row seat in the front pew for services. He missed those days as a boy listening to the preacher deliver the word and believing God was going to save him from all danger and heartache in life. He thought he was just a kid then, but now that he was a grown man, he felt God wasn't delivering on his promises. He wondered where God was when his dear, sweet mama was dying from cancer. Where was God to stop him when he committed that horrible crime? Where was he to protect his heart when Alisha told him she didn't want to be with him anymore? "Where were you, God, when I needed you?!" Clayton cried out as tears rolled down his face. His emotions ran wild as he remembered all the hurt and pain he endured as he listened to the sermon. He got on the treadmill and started his workout.

The preacher on the TV started to speak about forgiveness. He spoke about God forgiving you for your sins. The more Clayton ran, the more he thought about his sins and all the bad things that happened to him, as well as the bad things he had done, and silently prayed that God would forgive him for his sins. When he was done with his run, his muscles felt tight, so he decided to sit in the steam room for a while to relax.

He was glad he had the room built to help him relieve stress, and now was definitely the time for that. He really needed to get his head in the game and stay focused on the big event he had planned. After 20 minutes in the steam room, he felt better. He jumped in the shower and quickly dressed for the day. It was already 8:15, and he still had to make the coffee and donut run for Deva. He made sure he picked up everything she requested, or he would have to hear her bitch and complain during the entire meeting, and he was not in the mood. When he walked into the coffee shop, it was bustling with customers. He never realized how many people were up and about on a Sunday morning.

"It's a beautiful day at Starbucks. May I take your order?" The friendly barista greeted him. "Good morning. May I have a double shot venti on ice and a Grande venti caffe americano, please?" He said, making sure he ordered a large cup for himself. "Sure, would that be all?" The girl asked, smiling at him with crooked teeth. "Yes, that's all," he responded and handed her a twenty. "Keep the change, beautiful," Clayton said and winked at her, making her blush. "Thank you, and have a nice day. Come back and see me whenever you want," she yelled as he exited the store. Clayton had a charming effect on women, and he loved it. He could make any woman feel like she was the most beautiful creature on earth. He smiled as he got into his truck. You still got it, heartbreaker he said to himself in the mirror. After making the next stop for the donuts, he was pleased traffic was light as he sped down JFK Boulevard, and he made it to the salon on time. He pulled into the driveway and parked next to Geneva's Benz. He smiled, knowing she would be on time. He got out of the car, juggling the dozen donuts and coffee, hoping he wouldn't drop anything. Looks like you need some help, handsome she said as she exited her car. He wasn't aware she was in it watching him. That would be nice, he said, placing the coffee containers on the hood of his truck and grabbing his briefcase off the front passenger seat.

She walked over to him and took his briefcase from his hand. "I see you got my stuff," she said, kissing him on the cheek and grinning. "Yeah, I had to cut my workout short to make the run," he said jokingly, knowing he was going to stop for coffee anyway. "Whatever, man, you wake me up this early on a Sunday morning, you'd better have me plenty of caffeine and sugar," she said, laughing. They walked towards the elevators a few feet away. "Hey, did you contact Darrin and let him know we were meeting this morning?" he asked, remembering he forgot to call him on his way to the shop. "Yes, and I called Trevor and Sydney, too," she said, reassuring him the accountant and business manager were on their way as well. "That's great, sweetie. What would I do without you," he said, smiling as they got into the elevator. He truly valued Geneva as a friend and business partner, and he knew he wouldn't be a success without her. She helped to keep him balanced and on top of his game, and together, they were magical. "You know I'm your Gale to your Oprah," she said, grabbing his arm. "Come on now with that Gay shit again," he said, laughing. "I'm just kidding. You know I know you're a beast with the ladies," she said, hugging him around the waist.

"Speaking of ladies, what happened on your date last night?" She asked curiously. She figured he got lucky with Regina since he never returned her call last night. "It went great, Deva. She really is a fantastic lady, and I'm glad I invited her here and asked her out," he said, thinking about his date with her. "Oh, so you got a chance to tap that ass, huh?" She asked, amused. "It wasn't even like that. We really clicked with one another. We had dinner, sat, and talked for hours. I learned a lot about her, and she really made me interested in knowing more," he said, wishing he had remembered to send her flowers earlier that morning. He had been so preoccupied with Alisha's message that he had forgotten to do a lot of the things he was supposed to do that morning. "Well, I'm happy to hear everything went so well. You look like you had a really good time, and I'm happy for you, baby." "Thanks, Deva. I think she may be the one," he said, "Fingers crossed."

When they reached his office, all was serene and quiet. He loved Sunday mornings there. It displayed peace in an otherwise chaotic environment Monday through Saturday. Clayton walked over to his desk and placed the coffee and donuts down. He pushed the button on his computer to jumpstart the system. "So, do we have everything in place for the showcase?" He asked Geneva while she wolfed down one of the warm, soft donuts. "Yeah, everything seems to be good. I went over the cost of the Gala with Sydney, and he assured me that we were within budget and that all the numbers looked good," she said in between bites." "Great, I just need to find out from Trevor how much we have to spare for entertainment. I want to capitalize on the Philly talent and have some local groups perform," he said, thinking he could reach out to some of the booking agents he knew who frequented his establishment. "I would love it if you could get Boyz 2 Men or Jill Scott to perform," Deva said as she swayed, thinking of their music. "That would be dope. That's why I need to know what the budget is cause I'm sure they require a pretty penny for appearances," he responded, liking her ideas. "Well, Mr. Big Shot, you're gonna have a world-renowned chef catering. You might as well go all out and have the best Philly Entertainment," she responded sarcastically. Clayton sipped his coffee, ignoring her comment about Chef Ramsey. He logged into his computer and started looking over the profits from the day before. Everything was looking good until a large figure caught his attention.

"Hey, why is there an invoice for Price and Associates on the books?" he asked curiously. There was a charge for ten thousand dollars listed. "Because your new lady insisted on paying for her spa day and wouldn't take no for an answer when I told her it was complimentary," she said, forgetting to tell him. "Well, make sure that it's removed immediately. I don't want any traces of her visit being sent to Price," he said, slightly annoyed she even entered it into the system. "Fine, whatever, Clayton, it was an honest mistake, that's all," she said, noticing he was getting angry by the oversight. "A mistake that could have potentially made us look like we were trying to get over on our new attorneys. This deal means a lot to our future, Geneva, and we can't do anything to screw it up," he said, raising his voice and trying to get her to realize how important Price was to the success of their company. "Jesus, I said I was sorry; I'll have it removed today," she said, aggravated as she got up and walked out of his office. He hated getting into spats with her, but he had to sometimes put his foot down to get her to understand all that was at stake. He continued looking over the books to make sure there weren't any other discrepancies there.

Everything had to be perfect, and he wanted to impress Mr. Price with the accuracy of how he ran his business. When Geneva came over the intercom, he could tell she was still pissed at him for snapping at her. "Darin, Sydney, and Trevor are here," she said, sounding hurt. "Ok dear, I'll be there in a sec," he said playfully, trying to cheer her up. "I got your dear," she chuckled softly and disconnected. He didn't like it when there was tension between them, especially in front of other employees. She was his support system, and he depended on her for a lot. They never gave anyone the indication that there was any turmoil between them, and he made sure to keep it that way. Whenever they did argue, they did it privately and always worked it out in the end. He loved her like a sister and knew she felt the same love and loyalty for him. He decided to send her some flowers as well when he placed the order for Regina.

He stood up from his desk, turned off his computer, and grabbed his planner. He was excited to finalize the plans for the Gala. This event was the final key to his success, and he was excited. All his dreams were finally coming to fruition. He strolled down the hall from his office towards the boardroom. As he reached the double glass doors, Sydney emerged from the elevator. "Mr. Taylor, good seeing you, sir," the older white man greeted him enthusiastically. "It's a pleasure seeing you, Sydney. Thank you for coming over so early on a Sunday morning. I hope I haven't interrupted your plans for the day?" Clayton said apologetically. "Oh, absolutely not. The Mrs. is actually happy I left out this morning; she gets to keep the whole bed to herself," he said, laughing. "Ahhh, I see. Well, great, let's join the others," Clayton said as he opened the glass doors, and they went inside. Geneva had the boardroom ready for the meeting. There were copies of the proposals, pens, markers, and coffee sitting in front of each chair and a fresh fruit basket in the middle of the table, along with bottles of spring water.

"Gentlemen, welcome," Clayton said as he sat at the head of the long wooden table. "Shall we get down to business?" he added. He felt powerful and confident, and it showed in his stature. Being a successful young African American male was quite impressive, and it was apparent on his colleagues' faces. His office manager, as well as his account were two older white men that Clayton had hired from Ethan Price's previous law firm.

They were bread from money and suburban life, and he knew they would handle his finances perfectly. They had worked for him for over two years and were dedicated to his company. At first, they viewed him as just a thug who had a little money to invest, probably from the drug trade, but over the years, they realized he was a fierce businessman who would make them very rich. Clayton developed a friendship with the men over time, surrounding them with his culture, inviting them to shows, concerts and, every now and again, the strip clubs in North Philly so that they would have an idea of who he was as a man and the clout he had in the city. Even though, at times he knew they were on edge when in the company of Clayton's more hood friends. Trevor was the first to take the floor. "Well, sir, we are meeting capacity for the budget," he informed Clayton. "The cost to rent out the Bellevue Hotel ballroom and the 20 penthouse suites have actually come in under budget, and we have more than enough to splurge on entertainment," Trevor informed him. "Fantastic!!" Clayton exclaimed.

"Oh, and Clay, the materials and designs you ordered for your peeps is fire," Darrin said, interrupting the office manager. Clayton looked at his friend. He didn't appreciate him butting in while Trevor was giving him the reports. He knew Darrin wasn't particularly fond of him or Sydney, and neither of the men liked him being at the meetings, but they were all Clayton's business partners, and they needed to respect that. Darrin was from the streets and rough around the edges, but he was a damn good designer and one of Clayton's closest friends. "That's what's up, D. I knew you were gonna come out the gate smoking," Clayton said, knowing full well the white men in the room had no clue what they were talking about. Geneva laughed at the banter between the two, noticing Trevor and Sydney turning red and looking uncomfortable. "Gentlemen, what Mr. Taylor and Mr. Brown are referring to are the uniforms he had designed for the wait staff and employees of Tailored To You for the event. Sydney, how much do we have towards the entertainment budget after the design costs?" she asked, taking control of the meeting before Clayton and Darrin scared them any further with their hood talk. He cleared his throat and opened his portfolio to the budget sheet. "It seems we have close to a quarter million as well as a credit of four hundred thousand in case any incidentals shall occur," he said. "Wonderful," she exclaimed; that gives us ample wiggle room for any extras we would want to really make this event the best this city has ever seen!" Everyone was all smiles by the time the meeting ended, and Clayton was ecstatic with the results. After shaking hands with the men, he walked back to his office and took out one of his Cuban cigars, which he only smoked on special occasions.

He had given everyone the rest of the day off as well as a sizable bonus for all the hard work they had been putting in to make the Gala a success. It was a beautiful Sunday afternoon, so Clayton decided to head out to King of Prussia to visit one of his favorite jewelers. He wanted to get Geneva a gift for withstanding the difficulties and challenges they faced over the past year and show how much he appreciated her as his partner and friend. When he walked into Rothmans Jewelers, the staff were all smiles. He hadn't been there in quite some time, but they knew whenever he did show up, he was dropping a shit load of money. "Clayton, how have you been, darling?" The owner, Isabella Devereux, approached him, grinning from ear to ear. She was a beautiful woman in her late 60s, stout in stature but dripping with elegance. She had migrated to the States from Greece, married a rich oil tycoon as a young girl, and over the years, she started importing jewels. After 33 years of marriage, her husband left her for a young blonde. He was twice her age, and he fell in love with her enormous bra size. Isabella didn't let that stop her, though. She had gotten a large settlement from her divorce and decided to open a chain of jewelry stores in three different countries across the globe. Clayton was delighted when she was in town, and he got a chance to see her. "Isabella, it's always a pleasure to see you," he said as he planted kisses on both her cheeks. "The pleasure is all mine, darling." "You look amazing as always," he said, admiring her stunning outfit. She was always dressed beautifully in silks and diamonds.

She resembled a young Zsa Zsa Gabor in the way she floated around the room. "Ah, this is from a French designer I've been canoodling with for a few months," she said, taking him by the arm and walking him over to her private cubicle. "Isabella, I'm hurt. You're supposed to only have eyes for me," he said playfully, knowing she loved it when he flirted with her. "Darling, a woman has needs even at my age," she said, laughing heartily. "So, what brings you in today, my love? Another diamond trinket for your lovely lady?" she asked, curious to know if he was still seeing his latest conquest, Naomi. She knew he changed women like the weather, but that one seemed special. He had brought her into the store a few times since they were dating and had bought her quite a few nice pieces for her jewelry collection, but he had done that for several others in the past, so it would have been no surprise if the gift was for someone new. "Actually, no, I'm here to get a gift for Geneva. We've had such a fantastic quarter, and we're way under budget for the upcoming Gala, so I decided to buy her something nice to show my appreciation for all her hard work." "Isn't that delightful? You are so very good to the women in your life, my dear," she said, smiling seductively. "I try, Isabella. So, what do you have that would make her eyes sparkle?" he asked, looking at the beautiful jewels in the showcase. She picked a lovely emerald and diamond necklace that was absolutely breathtaking, and he knew he had to get it for her. "She could wear it to the Gala, no?" she asked, knowing about the huge event he was throwing next week. "Yes, that's perfect, and she is absolutely going to love it," he said, envisioning it around her neck.

"Wonderful, now we find something for your beautiful lady friend," she said as she walked over to another display case. "As a matter of fact, Isabella, Naomi is in Italy with her dance troupe, so she won't be attending the event," he said. Clayton was relieved his girlfriend was going to be out of town for a few months. Their relationship had felt stale to him lately, and all she had become to him now was a show-piece. They hardly spent time together anymore, and truth be told, he wasn't feeling her sexually anymore either. The flame that was once there had all but burned out. "Oh, poor dear, so you will be alone on your special night," Isabella said sympathetically. "No, actually, I've met someone new, and she's wonderful," he said, thinking of Regina. "I haven't asked her to escort me to the Gala yet, but I'm planning on it," he said hopefully. "Well then, you must buy her a gift to make her say yes," Isabella responded. "You don't think that would be too forward? We've only been on one date, and I wouldn't want her to think I was trying to buy her affection," he said matter-of-factly. "Oh, don't be silly. Beautiful women love beautiful things," she said as she flashed the diamond rings she wore on each finger. "Ok, Isabella, what do you have in mind?" he laughed, curious about what she might pick for him. She reached into the display case and pulled out a stunning sapphire and diamond bracelet. It was very elegant but not showy. "This is class," she said as she handed it to him. "It's just a gift to say I think you're special," she added.

"And you don't think she would be offended by it?" he asked, wondering if it would be too much too soon. He would love to spoil her, but he didn't want to move too fast and scare her away. He knew Regina was a very independent woman, and he liked that about her, but he also wanted to do nice things for her and make her feel special. "If she doesn't like it, then pa," she spat next to her. Clayton laughed, knowing it was a thing she did when she was dissatisfied about something. "Ok, you've convinced me. I'll take the bracelet and also pick out a pair of 2-carat diamond earrings for her daughter," he said, remembering Regina's child he knew she thought the world of. She had told him about Nyla and all the wonderful achievements she had accomplished at her new high school. He really enjoyed listening to Regina brag about her baby girl. "Oh, so this lady comes with a package," Isabella said, raising her eyebrows. "Yes, she has a daughter, and even though I haven't met her yet, I can already tell she's great," he said, smiling. "Aww, such a noble man. I can't wait to meet this lovely lady at the party, Clayton," she said and kissed him on the cheek. She took the necklace, bracelet, and earrings with her to the back room to clean and gift wrap them for him.

As he glanced around at the other lovely pieces, his cell phone rang. "Hello, this is Clayton Taylor," he said when he answered. "I hope I'm not interrupting you," Regina said shyly on the other end. Instantly, his face lit up. "Absolutely not. How are you?" he asked, happy to hear her voice. "I'm great. Just wanted to call and thank you for the lovely roses you sent," she said sweetly. "They arrived a little before noon by special messenger." "Oh, great, you got them. I was hoping you'd be home to get them. Didn't know what your Sunday schedule was like," he said, feeling good he had sent them to her. "Yes, it was a wonderful surprise. Thank you, Clayton." "You know, I'm surprised you called me but delighted at the same time," he responded happily. "I was just talking about you to a dear friend of mine," he added as he glanced over at Isabella wrapping his gifts. "Oh, really?" Regina said. "Well, I hope it was all good," she smiled widely. "Oh, absolutely nothing but good things," he said, enjoying the conversation. He loved the sound of her voice, seductive yet shy, and it made him feel like a teenager talking to his high school crush. "Well, I won't hold you. I'll let you get back to saying nice things about me," she chuckled. "I just called to thank you for the lovely flowers, is all."

"Well, you're more than welcome and just know there's more to come," he said, thinking about the bracelet he just purchased. "Stop it, Clayton, you're spoiling me already," she said bashfully. "Hey, how about dinner tonight?" he asked, hoping she'd say yes because he really loved spending time with her. "That sounds nice," she responded, "but how about I cook for you?" she suggested. "I can really get my chef boy r dee on when I want to," she said, laughing. "Oh, you can burn in the kitchen, huh?" he asked, intrigued. "Yes, but not as fancy as the dinner we had last night," she said, remembering the lovely restaurant he had taken her to the night before. "I'm sure it will be just as tasty," he responded seductively. "I'm sure," she added, laughing. "OK, well, I'm out running a few errands, and then I'll have to go home to change, so how about 8? Is that a good time?" he asked, flattered she was inviting him to her home. "Eight would be perfect," she said as she looked at the clock on her kitchen counter and saw she would have more than four hours to prepare a great meal for him. "Wonderful, I will call you when I get in and get the directions," he said, wanting to do backflips because she invited him to dinner. "That sounds great. I look forward to seeing you, Clayton," she said sweetly and hung up.

He was smiling so hard his cheeks hurt. He turned around to see all the ladies in the store looking at him, including

Isabella, and he started to blush. "She invited me to dinner," he said out loud as if he had just won the lottery. "Beautiful, darling," Isabella said, clasping her hands together in delight. "This woman, she makes you very happy, yes?" she asked. "Yes, she does, Isabella; she makes me feel like a kid again," he said, liking the effect Regina was having on him. "Well, you go and get ready for tonight and make sure you give her the lovely gift," she said as she handed him the platinum-colored jewelry bag. "Oh, for sure. How much do I owe you?" he said, reaching in his back pocket for his wallet. "It's fine. I will put it on your account. Now go," she said as she hurried him toward the exit. "Isabella, you are a doll," he responded as he hugged her tightly. She was a really good friend, and he respected her deeply. "I will see you at the event, right?" he asked as he opened the door. "But of course, darling. I wouldn't miss it for the world," she said excitedly. "Great, see you next week," he said as he rushed from the store.

He made the 20-minute drive back home in record time. He had a good 2 hours to get himself together before his date with Regina. When he got in, he headed for his bedroom and placed the necklace for Geneva in his closet safe until the night of the gala. He removed the gifts for Regina and her daughter from the glittery bag and examined the beautiful jewels before placing them on his dresser next to his wallet and keys. I hope she likes them he said out loud, smiling. He went to take a quick shower, then groomed his beard and gave himself a quick shape-up. He loved the advantages of his skills knowing how to take care of himself as well as making others beautiful. Clayton walked back into his massive dressing room, not knowing what he would wear. He definitely didn't want to be too formal and showy since dinner was at her place and not a three-Michelin-star restaurant, so a suit was out of the question. As he looked at the rack of expensive clothing, he noticed the dry cleaning his housekeeper picked up for him and was happy he had something casual to choose from. Carmella always took care of sports and casual wear for him, making sure they were cleaned professionally. He decided to wear the Valentino Garavani tee, a pair of off-white jeans and a fresh pair of Yeese's for dinner since he knew Regina had never seen him in it. It was gonna be a relaxed evening, and he wanted to look the part. He was sexy and confident as he looked at himself. "Damn, brother," he said, grinning as he admired his lay in the full-length bedroom mirror. He sprayed on his favorite cologne and headed for the kitchen.

He wasn't sure what she was serving for dinner, but he wanted to bring a nice bottle of wine with him to complement the meal. He decided on a bottle of Armand de Brignac Rose from his wine refrigerator and knew it would taste great with any meal. He went back into the bedroom, put the beautifully wrapped gifts and wine into the bag, and grabbed his keys and wallet. Just as he headed for the garage, his home phone rang. "Damn it!" he shouted as he went over to the phone in the kitchen. He wondered who could have been calling him on a Sunday evening since he had already seen Geneva and Darrin at the meeting earlier, and Naomi had sent him a text letting him know she wouldn't be able to talk for several days due to her hectic schedule on tour. "This better not be the hospital again," he said as he grabbed the phone from the kitchen counter. "This better be good," he said, annoyed with the person on the other end of the phone. "Clayton, please don't hang up," the woman said nervously on the phone. "What the fuck do you want?" he asked angrily into the receiver, instantly recognizing her voice. He knew it was Alisha, and he knew at some point he was gonna have to talk to her, but he didn't plan on it being today.

26

EVELYN

Evelyn woke up from her third nap of the day and still felt drained. She had taken several zanies and eight hundred milligrams of Motrin all day, and her head was still ponding. Her mind was twirling from seeing the twins a few nights before. She was glad her husband had spent his Sunday in the city to give her time to regroup. He had called her several times throughout the day, and she reassured him she was fine and not to worry. She needed to come up with a plan to handle the twins, and she didn't want to be distracted by Ethan. She had left two messages on Clayton's answering machine the night before, but he hadn't returned her call yet. She had even set up a meeting with Kendall, her old flame from her past, in hopes he could help her with her problem. She told him she would be coming to New York in a few days. Evelyn had to get her players in order to take down the twins once and for all. There was no way she was gonna let them interrupt and destroy everything she had built. She kept trying to get out of bed and get herself together, but she couldn't. Her head was spinning, and she wasn't able to get rid of the headache she had been suffering from since the night she saw them. She looked over at the nightstand and saw an empty bottle of chardonnay. She knew she must have drank along with an empty pill bottle.

It was almost three o'clock on Sunday afternoon, and she had to get it together. She hadn't been out of bed in almost two days. Ethan would be coming home later that night, and she didn't want him to see her still there. She decided to take a cold shower to perk herself up. Afterward, she felt a little better but realized she hadn't eaten much in days, which could have been one of the reasons her head was still killing her.

As she made her way through the house, she noticed all the staff was gone for the day. She was relieved to see that Henrietta had left her and Ethan's dinner in the oven for them. She didn't have enough strength to prepare and cook him something to eat, and she knew he was expecting Sunday dinner when he arrived home later that night. Evelyn made herself a cup of coffee, placed her food in the oven, and sat down at her kitchen island. She took out her cell phone from her satin robe and checked her messages. She saw that Ethan had called her again, twice as a matter of fact, and she had a call from the director of the children's foundation she started a few months ago. She pressed one on her keypad to dial Ethan's cell. "Hey, baby," he answered pleasantly. "How's my angel feeling today?" He said happily. "I'm feeling great," she lied. "I just wanted to check in because I saw you called me twice while I was napping." She tried to sound upbeat and cheerful, which was hard because of her splitting headache, but she didn't want to tell him that because she knew he'd worry.

"Oh yeah, I just wanted to hear your beautiful voice, is all," he said seductively. "I've been listening to these clowns all day in meetings, and my ears are bleeding," he chuckled, referring to the other partners of his law firm. He had been in litigations all weekend trying to secure contracts for Clayton's business. He was a huge client, and he knew after securing this deal, he would be a very rich man. He hadn't told Evelyn about his partnership with Clayton yet because of all that happened the night she went ill. "You working on something big?" she asked, trying to show interest in his work even though her mind was somewhere else. "Yeah, baby, it's mega, and it's gonna set us up for greatness," he said excitedly. "Awesome, well I'm gonna let you go, and I'll see you tonight for dinner," she said. "Absolutely, I can't wait to get home to see my lovely wife." Ethan was so in love with her, and no matter what she said, he kept silently praying she was pregnant. "All right, my love, I'll see you later," she said, smiling. Ethan always made her feel special. They blew each other kisses through the phone and hung up. "I'm gonna have to give that man some tonight," she said out loud as she thought about making love to her husband.

Evelyn ate some dry toast and took two more Motrin to try to soothe her headache. She wanted to be in a better mood when Ethan came home so that she could enjoy her evening with the love of her life. She knew he deserved that. He had been working so hard and would do anything he possibly could to make her happy. She looked over at the clock and saw that it was six thirty. Ethan wouldn't be home until at least eight, so that gave her some time to eat and hopefully let the Motrin kick in. While she was sitting there, she decided to try Clayton's number again. She really needed to talk to him before seeing Kendall, and she prayed he would answer this time. While she prepared to leave another message on his machine, she was surprised to hear his voice.

"This better be good," he said into the receiver, annoyed. "Please, don't hang up, Clayton, it's me," she quickly said nervously. There was silence for a few seconds before he spoke. "Alisha, what the hell do you want?" he asked angrily. "Clayton, I really need to talk to you; it's very important," Evelyn said. "Talk to me about what? What could you possibly have to say to me after all these years, huh?" She heard tears and frustration building in his voice. "Clayton, how have you been? It's been so long since I talked to you," she said, trying to calm his tone. "Really? How have I been? You're calling me to find out how I've been? You have some fucking nerve, you know that?" he spat into the phone. She knew small talk wasn't going to work, so she got right to the point. "Listen, I need to see you; something has happened that's not good," she felt herself trembling as she spoke to him. "What the hell happened, Alisha? You lost all your money? That nigga out there in New York whopping your ass? Huh? And you thought you could call me to fix your problems again?" he said, angry and hurt as all the feelings he had for her crept back into his head. "No, it's nothing like that, honestly," she said as tears started to fall from her eyes. She didn't realize he was still so hurt since their last encounter over ten years ago. "Clayton, I'm so sorry for what happened to us a long time ago. I never meant to hurt you; I just needed to move on and get away from my past. Really, it had nothing to do with my feelings for you. I loved…" "Shut up," Clayton interrupted her before she could get the rest of her words out. "What were you gonna say, Alisha? That you loved me?" "Yeah," she said softly. "Bitch, you didn't love me, you used me. And I fell for your shit, believing we could have had a future together," he yelled. He felt his blood starting to boil. "Clayton, please, it wasn't like that. Honestly," Evelyn cried. He had never called her a bitch before, and she knew he was really mad. "Look, I'm busy, so what is it that's so important that you decided to interrupt my life again with your bullshit?" He wanted to get off the phone with her now. He couldn't take hearing her voice any longer. He still loved her, and his heart was breaking all over again. "Ok, wait, please. I needed to tell you something," she said in a hurry before he hung up on her. "The twins are out of jail, and they saw me, and we are in danger," she said frantically. "What the fuck do you mean they out of jail? We put those mother fuckers away for life; what do you mean?" he asked, confused. "Clayton, I saw them. They are out, and you know they gonna be coming for us," she said, sounding scared.

"Us? What the fuck do you mean us? They saw your ass in New York, not me, and they don't know where I am," he said. "I'm not in New York anymore. I live in Philly. I've been here for years; I just didn't tell you. I knew you were here running a successful business, and I didn't want to interfere with your life." "Wait, hold the fuck up. You live in Philly?" he asked, surprised. "Yes, and I saw them here just the other day," she told him. "They followed you here from New York, and now you brought them to me," he said, furious, thinking she was trying to set him up. His head was filled with so many questions. He was trying to comprehend what she was saying to him. "No, Clay. I've been in Philly for a while now, and I don't know how they knew I was here, but they saw me." She didn't want to tell him yet that they were with her husband. She didn't fully know the situation, and she didn't want him to try to get Ethan. Clayton didn't know anything about her new life or identity, and she wanted to tell him in person if he would agree to see her. "Look, can you please meet me somewhere tomorrow? Please," she begged. "I can't believe this shit. You call me out of the blue and tell me that these niggas are in my city and my life is in danger, and can I meet you somewhere? You have got to be kidding." He couldn't believe the conversation he was having with her. "I need to see you and tell you what's going on, please, Clayton," she sounded desperate. "Well, look, today ain't the day. I have plans, so hit me up tomorrow, and we can talk," he said, frustrated. "OK, I'll call you tomorrow morning. I can't wait to…" He hung up suddenly before she could finish. Evelyn sat there crying yet relieved Clayton agreed to meet her. She had to talk to him and figure out what they were gonna do about the twins. Her body trembled as her mind flashed back to that terrible night.

"Why the fuck did you shoot her, Alisha? Why?" Clayton yelled at her when they got back into the car. Alisha was in shock. Her clothes were covered in blood, and she still had the gun clutched in her hand. She tried moving her lips, but no sound. "Alisha, talk to me, please," he cried as he grabbed the gun from her. Clayton started the car and sped away from the house as quickly as he could. He drove for what seemed like hours before he pulled over on the side of a dirt road. The whole time he was driving, Alisha never said a word. Tears just fell from her eyes as she sat in silence. "She's dead, Clayton. I killed her," she said over and over as she shook violently when the car came to a stop. "I didn't mean to do it, Clay. I'm so sorry," she cried loudly.

Alisha had shot the only friend she had in that house of horrors. Kim meant so much to her, and she was the last person Alisha ever wanted to hurt. "Calm down, baby, and tell me what happened," Clayton said as he wrapped his arms around her. "It all happened so fast, Clay. She tried to take the gun from me, and I just panicked and shot her. God knows I didn't mean to. I'm so sorry. God, I'm so sorry," she began to sob again. "It's alright, Lee Lee, it's gonna be ok," he said as he held her tightly. "What are we gonna do, Clay? Jacob and James are gonna kill us once they get back to that house and see Kim dead and all of their shit gone. They coming after us for sure," she said, scared for her life. "Look, we just gonna take this shit to Smitty and go, that's all. He's waiting for us to deliver, and then you and I can leave this fucked up town and start over right. Isn't that what you want?" he asked as he held her face gently. "Yes, Clayton, that's all I want. Take me away from here," she sobbed quietly.

Once he calmed her down, Clayton started the car and drove over to Smitty's house as planned. He went through the back entrance so nobody could see him. He had the trash bag full of drugs when he went inside and his 22 pistol in his pocket. Alisha stayed in the car as a lookout until he returned. "Hey man, what took you so long?" Smitty asked as he entered his living room. "Look, shit went a little crazier that we planned," Clayton told him. "You got the money ready?" he asked, anxious to get his bread and leave. "Calm down, young buck. I need to see what you brought me first," Smitty replied in a smug tone as he inspected the contents of the bag. "It's thirteen bricks of coke and horse, at least two million dollars' worth," Clayton said, not really sure of the street value, but he knew it was probably worth ten times as much. "Two million? You must be out yo rabbit ass mind nigga, that's only worth half a mil," Smitty said in a self-satisfied voice. "Look, man, the deal was two million dollars, and I want my money," Clayton said, getting pissed at this asshole for trying to back out of the deal he promised. "I know what I said, but my money is looking a little funky right now, young blood, you understand, right?" he said, trying to con Clayton.

Smitty was surprised and impressed he had robbed the twins in the first place. He was for sure certain the young, scrawny kid wouldn't make it out of their house alive. He never intended to give Clayton any money; anyway, he thought he would just play along to see if he would really do the heist. "Listen, come back tomorrow, and I'll have yo money, ok? I'm waiting for my bitches to bring me their green from tonight, and then I'll have your paper for you," he told Clayton, thinking he could bullshit him to leave and he would keep the drugs. "That wasn't the plan, Smitty. You told me you'd have the money when I got here, and now you trying to play me. That's not what we agreed upon, nigga. Now get me my paper so I can get the fuck outta here," he said firmly. "I ain't giving you shit, boy, now get yo ass outta here before I call the police. Better yet, I'll call the twins," Smitty said, laughing as he poured himself a drink, thinking he was scaring the young boy. Just then, Clayton pulled the gun he took from Alisha from his back pocket and put it in Smitty's face. "Mother fucker, you trying to play me like some punk, huh?" Clayton asked angrily. "Where the money at, you fat piece of shit," he said as he clocked the gun. "Come on, man, you don't want to do this. My soldiers are gonna come in here and put a bullet in your brain, man. Come on," Smitty said, placing the glass down, frightened. "You ain't got no soldiers, remember, nigga? You the only dick that would ever be under your roof," Clayton said, remembering what Smitty always said about any dudes living in his house. "And I know all your pussy is out on the streets making money, so cut the bullshit and give me my bread before you take your last breath," Clayton scowled. "Alright, alright, the money's in the safe downstairs. I'll give it to you, man. Chill," Smitty said as Clayton saw him start to sweat. "Come on, nigga, let's go get this money." Clayton grabbed him by the arm and pushed him towards the basement stairs. He knew from the times he was there with his mama that Smitty kept his money down there. He had watched him a few times take large sums from his worker's earnings and put it in the safe. When they got down there, Clayton made him open the large metal safe. Smitty hesitated, knowing he had protection inside before he reached in and pulled out a thirty-eight pistol. "You ain't gone rob me like some bitch," Smitty said as he tried to shoot the gun. Clayton peeped the game and fired two shots into Smitty's temple before he could turn around. He watched Smitty's body fall to the floor. He then took an old gym bag that was lying in the corner and filled it with money from the safe. It was a little over two million dollars, the exact amount he was going to give to Clayton for the drugs. Smitty wasn't a big-time dealer. He used to buy just enough to supply his workers and Jons from time to time, but once he found out Clayton and Alisha planned on robbing the twins, he made a deal with Clayton to buy the take. He wanted to up his game and become the next big-time dealer in the South. He never had any intention of paying Clayton and Alisha for the drugs. He thought he could threaten them and scare them into giving it to him. He had no idea Clayton had a piece and that he was not afraid to use it. Clayton left Smitty's body lying on the floor and the drugs upstairs as he made his way out of the house. He had no use for the drugs, and he knew of no one who would buy that much weight from him except Smitty. When he got back in the car, he saw Alisha sitting there looking terrified. She quickly grabbed him and hugged his neck tightly. "I thought you weren't coming back," she said when he got back into the car. "It's cool. He tried to play me, but I got the money," Clayton said as he handed her the bag. She looked inside, amazed at all the money she had seen. "Clay, this is more than two mil." "Yeah, I know. Smitty had a change of heart and decided to give me more," he said, not telling her he had to kill that mother fucker too. "We got to get out of here before anyone gets home," he said, looking around to make sure no one was in sight. "I love you, Alisha, and I'm gonna take care of you no matter what," he said as he kissed her softly on the lips.

The chime from the doorbell startled Evelyn from her thoughts. She heard Ethan entering the garage. She quickly got up and ran into the powder room to put some water on her face and check her hair to make sure she didn't look disheveled when he came in. She had been so deep in her thoughts she hadn't realized it was close to eight o'clock. "Honey, I'm home. Where are you?" Ethan said as he entered the kitchen. "Here I am, baby," Evelyn said as she walked back into the room. "I am so happy to see you," she said as she hugged him tightly and kissed him long and hard on the lips. "Wow, that was nice," he said as she took his briefcase and placed it on the kitchen counter. "I want you to go wash up and then come eat your dinner. Then meet me in the bedroom," she said seductively as she untied her robe, exposing her naked skin. Ethan instantly got a hard-on. He had been wanting to make love to his wife all weekend and was excited to see that she felt better and was in the mood. "Well, shit, don't threaten me with a good time," he laughed as he ran towards the steps taking them two at a time. "Warm up my plate, babe. I'll be back in a few minutes," he yelled down from their bedroom. He was super excited to finally be able to spend a romantic evening with her and was happy she was finally in good spirits. Little did he know the anguish she was facing about the twins. Evelyn removed his plate from the oven and poured him a glass of wine. She wanted to get him relaxed and ready for her. Even though she still had a splitting headache, she was gonna fuck her husband tonight to put him at ease. She didn't want him asking any questions, and the only way she knew to keep him quiet was to fuck his brains out.

27

ETHAN

Ethan was exhausted when he left the office. He had been working on the legal documents all day for the opening of Clayton's salons. One of the associates from his firm had come in to assist him, but there was still so much to do. He thought about calling Regina and asking her to come in, but he didn't want to disturb her on a Sunday. She had already been gracious enough to go by Clayton's salon on Saturday, but he couldn't ask her to work on both of her days off. He knew she had a daughter and was probably spending the day with her. There were a lot of legal technicalities he had to fix, and it had to be done by him since he was the senior partner and owner of the firm. Even though he was tired, he was excited to get home and spend time with Evelyn. He had called her before he left the office, and she sounded happy, which was great for him because maybe he could finally get laid. He had been wanting to make love to his wife for days now, but she was going through some type of mental break-down that he just didn't know how to cope with. She seemed hormonal and cranky, which led him to believe she might really be pregnant, but maybe he could be wrong, and she was going through a change of life. Either way, she was withholding sex from him, and that was definitely not like her. Evelyn was one of the most sensual sexual beings he had ever been with. From the first time he made love to her, she wanted it more than he did. That made him smile as he thought about the first time she gave him head. They had only been dating for a short time, and he wanted more than anything to fuck her. They had been out at a nightclub in Society Hill and drinking. She had her driver pick him up from his office earlier that night, and when he got into the limo, she was wearing a skin-tight black dress and six-inch stilettos.

He remembered begging her all night as they drank shots of tequila. "No, no. I'm not ready to give you my special package yet," he recalled her telling him as he rubbed between her thighs when they got back into the car. "But I will give you a treat," she said as she unzipped his pants. Next thing he knew she was leaning over and taking his piece in her mouth. It felt wonderful, and Evelyn was a pro. She sucked him off so good he came in minutes, and that's not something he normally did. Ethan wasn't necessarily a man whore, but he did have his share of women back in the day and always had control of his rod, but he had to admit none of them compared to Evelyn. She was skilled in everything she did sexually, and he knew she had him pussy whipped. She got a kick out of putting it on him, and she never seemed to get tired. He loved her sexual energy. When he pulled into the garage of their home, his excitement couldn't be contained. He had a stiff one in his pants from thinking about her all the way home, and he couldn't wait to see her.

When he walked inside the house, he called out her name. "Here I am, sweetie," she said as she entered the kitchen. "Oh, how I've missed you," Ethan replied as he hugged her tightly. "I've missed you too. Now go wash up while I heat up your dinner, and then get ready for a hot, passionate night," Evelyn said, getting him more excited than ever. "Sure thing, baby, don't threaten me with a good time," he replied as he ran up the stairs. He was so happy his wife was back to normal, and he couldn't wait to make love to her. He quickly took a shower and went back down to the kitchen to eat his supper. "How was your day, dear?" Evelyn asked as she watched him eat the platter Henrietta prepared for him. "It was great. I'm working on a huge case for a new client that's gonna be both lucrative and exciting," he said. "Really?" Evelyn said. "Yeah, we actually are going to attend the gala for the main event next week," he added, remembering he forgot to tell her about Clayton's big party. "Well, that sounds great. I'm looking forward to spending time with my husband," she said as she kissed him on the cheek. Evelyn was used to going to different events with her husband and knew he loved having her on his arm as a showpiece. Ethan finished his dinner in record time and left his plate on the counter. He was anxious to be with his wife. He got up from the stool and then carried Evelyn up to their bedroom. As he lay her on the bed, his passion rose to the tip of his penis, and he almost came just from looking at her. He was glad he took a little blue pill when he got out of the shower because he was gearing up for a long, seductive night. He made love to her for hours, releasing all his stress and emotions onto her body. When they were done, they were both content and happy. "Aww baby, you were an animal tonight," she said playfully. He laughed, knowing he did fuck her like a beast. "I really missed you, that's all," he said as he pulled her closer in his arms. "I missed you too, E. I promise not to make my husband suffer that long again," she said as she relaxed next to him. "You'd better not," he said, pouting in a childlike voice. "I've just been so tense, that's all. I have a lot on my mind," she said as she played with the hairs on his chest. "But I must admit you certainly relaxed me tonight," she giggled. "That's good to know, babe. I'm glad I can still rock your world like I used to." Evelyn noticed him getting hard again. She loved how he could easily be aroused simply from her touch.

They hadn't done much foreplay before they got started. Ethan was rock-hard and dove right in as soon as they got to the bedroom. He did actually wear her out for once, and she wanted to take a little breather before round two, so Evelyn decided to give him head since that didn't take too much effort on her part. She eased her head towards his manhood and put it into her mouth. "Damn baby, I wasn't quite ready yet," he chuckled. She sucked lightly and gently as he massaged her shoulders. "Aww, yeah, that's it, baby, that feels good. Your shoulders do feel tense; maybe I'll send you to my new client's salon for a deep tissue massage and spa day," Ethan said as his wife continued to give him pleasure. As he spoke, Evelyn started to suck harder and faster. "I think you'll like the place; it's called Tailored To You." Just then, Evelyn realized Ethan was talking about Clayton's spa!

She pulled and sucked her husband fast and hard, taking his whole cock into her mouth. She didn't want to stop and get him suspicious, so she continued even though she was upset that he hadn't told her about his newest client. She was sucking so furiously that before she knew it, he was ejaculating with tremendous force into her mouth. He held her head there as he let out a mighty roar. "Got damn it, Evelyn!" he cried as she pulled away with his seaman still in her mouth. She quickly jumped up and ran into the bathroom. She spit all of his juices into the sink and coughed while she ran the water. "What the fuck was happening?" she asked to herself. "Clayton was her husband's new client? Did he know? Was that the reason Clayton was so angry with her on the telephone?" She needed answers, and she needed them now. Evelyn grabbed the mouthwash, gargled it, and then drank some water.

When she went back into the bedroom, Ethan was snuggled up with a pillow and snoring. She had physically drained him with her lovemaking. She was furious. She wanted to wake him and ask him what the fuck was going on with his business deals, but she wasn't sure if he even knew what the hell he was doing, so she decided not to wake him. But she definitely needed to get more information from him about Clayton and the twins as soon as possible. Evelyn grabbed her phone from the nightstand and went back into the bathroom. She dialed Kendal's number again, but this time, he didn't answer. She was going to leave a message but decided against it and sent a text instead that simply read: I need to meet ASAP. A matter of life or death.

28

REGINA

Regina was all grins when she hung up the phone with Clayton. She had been thinking about him all night and, after receiving the flowers, knew she wanted to invite him over and make him dinner to say thanks. She knew it could never make up for the wonderful evening she had shared with him the night before or for the lovely gifts he had showered her with at the salon, but it was a start. Regina got up from the kitchen counter and checked the crockpot with the roast she had been cooking since that morning. She decided she would make her mother's famous pot roast with potatoes and grilled vegetables for dinner. She knew she couldn't go wrong with her choice since she knew the recipe like the back of her hand. That was one of her favorite meals her mother made for her as a child, and she made it often for Nyla, who enjoyed it just as much. Everything was going smoothly, and she was excited. Her daughter was at her friend Asia's house, so she and Clayton could have some time alone. She felt like she was moving really fast with him, but she couldn't shake the attraction she had for him. He was unlike any man she had ever met, and she felt so comfortable and at ease with him. Clayton made her feel safe, and she opened up to him, which was rare for her. Regina went over to the bookshelf and plugged her phone into her Bluetooth speaker. She looked through her playlist and decided to play her '90s collection she had stored on her phone. She pressed shuffle, and Tyrese, a sweet lady, filled the room. She sang along as she fluffed the pillows on the sofa, wiped off the coffee table and sprayed all the fabric with Febreze. She wanted everything to look nice when Clayton arrived. Her place wasn't fancy, but it was nice and cozy, just enough for her and Nyla. She was happy with the location she lived in and felt safe. Knowing she still had time before Clayton arrived, she decided to take a relaxing bath. She went into the bathroom and turned on the water. Steam immediately fills the space from the heat. When she climbed into the claw foot tub full of bubbles, her body sank into the warm, scented water. She was happy her body was still loose from the wonderful massage she received at Tailored To You, and she was floating on cloud nine. She had never had a professional massage before but made a mental note to add that one to her monthly regimen. A woman has a right to treat herself every now and then, she thought. As she lay there enjoying her soak, she noticed her playlist had changed. She could hear Keith Sweat echoing from the speakers. Let me lick you up and down till you say stop. Regina smiled, wondering how it would be to sleep with Clayton. "He was probably hung like a horse," she said out loud and laughed. "I ain't had no good dick in years." The song continued to play as she thought about him doing the things Keith sang about to her. Regina closed her eyes and thought about her first sexual encounter, realizing it was bittersweet. She was only seventeen years old, still a virgin and inexperienced. It was with Tony, her first true love, the man who would take her virginity and make her a woman.

She had met him at the county fair and was instantly attracted to him. He was different from the other guys she had dated. One of the biggest differences was that he was white, but he had a swag about him that Regina couldn't resist. It was a hot, breezy night in Philly, and he approached her as she waited to get on the Ferris wheel with her friends. "You are the prettiest girl here," he said to her. "Thank you," Regina smiled widely. "Can I get on the ride with you?" he asked her, and she said yes. They ended up spending the rest of the day together and exchanging numbers, and to her surprise, he lived right in her neighborhood. That was odd to her since she thought only people of color occupied the homes where she was from. He called her the next night and invited her over to his place. Regina knew that he was older than her but figured only by a few years and never imagined he would have his own apartment. Half the guys she knew, even the ones well into their twenties, still lived with their mommas. When she got to his place, she was surprised to see all the beautiful artwork and plaques he had on his walls. Then she noticed his degree from Penn State and realized he was a school teacher in the Neighboring school district. Regina was mortified. This was a grown man's house. She was with a teacher, and this was his bachelor pad, and she was just a junior in high school. She had lied and told him she was nineteen, thinking that was close to his age and maybe he was in college; she never realized he was a full-blown man who could go to jail for dating a minor. She was already nervous being there but to now know this about him made her feel even more uneasy. She wanted to confess that she was only seventeen, but after seeing all the trouble he had gone through for their date, she decided to wait and see how the night would play out. She figured if things got too heavy, then she'd confess her age. He was so nice to her, and she was enjoying his company.

He had cooked her dinner, and they ended up drinking three bottles of wine, which made Regina tipsy. She had never drank wine before, just wine coolers and beer she'd sneak from her mom's refrigerator when she wasn't home. The wine had a different effect on her than she was accustomed to. She felt warm and tingly inside and relaxed. All of her nervousness and inhibitions had seemed to melt away. She felt like a grown woman and forgot she was only a child playing make-believe. After dinner, he suggested they watch a movie, and next thing you know, they were kissing passionately. He started to gently rub her breast and slowly moved his hands down to her hips. She could tell he was experienced by the way he caressed her body. Regina felt her lust and excitement start to rise within her. She had never had sex before, but she knew what it felt like to be aroused. She had seen plenty of dirty movies and had even let a boy finger her when she was twelve. Besides, her cousin Val explained the birds and the bees to her in detail during one of her many visits to North Carolina.

"Tony, wait, there's something I need to tell you." She pulled back from his embrace. "What's wrong? Am I moving too fast?" He asked, not wanting to frighten her. "No, it's not that

I want to do it. It's just that I'm a virgin, and I don't want to disappoint you," she said as she hung her head, knowing she should reveal her age to him. "Disappoint me? Are you kidding? I'm honored that you're willing to give me your virginity," he said, delighted she wanted to sleep with him. She wanted to tell him right then that she was just a teenager, but something inside her wanted to be with him. She had been with other boys in the past but had never gone all the way. The others always seemed childish and clumsy, but not Tony. He was a real man, and she knew he would take his time and treat her like a lady. "Listen, how about we take it slow? I want to make your first experience the best." He took her by the hand and led her to his bedroom. He went into the bathroom, turned on the shower and lit some candles. He then came back into the room and slowly removed Regina's clothes. She was glad she wore the new bra and panty set she bought from Straw Bridges the week before. "You look so beautiful," he said as he admired her toned coco brown body. He then laid her down on the bed and gently started to kiss her. She had never felt like this before. Her body trembled with anticipation. He removed his lips from hers and slowly started to kiss her neck and then her shoulders until he found her Nipples and suckled gently. Regina felt her body start to shake as she climaxed from his touch. Tony then slowly licked his way down to her soft, moist, fleshy middle and devoured all of her sweet essence that flowed between her legs. She felt her body start to twitch and jerk as she came into his mouth. He then lifted her up and took her into the bathroom. They got into the shower, and the warm water rushed over their bodies. He then kissed her again as he held her tightly in his arms. Gently he massaged his rock-hard cock against her. He whispered in her ear softly, "Are you ready?" Regina grabbed hold of him as he entered her. She felt a piercing pain shoot up her spine as she felt her inner walls being ripped. Slowing, he thrust inside her as she felt her childhood being diminished and womanhood enveloping her. He started to speed up the rhythm as she moaned louder and louder. "Yes, Tony, don't stop," she cried as he stroked her faster. Just as her pain transformed into sheer pleasure, he yelled, "I'm about to come, bae. Do it with me," and Regina wrapped her arms around his neck, and they both climaxed together.

They lay against the cool shower wall spent from their love-making. "Are you alright?" he asked as tears rolled down her cheeks. "I didn't hurt you, did I?" he asked with concern. "No, not at all. It was beautiful," she said reassuringly. "It's just that I have never been with anyone like that before, but I am so glad it was with a man like you," she said as she rested her head on his chest. Tony beamed with joy. "Well, do you think we can go another round?" he asked, wanting her again even more. "That would be awesome," Regina said as she started to stroke his man piece. He turned her around this time to face the wall and entered her from the back, taking in her round hips and soft ass as he pounded her with more force the second time around. They ended up making love in the shower three times before getting out. He had washed her hair and her body, and by the time he lay her in bed beside him, Regina felt like she was floating on a soft cloud.

"Here, take this aspirin," he told her. "You might be a little soar by the morning," he chuckled. She took the pills and drank the bottle of water. He sat next to her side of the bed. She lay there with him for hours in his arms and listened as he softly snored. This was the best night of her life, but she knew she could never see him again. He was a twenty-five-year-old man, and he had just taken the virginity of a seventeen-year-old girl. He could be arrested and thrown in jail, and his whole future would be ruined because of her and she didn't want that she cared for him too much. When Regina felt sure he was totally asleep, she got up from the bed, got dressed, left him a note thanking him for an incredible night and left his apartment. She walked home feeling sad. She had finally met someone she cared about and that she had given her body to, but there was no way they could be together. She felt hurt and alone, but more so than anything, she felt like a woman.

29

CLAYTON

Clayton got into his BMW, and he was furious. He kept playing the conversation over and over with Alisha in his head. This bitch has the audacity to tell me she needs me? He said out loud as he started the car. He couldn't believe all the shit she had told him. She was living in Philly, had been there for years, and, more importantly, the Twins were back in the picture. He couldn't understand what was happening to his life. He drove down Kelly Drive in a trance, trying to process his new information. This bitch is trying to set me up, he kept repeating to himself. There was no way he could Phantom everything that was happening. Anger started to build inside him. Alisha always knew how to get under his skin, and even after years of no contact, she still had that power. He really didn't want to see her again but had to meet her so that he could find out what the fuck was going on. He had to call Darrin and let him know since he was familiar with his past, and Clayton knew if any shit went down, Darrin would have his back. He didn't know what he would be walking into when it came to Alisha, but he wanted to be ready just in case. It was her fault he was in all this mess in the first place.

She had convinced him that they could come up from robbing the twins and have enough money to live a happy life together, but that had all been a lie. Everything that came out of Alisha's mouth was a lie. She was a manipulator and a con, and Clayton refused to get caught up in her trap again. Suddenly, his phone vibrated, and he looked at it to realize he had missed his exit to Regina's house. He had programmed her address on the GPS in his phone so that he wouldn't get lost. He made a U-turn and headed back onto Kelly Drive. He was supposed to come off the highway at the Philadelphia Zoo but was distracted by the thoughts of Alisha. "Damn it, I'm gonna be late fucking with this bitch," he said out loud, hitting the steering wheel. He was looking forward to seeing Regina. When he got off the exit, he pulled into a gas station on the corner. He picked up his cell phone and dialed her number. "Hello, handsome, you downstairs?" Regina asked seductively. "No, I'm actually just a few blocks away and wanted to call and make sure you didn't need anything before I got there," he said, hoping he didn't sound distracted or frustrated. "Nope, I'm good. All I need is you," she said, surprising herself at how comfortable she was with him. "Great, I'm gonna run into the Sunoco and grab some mints, and I'll be right there," he said, feeling better just from hearing her voice. "Ok, I'll see you soon," she said happily and hung up. He was glad he had called her; she made him feel good, and he was suddenly excited to see her again. He needed to be in the company of someone that made him feel special, and he was glad he was going to see Regina.

She was a great lady, and when he was with her, he forgot about his past and the hurt he endured when Alisha left him. He loved the way she smiled and how sexy she looked when he came into her spa suite to welcome her to his business. He felt genuineness about her, a comfortable space in which he could feel safe and just be himself. He was happy he had gotten her the bracelet and earrings for her daughter. He just hoped she wouldn't think he was moving too fast. He had only been on one date with her, but something inside him felt like she was the woman of his dreams, and he had known her for a lifetime. Someone he could share his life with and finally be happy. She was the total opposite of Alisha. Regina was kind and Quiet. She seemed to have a lot of mystery about her that intrigued Clayton, and she made him want to know more about her. Unlike Alisha, who was manipulative and demanding. She was a selfish bitch that only thought about herself and didn't care who she hurt to get what she wanted. He was relieved he had cut ties with her long ago. She was toxic to him, and he hated her for causing him so much pain. He desperately needed a good woman in his life, a rider, a Bonnie to his Clyde, and so far, no woman had ever made him feel that way, not even Naomi, whom he cared about deeply until he met Regina. He knew she was the one, and there was nothing that was gonna stop him from making her his lady. After sending Darrin a text to let him know to be on standby, Clayton exited the car and went inside the gas station. He grabbed a few packs of Mentos and a pack of gum before heading to the counter. "Six seventeen," the Indian man said from behind the glass partition. "Wait, give me a pack of magnum condoms, sensitive," Clayton said before he paid. The man grabbed the package from the shelf, placed his items in the bag and smiled. "That'll be nineteen thirty-four. someone's getting lucky tonight, huh?" He asked with a grin as he reached for the money. "I hope so," Clayton replied, placing a twenty on the counter. He grabbed his bag and left the store.

He hadn't been thinking about sleeping with Regina tonight but figured he should be prepared just in case. He was definitely attracted to her and would love to make love to her, but he didn't want to rush her. She made him feel ways he hadn't felt since he was a teenager with Alisha, and just the thought of being with her sexually made his dick hard. He loved her shape, the twinkle in her eyes when she smiled, the fullness of her lips and the curve of her hips. She excited a part of him deep down that went beyond his loin. He thought she would be the perfect lover that their bodies would be in unison and move to the same rhythm. The more he thought about Regina, the more his thoughts about Alisha vanished. He was glad about that since he wanted to be in a good headspace when he saw her. He wanted nothing more than for the evening to go smoothly.

As he pulled up to her apartment building, he actually started feeling nervous. She did something to him that was hard for him to comprehend, but he liked it. She made him feel like a schoolboy, and he had to admit that he liked the feeling. He had a pep in his step, and he smiled harder than he ever had. He decided to sit in the car for a few minutes to allow the blood to circulate away from his penis. He didn't want to show up at her door with a hard-on. He reached behind him in the back seat and retrieved the bag of gifts he had gotten for her and her daughter, along with the wine. He took one condom out of the box and placed it in his wallet, then got out of the car. He popped a few mentos in his mouth to ensure his breath was fresh. As he made his way to the double glass doors of her building, he took out his cell phone and dialed her number. She picked up on the first ring, "Hey, where are you?" She asked. "I'm downstairs and realized I didn't know your apartment number." "Oh, it's apartment three seventeen," she responded, happy that he had finally arrived. "Got it. I'll be right up." He walked in, noticing how well-kept the apartment building looked. He walked over to the desk where an elderly gentleman sat watching a TV monitor. "Good evening," Clayton said to the man. "Hello there, sir. How can I help you?" he asked, looking up from the screen. "I'm here to see Ms. Allen in apartment three seventeen. She's expecting me." "Sure thing, the elevator is right around the partition," he said, pointing in the direction. "Thank you," Clayton said graciously. "I'll keep an eye on that pretty car of yours, too," he said as Clayton turned the corner. "Thanks, buddy. I got you when I leave," he responded, making a mental note to tip the kind man. When he got on the elevator, he was instantly filled with anticipation. He was excited about seeing Regina and hoped she like her presents.

The elevator stopped on the third floor, and when he got off, he noticed how serene and quiet it was. Her apartment was only steps from the elevator, so he didn't have to walk far. He again checked his breath and looked down at the outfit he had selected for the night and was pleased. He looked and felt comfortable and knew it was the right pick for a nice dinner at home. Just as he was about to knock, Regina opened the door. She looked so beautiful. She was wearing a soft pastel maxi dress she had bought herself as a gift from Nordstrom's. "Hello there, handsome," she said as she reached out to give him a hug. She was happy to see him. "Wow, you look fantastic," Clayton replied. "Why, thank you. You're not looking too shabby yourself," she said with a smile. When Clayton entered the apartment, he was quite impressed. Regina had a beautiful place filled with interesting artwork and lovely paintings. As his eyes scanned the room, he noticed pictures of her and her daughter, as well as photos of her with others he assumed were family or close friends. The photographs were sitting on a lovely bookshelf filled with a collection of vintage books.

To the right of the apartment, he assumed, were the bedrooms and bath, and to the left was the kitchen. There was a large island in the middle with a granite countertop and metal stools around it. In the living room, she had a large sectional in the middle of the floor with a hand-carved wooden coffee table. Surrounding the sectional area were beautiful, large, colorful throw pillows on top of a lovely Persian rug. Everything about the room had class and the comforts of home, unlike Clayton's place, which was large and stark yet ultra-modern. His place was definitely a bachelor pad and masculine, whereas Regina's place was warm and cozy. "Something smells fantastic," Clayton responded as he walked over to the kitchen counter to set his bag down. "Thank you. I hope you're hungry," Regina said as she went over to check on the stew. "I'm starving. I haven't eaten all day, so I'm ready to throw down," he said jokingly. "I love a man with a hearty appetite," she said as she winked at him. "I bought a bottle of wine. I hope you like it," he said as he removed the expensive bottle from the decorative bag. "Where's your daughter?" he asked, noticing the gifts he had gotten for them when he removed the bottle. "Oh, she's at a friend's for the evening. She didn't wanna hang out with a couple of old heads tonight," Regina said, laughing. "Old heads? She must be referring to you," Clayton said with a grin. "Whatever, man," she smiled. Even though she was really liking Clayton she wasn't ready to introduce him to her daughter just yet. She wanted to give it some time and see where their dating would lead.

She prayed it would lead to something serious because, so far, he was definitely hard to resist. "I brought rose. I hope it pairs well with your meal," he said, realizing he should have bought two bottles. "That's great. I also have a few bottles of red and a Chardonnay, in case we need them," she replied. "Oh, so you're gonna try to get me boozed up to take advantage of me?" He asked, laughing. "Of course I am, just in case you don't like my food," she said playfully. They enjoyed a good laugh together. He felt so comfortable with her and liked the teasing and banter between them. "I'm sure I'll love it. Hey, you got a corkscrew?" he asked, wanting to open the bottle he had. "Sure, it's right there on the counter," she pointed. He got up from the stool he was sitting on, watching her. As he walked past, he got a whiff of her perfume. She smelled great. She wore the same perfume his mother wore back in the day when he was a kid. "Is that Chanel you're wearing?" he asked, remembering the scent. "Yes, it's a classic," she said, smiling at the fact that he recognized the smell. "It's a nice scent. My mother used to wear it," he said as he thought about her. "Oh, really? She has great taste. Maybe I'll have to send her a bottle for Christmas," Regina said, forgetting his mother had passed away years ago. "She's deceased," Clayton said in a low tone. "Oh God, I'm so sorry, Clayton. I forgot," Regina said, feeling awful about what she said. She reached out for his shoulder to comfort him. "It's fine. I wasn't trying to ruin the mood; I just like the way you smell, and it brought back really good memories for me, that's all," he said as he hugged her around the waist. "Well, thank you for the compliment. Now let me get back to cooking," she said, pushing him away lightly on the chest to release his grip and glad that the evening hadn't gone dark. !Ok, fine," he jokingly pouted. He opened the wine and poured a glass for the both of them. He heard Anthony Hamilton playing softly in the background. "Do you need any help?" He asked as he walked back up behind her. She could feel his warm breath on the back of her neck. She started to feel a tingling sensation between her legs, and she closed her eyes for a moment to savor the feeling. "No. Now, will you go sit down or go change the music?" she said, getting aroused by his close presence.

"Ok, ok, I just wanted to help. I'm a beast in the kitchen. You don't know what you're missing," he said, throwing up his hands. He walked over to the bookshelf and picked up her cell phone. He clicked on the Apple Music app and went to her playlists. He was surprised at her collection of music. "Hey, you're really into oldies, huh?" he asked, noticing all the incredible artists from the 60s, 70s and 80s she had stored in her phone." Yeah, I'm sort of an old soul at heart," she responded, happily smiling. He liked her music collection.

"Me too. I'm really into Sam Cook and Otis Reading. Unfortunately, I don't come across many women who are into great music," he said as he selected Sam Cook's greatest hits to play. "All the women I know are into Meek and the Migos or Cardi B- they don't appreciate music like this," he said as he sat back down at the counter. Sam Cook started to croon, "Darling, you send me as Clayton started to sing along." "Oh, wow, you're serenading me now," Regina laughed. "Maybe we are a couple of old heads." "Yeah, don't I sound great?" he asked as he got up and took her by the arms. "Clayton, come on, I'm trying to finish dinner," she said, trying to sound annoyed when, in actuality, she was loving the attention. He took her by the waist and started to dance with her as he sang in her ear. She was swooning. She felt like she was floating on a cloud as he held her in his arms. He smelled amazing as well. Regina didn't recognize his cologne but knew it had to be expensive. After the song ended, she was expecting him to let her go, but he held onto her and waited for the next track to play. "I thought you said you were starving," she asked him softly in his ear. "I was till I felt you," he whispered seductively. Just then, he gently kissed her lips.

His were as soft and moist as Regina had expected. Their kiss lasted for what felt like an eternity, and when they stopped, they looked into each other's eyes with desire. "Regina, I really like you and have every intention of sticking around if you let me," he said seriously. "I like you too, Clayton. I'm just scared of getting hurt or used. I've been through a lot in my life, and I have a daughter to protect," she said honestly. "I know, and I wanna take care of you, treat you like a queen, and lavish you with the finest things in life." He was being as sincere as he possibly could and hoped she believed every word he said to her. "I'm just an average woman, and I'm sure you have someone special in your life already," she said as she released herself from his grip and walked back to the kitchen. "I'm not gonna lie to you; I was seeing someone, but from the first day I saw you, I knew it was you I wanted to be with. Them other chicks out there are just fishing for a good dude to provide for them, but I know there's something different about you, Regina. Something pure and sincere, and I was instantly attracted to that, to you," he said, pleading his case.

He really liked her and wanted to be with her, and he was confident she felt the same for him. "Clayton, we have been on two dates. How do you know I'm the one you wanna be with?" She asked. "Because when I touch you, I feel your soul inside me," he said softly. No one had ever said something so beautiful to her before, and it made her tear up. "Why are you crying?" He asked as he walked over to her and placed his hand on her cheek. "Because this is like a fairytale. A rich, successful, handsome guy wanting to be my Prince Charming. Shit like this don't happen to me," she said sadly. "Well, believe it, baby, because I'm here for the long haul if you'll have me," he said as he kissed her again. "Ok, I'm gonna trust you, Clayton," she said, looking into his beautiful eyes. At that moment, she knew she could trust him. A sense of safety and peace came over her. Something she hadn't felt in a long time, and she liked it. "Ok, come on, let's eat because I really am starving," he said as he grabbed the plates and sat them on the counter. Regina placed the garlic bread, salt and pepper onto the counter and filled both their bowls with the wonderful stew. Clayton asked if she had any candles and sat them in the center next to the bouquet of flowers he had sent her earlier.

"This stew is the bomb, baby. Damn, I didn't know it was gonna be this good," he said between mouthfuls. "Thank you. It was my mother's recipe. She was always proud of how good it tasted. I would devour almost a whole pot when I was younger," she added. "You must have been a fat kid," he said jokingly. "Shut up. I was not fat; I was just big-boned," she said, thinking of her looks when she was a young girl. "No, actually, I was always skinny. I later found out I had a super-fast metabolism, and it was impossible for me to gain weight." "Well, it must have slowed down now cause you packing some junk back there in that trunk," he laughed. "You are so corny," she said, swiping him with her napkin. "No, all jokes aside, how did you come by the figure you have now?" He was interested in getting to know everything about her. "Well, as a teenager, I took a lot of dance classes and then, older, started working out at the gym to get toned," she said, making a fake muscle with her arm. "I'm super strong," she laughed. Their conversation went on for almost an hour as they enjoyed their meal and the delicious wine Clayton had brought. As Regina got up to place the dishes in the dish-washer, she noticed the bag still on the counter.

"Hey Clayton, can I keep this beautiful gift bag?" she asked him. He had made his way into the living room and was relaxing on the sofa. "Sure, and you can also keep what's inside," he said, nervous at what her reaction would be when she saw the jewelry. "What's inside?" she said anxiously, like a kid at Christmas. "Take a look and see." She picked up the bag and took it into the living room. "Clayton, what did you do?" she asked. She sat down on the sofa and removed the two elegantly gift-wrapped boxes. "Oh my God, Clayton, what is this?" she asked again. "It's just a little something I got for you and your daughter," he said, pleased with himself. When Regina opened the smaller of the two, she saw the most beautiful diamond stud earrings she had ever seen in her life; they were huge and sparkled like glass. "These are amazing," she gasped. "They are for Nyla," he said happily. "I hope I didn't go too far buying them for her," he said, hoping she would approve. "No, not at all. They're beautiful, but you haven't even met her yet. You sure you wanted to get her such an expensive gift?" "Of course, and I know if she's as lovely and special as her mom, they will be well deserved," he added. He wanted her to know that he wanted to take care of her as well as her child and to give them a life they would enjoy. "Thank you, Clayton; this is the nicest thing anyone has ever done for my baby, including her father," she said, thinking of her deadbeat ex.

"I'll make sure Nyla thanks you herself as well. She's gonna flip when she sees these," Regina said, placing the box back into the bag. "Now on to you," Clayton said in anticipation. "Close your eyes, and let me do the honors." He took the box from her hands. He noticed he was nervous as he saw his hands slightly shaking. "Pull it together, dude," he said to himself. When Regina closed her eyes, she was excited. "Ok, I'm ready," she said. "You're not peeking, are you?" he asked. "No, no," she said excitedly. When he placed the bracelet on her arm, she opened her eyes and started to cry. He was hearing her say she loved it, but she was crying. "I absolutely love it," she said, then wrapped her arms around his neck and planted a long, seductive kiss on his lips. She thought to herself if she wasn't gonna give him some before, she was definitely gonna give him some now.

He placed the bracelet on her wrist and admired it as she twirled her arm. "This bracelet must have cost more than my apartment, Clayton," she said, still in amazement over the gift. "No, it wasn't that much," he lied, knowing it was gonna set him back a pretty penny once Isabella sent him his bill. Including Geneva's necklace, these gifts set him back at least two hundred grand. But it was well worth it, especially after seeing the joy on Regina's face. She glowed when she was happy. "Don't you worry about that; a fine woman deserves fine things, and I'm gonna make sure you have it all," he said, knowing he was going to shower her with whatever she wanted. "You know the Gala for the launch of the new salons is next week, and I wasn't sure if Price was going to ask you to come, but I want to make it official and ask you to be my date. Will you accompany me?" he asked, feeling nervous about asking her. "Seriously? Do you really want me to go with you? Wow, you're really making this a Cinderella moment. Clayton, I'd love to go with you!!" she exclaimed as she hugged him tightly. "That's great, and if you need something to wear, I will arrange for some designers to come by and do a fitting for you if that's ok," he asked, not wanting to be too pushy. He just wanted her to be happy. "Designers? Seriously? I wasn't even thinking about what I would wear," she exclaimed. "Listen, don't worry about that now. We have plenty of time to sort out the details. I'm just glad you accepted my invitation," he said, thrilled she said yes.

He gently took her by the waist and cradled her in his arms as they listened to the music that filled the room. After a few minutes, Regina took his hand and led him toward her bedroom. "Are you sure?" He asked, wanting to make sure she didn't want to sleep with him because of the gifts and invitation to the Gala. "Yes, Clayton, of course, I'm sure," she said when they made it to her bedroom, and she slipped her dress from her shoulders. She wore a beautiful peach-colored lace bra with a matching thong that complimented her bronzed skin and sandy hair. She looked amazing. Clayton stood there in amazement as he watched her turn down the comforter on her queen-sized bed. The room smelled like lavender and peppermint, just like at the Solon, and it glowed from the candles she had placed on the night-stand. "Well, are you just gonna stand there, or are you gonna join me?" she said as she slipped under the covers. "Of course," he added as he removed his shirt, shoes and the rest of his clothing. He laid everything neatly on the chaise she had in the corner next to the dresser.

He climbed into the bed, and the sheets felt cool on his skin. He had removed the condom from his wallet and placed it on the nightstand next to the bed. "I didn't expect you to be a boxer kind of guy," she said, admiring his underwear. Clayton chuckled. "Yeah, not tightly whiteys for me." He slowly started to rub her thighs and leaned in to kiss her. Her body started to feel tiny electric shockwaves go through it. She moaned softly as he caressed her breasts. His dick was harder than the rock of Gibraltar. She felt it pierce her side as he leaned into her. She was pleasantly surprised at its girth. She reached down to take it in her hand. "Damn, baby, you working with some serious equipment," she laughed. "Don't be scared; he won't bite," he joked. He laid her down on the mountain of pillows she had on the bed and started to kiss her body, removing her thong without missing a beat. He started at her neck and worked his way down to her soft, plush middle. She arched her back as he used a serious tongue game on her insides. She had never had a man devour her so passionately as Clayton did. One after another, she felt her body erupt with pleasure.

She felt her legs start to shake violently as she let out a loud scream of ecstasy. She knew she must have had at least five orgasms in a row. She pleaded with him to stop, but the more she begged, the hungrier he seemed. As he made his way back up to kiss her, he grabbed her wrists to hold her down as she squirmed with delight. "Did that feel good, babe?" he asked seductively in her ear. He felt her breathing heavily as her chest went up and down. "That was amazing," she said, breathlessly. "Now it's my turn," she said as she flipped him onto his back and climbed on top of him. He had never been with a woman as aggressive as Regina, and he liked it. She started licking his chest and planting kisses down his sides until she made it to his rock-hard dick. She then wrapped both hands around it and licked the tip.

Clayton felt his toes curling as he anticipated her next move. He felt her reach over into the nightstand, and before he could ask what she was doing, he felt both a cool and warm sensation on his genitals. Regina had put his piece into her mouth with a peppermint candy and was sucking long and slow. He could feel a rush of excitement deep within him as she sucked harder and deeper. It was both sensual and erotic as she swirled her tongue around his manhood and slurped his sweet juices. He could feel her breath as it tickled his genital hairs. She tugged and pulled as Clayton moaned deeply. He gently took her hands and lifted her from his throbbing penis. He needed her to stop before he exploded in her mouth. He reached over and placed the condom over his penis and languidly pushed it inside her. He could feel her inner muscles clench him in a feverish motion each time he stroked her. With each thrust, he could feel her body erupting. He took her breast in his hand and closed his teeth around her nipples, sucking gently. "Damn it, Clayton, this feels so good," Regina cried out. "Please don't stop. Keep fucking me," she exclaimed. He then wrapped her legs around his back and grabbed hold of the headboard so that he could go deeper inside her. Regina started to move in rhythm with him. First, in slow melodic tones, then he speeds up and plunges deeper into her womb, causing her to scream in ecstasy as both of their bodies stiffened and they felt each other release orgasms. Clayton lay still, breathing heavily as Regina's body trembled with pleasure.

The way she felt was indescribable. He then leaned over and kissed her glistening wet skin. "Are you alright?" He asked softly. "No," she said as tears started to roll down her cheeks. Clayton sat upright in bed and looked at her. "Did I hurt you? "He asked, concerned that he was pushing too hard. "No, it's not a bad thing. I'm just messed up emotionally, that's all," she said, feeling foolish. Regina had never experienced a sexual encounter like that before. She had let all her inhibitions melt from her and felt exposed and vulnerable. Clayton had made her feel freer than she had ever felt in her whole life, and she was scared of what the outcome would be of their relationship. "Baby, what is it? What can I say to make you believe that you are the one and I'm not going anywhere?" He asked, trying to put her mind at ease. "Honestly, Clayton, I don't know," she whispered. He then took her in his arms and cradled her. "As of today, you don't have to be afraid. I'm here. I will protect you and take care of you and your daughter. I'm your man, Regina, and you are mine forever," he said, then kissed her passionately. This was the feeling she had always longed for, and she finally felt relaxed. Clayton lay there stroking her hair and feeling good. He finally felt like he had found a woman that he could love forever. Now, all he had to do was take care of Alisha and the twins, and he could finally be happy once and for all.

30
ETHAN

When night turned into morning, Ethan was feeling on top of the world. Evelyn had sexed him into a coma, and he felt good from head to toe. He was refreshed and full of energy when he finished showering and decided to go for a run before heading into the office. When he got back home, he noticed Evelyn was gone. She had left him a note telling him she was going to her gallery for a few hours and then having lunch with some friends and that she would see him later that night for dinner. After he got dressed, he checked his answering service. "Hey brother, this is James, one of the twins. I was wondering if we could set up a time to have a few drinks and discuss some additional business deals this week. Hit me up and let me know when's a good time, and be sure to bring along that beautiful wife of yours; we'd love to meet her," he said. Clayton grinned as he saved the message. "Damn, these niggas wanna do more business with me, and I'm in the clear and don't owe them any money. I am the man," he said out loud as he did a dance across his bedroom floor. He was extremely excited about his new business ventures that he was about to secure and knew his bank account was gonna be fatter than ever. He would finally have the capital to expand his practice and be a well-known successful attorney in several states. Nothing could stop him, and he was on his way to the top. When he got to the office, he saw that Regina wasn't at her desk, but she had all the files for Clayton's mergers completed and on his. He was pleased with his paralegal and made a mental note to give her a bonus for doing so well with his clients and also to invite her to the gala Clayton was throwing that weekend. She had come up with some great ideas for him to run by Clayton, and he knew the other partners would be pleased with the attention and notoriety the firm would receive. He hoped she wasn't too pissed at the fact that he had told Clayton she would be available to him day or night.

He was well into his third cup of coffee when his cell phone rang. It was Evelyn. "Hello, beautiful. Where are you?" He asked, hearing a lot of noise in the background. "Hello, darling. I'm in New York. I decided to come into the city, do a little shopping, and have lunch." She wanted to be truthful with her husband, but, of course, she would never tell him that she had gone there to meet another man. She wasn't exactly lying to him either since she did just put a hurt on his black American Express card. She had gone to several shops in Manhattan that she hadn't been to in years, and she actually enjoyed treating herself. "Well, make sure you get something lovely for the gala we're attending this weekend, ok?" Ethan said excitedly. "Gala? What Gala?" she asked, trying to match his energy. "Well, you know the new client I was trying to tell you about last night, Clayton Taylor, before you sexed me unconscious?" He grinned at the memory of their love-making. "Well, he's throwing a big soiree' at the Bellevue to celebrate the expansion of his businesses and guess who's the major law firm and lead attorney he hired to make it all happen? That's right; your man, baby. Me!" Ethan said glee-fully. "Oh, my goodness, really, baby?" Evelyn was truly shocked by the news he had just given her. Her mind was filled with so many questions, but she knew now wasn't the time to ask. "Oh, ok, sure. I'll look for a dress for your special evening," she said, still stunned but trying to sound noncha-lant about the news.

There was no way she could let her husband know that she had any connection whatsoever to Clayton Taylor. She real-ized she was going to see her first love face to face after many years and with her husband, so she had mixed emotions about their reunion. She knew she needed to meet with Clay-ton, and she was trying to come up with a way to get him to see her, but how convenient it was going to be that she would get the opportunity to talk to him and tell him she had connections that would take care of the twins. Evelyn also wanted him to know how truly sorry she was for all that had gone down between them. His event wasn't the place she wanted this to happen, but she thought that telling him at his party may be some good news, and then maybe it would ease some of the hatred he had for her. She wasn't sure of how he would take in all this information, especially her being married to his attorney, and she wasn't sure if he was still harboring any romantic feelings for her after all these years, but that was just something she would have to deal with when she saw him.

"I've got the fashion designer Darrin to design my tux for me," Ethan said, interrupting her thoughts. "Clayton put me on to his work." "Oh, that's wonderful, honey. I'm sure you're going to be the sexist man there," she said sweetly to her husband. "Yes, and I'm going to have the most beautiful woman on my arm," he said seductively. He truly loved his wife and felt like he was the luckiest man in the world to have her. "Aww, honey, you're so sweet. Well, I must go now and find something gorgeous. I love you, and I'll see you tonight," she said, hurrying him off the phone. "Ok baby, I'll see you tonight, and please try not to max out my credit cards," he said jokingly and hung up. He smiled at the thought of her swiping away at five-story, Armani and Gucci. Ethan knew his wife could put a hurt on his credit cards, but he didn't care whatever made her happy. After signing and proofing all his paperwork, he decided to go for a steam in the gym located in his office building. He hadn't been there in months and thought it would be a good idea since he had some time before his next meeting. He rode the elevator to the twenty-ninth floor and was surprised to see so many of his colleagues there at that time of day.

"Ethan, man, how are you? Christopher said to him when he entered the locker room. Christopher Martin was a successful prosecuting attorney who had started his own law firm about three years before Ethan and had begged him to come to work for him. He knew Ethan's potential as a business attorney but doubted his ability to be a successful criminal lawyer. He watched Ethan's practice grow into a multimillion-dollar business and was secretly envious of his success. "Chris, what's up? How's it going?" Ethan asked. "It's been great. I haven't seen you in a while. How's it going in the world of criminal activity?" He said jokingly. "Quite good, actually," Clayton said, taking note of his sarcasm. "Someone's always committing a crime somewhere," Ethan said.

As they continued with small talk, a few more lawyers from different firms came in, surprised to see Ethan there. They were all colleagues and saw each other frequently, but Ethan hardly ever made an appearance. They all had a few drinks during their steam and made promises to get together for lunch soon. When Ethan left, he felt great. He needed that time to unwind, and by the time he got back down to his office, Regina was there busy at work. "Hi, Mr. Price. Your one o'clock is in the conference room, and here are the notes of her case," she said, handing him a notepad. "Regina, you are the best. Make sure I see you after my meeting; I have some things to go over with you," he said, smiling at her. "Sure thing, sir," Regina replied and continued typing a brief. Ethan looked over the notes and saw that the client in his office was there to hire him to represent her son on a murder trial. He was only sixteen years old and had killed his girlfriend in a fit of jealousy.

"Hi, Mrs. Brooks, I'm Ethan Price. Sorry to keep you waiting," he said, shaking her hand and taking a seat at the head of the table. "Hello, Mr. Price; thank you for seeing me on such short notice. I was referred to you by Vincent Shaw," she said quietly. "Aww, yes, Vincent, how is he these days?" He asked, knowing she was referring to Snake, his old boss from the hood. "He's fine. He told me to come see you and that you would help with my son's case." Ethan looked at her meager attire and instantly knew she had no means to pay him for his legal services but was sure Snake would be footing the bill. Her son must have been one of Snake's soldiers, and Ethan knew he always took care of them like family. "Yes, of course, I'll do whatever I can to help you," Ethan said, looking at the notes Regina had written for him. "So, your son, is he currently on the street or in lock up?" He asked, trying to be gentle with the questions he asked. She was an older woman in a very distraught state sitting there, and he knew getting the details out of her was going to be hard. "He's locked up in youth study center right now, but if I don't get him bail soon, he's gonna be sent to Holmes Burg or Grater Ford prison pending his hearing," she said with anguish piercing her words. "Has he had a bail hearing, Ms. Brooks, or has the public defender gone to see him yet?" Ethan needed to get as many details as possible so that he would know what he was up against. Now really wasn't a good time for him to be taking on a case like this, especially with him being in the public eye recently with a client like Clayton Taylor.

He was getting so much publicity because of him, and his law firm was really pulling in a different type of clientele. Even though criminal law used to be Ethan's main passion, he was living a different lifestyle and rubbing elbows with the elite. "He had a man come see him," she said as she pulled a card from her purse. She handed the card to Ethan. "He told him he wasn't gonna get no bail and that his trial wouldn't get started for at least a year or two and that he was gonna have to sit in jail the whole time," she told him as tears ran down her cheeks. Ethan looked down at the card she gave him and saw it was Christopher's card, his colleague he had just shared cocktails with in the gym.

Chris was one of Philadelphia's most notorious prosecutors and had a way of scaring even the most seasoned criminals into confessing their crimes. Ethan handed her some tissues and told her to take a minute to compose herself. Then, she exited the room. He needed to get a cup of coffee and find out if Regina had any additional intel on this case. When he walked back into the front office, Regina was having her lunch. "Hey, sorry to bother you, but you didn't tell me I was in for such an interesting client today," he said, motioning toward the conference room. "Oh, yeah, Mrs. Brooks. I feel so sorry for her situation. Her son, who's the only breadwinner of the family and lost it when he caught his girlfriend Boo'd up with someone else. Apparently, she had been messing around with him for quite some time, just not publicly, but when he caught her down on South Street and hugged up with the guy, that's when he approached them, and then a fight ensued. Mrs. Brooks' son pulled out a gun and fired it. His girlfriend stumbled in the way of the bullet, and it struck her in the chest. He was so messed up that she was the one hit that he tried to shoot himself afterward, but the gun jammed right in the middle of the street. He just sat there, rocking her lifeless body back and forth till the police came. Apparently, the other guy fled as soon as the girl was hit. That's pretty much all I found out about the situation right now, but I have an appointment with the DA's office and first officers on the scene today at 4 to get more information." Regina was on top of everything. Ethan was so grateful for her and knew he wouldn't be a success without her. "Thanks, Regina; I'm gonna go back in and see if I can console her and let her know we're gonna do all we can to help her son. Set up a meeting for me with Chris, too; he's apparently the lead prosecutor for this case. See if we can get him to agree to a bail hearing, at the very least. Thanks again," he said as he headed back towards the conference room. "Sure thing, boss," Regina smiled.

She loved working for Ethan because she knew he cared about his clients and put great faith in her to assist him. She was confident he'd win the case just like the many others he'd won over the years since she'd been working there. About thirty minutes had passed before Mrs. Brooks came walking up to Regina's desk with a smile. "You have a great boss, young lady." "Thank you," she said as she shook Regina's hand. She didn't know what Mr. Price had told her, but, whatever it was, it made this woman happy that he was representing her. "You're welcome, Mrs. Brooks," Regina said to her as she left the office.

Ethan walked in, grinning from ear to ear. "What just happened in there?" she asked when he took a seat across from her desk. "I told her she had nothing to worry about and that I would have her son out of jail within twenty-four hours." "Oh, really?" Regina asked, curious of what he had up his sleeve. "And just how are you gonna do that?" she said."Well, when Mrs. Brooks finally told me everything that happened, I found out that it wasn't actually her son who fired that fatal shot. It was the police, and she happened to have a video on her son's cell phone to prove it, so I made a phone call to Chris's office and made them aware that I was his attorney and that I had incriminating evidence against the

Philadelphia Police Department, and that if they didn't release him today on bail that they were gonna have a hell of a lawsuit on their hands." "Mr. Price, you are great," Regina said, leaning in to give him a high five. "Just doing my job, Ms. Allen. Just doing my job." Ethan got up and went back to his office. He knew he could give the case to one of his junior partners to handle once he met with Chris and worked out the details. He got a thrill from working cases like this but knew he had to stay focused on Clayton Taylor. Being in the trenches was cool, but right now, he had bigger fish to fry.

31
EVELYN

Evelyn sat at the Starbucks, sipping a latte while waiting for her meeting with Kendall. She had decided to meet him on Fifth Avenue in the fashion district, so if she was seen there by any of Ethan's colleagues, she could just tell them she had traveled to New York for some retail therapy. She was dressed inconspicuously yet stylish and fit right in with the elite crowd of New York. She hadn't been back to the city alone since her split from Kendal but felt right at home. She kept her distance in case she ran into someone from her past because she knew it would be too painful. She had only decided to meet Kendal there today because it was so last minute, and she needed to see him right away. As she stared out the big picture framed window, she watched as women hurried down the street carrying their expensive Hermès Bur-kin bags and bogged down with packages from Sax and Neiman Marcus. She saw businessmen on their cell phones negotiating major business deals and New York's finest patrolling the sidewalks. There was traffic a mile long, with taxi cabs and limos honking their horns at pedestrians who crossed the big inter-sections illegally.

"Have you been waiting long?" She heard a familiar voice say behind her. When she turned around, Kendal was smiling widely down at her. "I could never wait too long for you," she said as she got up and wrapped her arms around his neck. "It's so good to see you, Kendal," she said sincerely. "You look wonderful." "Thank you, baby, you're not looking too shabby yourself there," he said, admiring her black Chanel suit and red bottom shoes. "As a matter of fact, you look better than I imagined," he added. "Thank you, Kendal. Would you like a cup of coffee?" she asked. "No, I'm good. Let's have a seat in the back where there's more privacy so we can talk," he said, gesturing to some empty tables in the back of the coffee shop. "Sure," Evelyn said, grabbing her Louis Vuitton bag from the chair and following him.

She noticed two men dressed in black suits follow them as well. "I see you still have security watching your back." "Yeah, you can never be too careful," he smiled. "So, what's going on, gorgeous?" he asked as they took a seat in a far corner. "Well," she sighed. "I'm afraid the twins are back in my life, and I don't know what to do." She seemed genuinely shaken as she told Kendal of the meeting her husband had with them and seeing them at the restaurant that night. "Do you think Ethan knows about the take and the shit that went down?" He asked, wondering if her husband was setting her up. "No, not at all, she said defensively. "Ethan is a square. He doesn't know about my past or anything else for that matter; I think he must have represented one of their workers or something. That's how he became associated with them," she said, protecting her husband. "They were just as shocked as I was when I got out of the car. They were never expecting to see me, and I sure as hell never thought I would ever see them again. But now that I have, they know I'm with Ethan, and I'm afraid they are gonna try to do something to him to get to me," she said, frightened. "Ok, calm down," Kendal said, taking her hands in his. "What is it you want from me?" He asked. "I want no, but I need you to make them go away. I need you to get rid of them once and for all, Kendal," she said frantically. "I know I'm asking a lot from you, but you said you'd do anything for me forever, and right now, I need you to kill those bastards," she said, her fear turning into anger. "Ok, E, I got you. Just let me know when and where, and I got you," Kendal said, looking at her lovingly. His feelings for her never went away, and he realized that just seeing her again, he was still in love with her.

"Do you still think about me, Alisha?" he asked. "Of course I do, Kendal, and I wished we could have stayed together, but I just didn't want to live that lifestyle anymore, that's all. No matter what, though, I'll always be your queen, and you will forever be my king," Evelyn said as she caressed his face. "That's all I needed to hear," he said as he kissed her hand and stood up from the table. "Listen, hit me up with the details, and I'll take care of your problem, ok? And if that husband of yours gets out of hand, I'll take care of him, too." Evelyn smiled, knowing he was dead serious about everything he said. "Ok, Kendal, but no worries, I can handle Ethan." She felt better that Kendal was going to take care of her twin problem. She just had to set up the time and place. "I'll be contacting you soon," she said as she reached into her purse for an envelope containing a hundred thousand dollars. "Here, I want to give you something for your trouble," she said, handing him the money. "Naw, babe, this one on me." He winked at her and headed towards the door.

Evelyn sat back and watched him as he climbed into a silver Bentley with his two goons. She was glad he still had feelings for her and was willing to keep his promise to always protect her and keep her safe. She hated having to ask him to commit murder but knew he was just returning the favor. She had done a lot of evil things for the sake of love for Kendal, and now it was his turn. He was gonna take care of her problem, and then her life could go back to normal, and she could finally enjoy her husband. She knew she had to reach back out to Clayton to let him know that everything was gonna be ok since he never returned her call or met with her as he agreed to, but she first needed to talk to Ethan and find out what he knew and what was really going on. Evelyn put on her designer shades, grabbed her purse, and decided to really do a little shopping while she was in New York. She felt good about her meeting with Kendal and decided to treat herself with some outfits. She walked outside and stood looking up at the sun that shone bright in the New York sky. She was finally starting to feel at ease. Little did she know the worst was yet to come.

32
REGINA

"Umm, I have to get ready for work," Regina said as she snuggled in closer to Clayton. They had made love three times that night and fell asleep in each other's arms. "Call out today, and let's just stay right here," he said, his voice sounding extra deep in the morning. "Oh, baby, I wish I could, but contrary to what you may think, you are not Ethan Price's only client. I have work to do," she said, stretching her body on his. "Well, you can quit and just relax with me every day," he said, nuzzling his face into her neck. "You're my lady now, and there's no need for you to go to work." "Well, as appealing as that sounds, I have a career that I love, a boss I respect and admire, and a teenage daughter I have to take care of, so with all that being said, I have to get ready for work." She rolled over and sat up on the edge of the bed. Clayton smacked her softly on the backside as she stood up. "OK, ok, I'll go, but I'd better see you later today so that we can finalize the details of our date on Saturday night." He got up and went into the bathroom, where Regina was turning on the shower. "Have you figured out what to do with

Nyla that night?" he asked. "Yes, you will see me later, and we will discuss the details of our date. My daughter will probably spend the weekend with her bestie, so I know she'll be safe and will have fun," she said, wrapping her arms around his neck and planting a big kiss on his cheek. "How about a little treat before work?" he asked, poking her with his growing manhood. "No, you horny toad, I'm already running late as it is," she said as she pushed him away. "Come on, Regina, he's hard and ready," he pleaded. "Ok, but we gotta do it in the shower," she said happily as they both stepped into the steamy enclosure. They made love once more in the shower before they both got dressed and headed out for work. She left twenty dollars on the kitchen counter for Nyla when she came home from school so that she could grab some snacks to hold her over before dinner. Her daughter had texted her that night and asked if she could stay at her friend's house till the morning and go to school from there. Regina had agreed since she wanted to spend more time with Clayton. When he dropped her off at her building, he gave her a long, sensual kiss and told her he'd call her later. This felt so good to Regina. She was finally feeling safe and happy and was in a relationship she felt would last and have a fairytale ending.

When she walked into the office at eight am, she was relieved to know that Mr. Price hadn't gotten there yet, so she immediately turned on her desktop and finished the contracts he needed for Clayton's business. She was very seldom late for work, and the times she was never due to a man. Her boss had no idea she was dating Clayton, and she wasn't quite ready to reveal that secret. She needed to stay on top of her job and make him none the wiser, well, at least until Saturday

when he would see her at the Gala. She always had a professional demeanor with the clients that hired Mr. Price, and she
didn't want him to think she was turning into a gold digger
and poaching his wealthiest one of all. She had gotten almost
all the documents completed in time before his one o'clock
appointment would arrive. She placed everything he would
need on his desk in his office and decided to go downstairs to
the building cafeteria for some fresh coffee and donuts. When
she got back, she saw his client sitting in the reception area
waiting. "Hello dear, I'm here to see Ethan Price," the kind,
old woman said when she saw Regina walk in. "Yes, hi, Mrs.
Brooks, right?" Regina said, coming around to the front to
greet her. "Yes, I'm here about my son, Timothy." Regina
had already been aware of her case. As soon as she got in
that morning, one of the receptionists gave her a brief of the
events. "Of course, may I get you a cup of coffee or tea or
something?" she asked her. "No, dear, I'm fine," Mrs. Brooks
said kindly. "OK, well, I'll take you to the conference room to
wait for Mr. Price, and if there's anything you need, please
don't hesitate to ask." Regina sat down her breakfast treats
and took Mrs. Brooks to a room next to Ethan's office. "He
should be with you shortly. Make yourself comfortable," she
told her. "Thank you." Regina closed the door and went back
to her desk.

While she was finishing up on some much-neglected paperwork, Ethan came in. He smiled and looked happy to see her.
"Hello, Ms. Allen," he said cheerfully. "Hi, Mr. Price. Your
one o'clock is waiting for you in the conference room," she
said as she handed him some notes she had taken from the
information she had gotten from the receptionist. "Great,

thank you." As he looked them over, he realized this was one of Snake's people, and it couldn't be good. "Ms. Allen, remind me to have a few moments with you later today," he said as he walked back towards his office. "Yes, sir," she said, unsure of what he wanted to discuss. Had he found out about her and Clayton, or did he see the invoice for the spa visit? She wasn't sure, but she silently prayed that it wasn't bad. When Ethan left, she decided not to focus on what he wanted to talk to her about and started to visualize what she would look like and wear to Clayton's party. She had never attended a big fancy party like that before and suddenly started to feel extremely nervous and anxious. She picked up the phone to call Monica. She knew she would put her on to the latest fashions and do's and don'ts for her big night. Besides, she hadn't spoken to her favorite Neice in quite some time.

Monica answered on the first ring. "Well, damn, ain't this a surprise!" she said loudly into the receiver. "Hey, boo, how's it going?" Regina asked, already prepared to hear the latest gossip and ratchet stories about her love life. "How's it going? I haven't talked to you in damn near a month, and all you can say is, how's it going? You got some nerve, auntie." Regina could tell her feelings were hurt. "I'm sorry, Mo, I've been so wrapped up with work that I haven't had the time to connect with you. Please forgive me," she said sincerely. "I miss you, though." "I miss you, too, bitch," Monica said and started laughing. She couldn't stay mad too long at her favorite aunt. "Well, Chile, let me tell you about that bastard Kenny, I am so through with him. He had the nerve to ask me to do a three-way with him! Well, honey, you know I kicked his ass out of my apartment and fast. The nerve of him trying to turn me into a dyke for his enjoyment," she said, cracking up. "If I'm gonna taste the twat it's gonna be on my terms," she stated. "Well, you know I had to go get me some new dick and quick." "Girl, you are too much," Regina interjected.

She wanted to know how Monica was doing, but she wasn't quite ready to hear about her lesbian escapades or insane love life. "Mo, listen, I need a favor," Regina said, changing the conversation. "What is it, auntie? You know I got you. You need me to kick a bitch ass really quick?" "No, silly, it's nothing like that. I am attending a big party this weekend and was hoping we could get together and go shopping. I need you to help me pick out something nice." Regina said. "Aww shit, what is it? One of those stuffy black tie affairs full of the old rich white lawyers," she said sarcastically. "No, it's the Tailored To You main event Gala at the Bellevue, and I have been personally invited by Clayton Taylor himself," Regina said, beaming. "BITCH shut up! Are you serious? That's all anyone who's anyone has been talking about. That party is gonna be LIT!! Oh, Regina, you gotta get me an invite, girl, please. I need to be in the room with all that money that's gonna be there!" Monica screamed. "Ok, I'll see what I can do, but you can't be in there acting a fool, girl. I have a reputation to uphold, and I don't need you making me look bad," Regina kidded. "I promise to be on my best behavior, scout's honor. But wait, how in the heck did Taylor invite you personally?" She asked curiously.

Regina realized she hadn't told Monica that she had started dating Clayton the day she went to visit his salon. "That's a story for another time. So, are you gonna go with me to find the right dress or what?" she asked, hoping to drop the interrogation at the moment. "Absolutely! You just tell me the place and time." "Cool, ok, let me check my schedule and find out what time I'm getting outta here today, and I'll give you a callback, ok?" She was happy she had made peace with Monica and was actually looking forward to seeing her and hanging out. "Ok. Gee, I'm so excited," she said and hung up. Their relationship had been strained since Regina had moved out and gotten her own place, but she loved her niece and wanted her to know nothing, or no one would ever take the place of family.

She hung up the phone and started to eat her hoagie she picked up at the new WAWA food market located down the street when Ethan came up to her desk. "You didn't give me a heads-up about my new client." He smirked as he motioned towards the conference room. "Yeah. Mrs. Brooks desperately needs your help, and I know if anyone can win this case for her son, it's you." "Thanks, Regina," he said kindly. He poured himself a cup of coffee and asked her to set up some appointments for him, then returned to the room to help Mrs. Brooks. When they came back out thirty minutes later, they both were all smiles and Regina knew he had worked his legal magic. There was something about the way Ethan handled his clients that made them feel at ease and confident in his legal ability. Regina admired and respected his work and was proud to be a part of such a prestigious law firm.

After Mrs. Brooks left, Ethan seemed relaxed when he sat down to give her the strategy he was gonna use to win. "Mr. Price, you are awesome," Regina said, giving him a high five. When he went back to his office, she felt relieved about whatever it was he needed to talk to her about. Since he hadn't mentioned anything while he was sitting at her desk, she knew it couldn't be too important. After she had her lunch, she sent Clayton a text telling him what an amazing time she had with him and to let him know how excited she was to go to his party that weekend. Just as she was about to go to the lady's room, a man came in holding two bouquets of long-stemmed white roses. "Delivery for a Miss Regina Allen and a Mr. Ethan Price," he said, reading the form. "I'm Ms. Allen, and Mr. Price is my boss. Thank you, you can leave them right here on my desk," she told him. He sat the flowers down and asked her to sign both invoices. Doing so, she noticed that one was from Clayton and the other was from Ethan's wife. When the delivery man left, Regina decided to be nosey and read Ethan's card before taking the flowers to his office. "Last night was magical. I can't wait to do it again soon. Love, E." Regina smiled at the thought of her boss being romantic with his wife. She had never met her in person, but she knew a lot about her from Ethan's many compliments and gift choices she picked up for her. She was a very myste-rious woman, and Regina was excited and intrigued to finally get a chance to meet her in person at the party.

33
CLAYTON

When Clayton got to his office, he was floating on air. He had had the best night of his life with Regina. After he dropped her off, he went to the gym for a light workout since the majority of his energy had been spent making love to her all night. She had an insatiable appetite for sex and really wore him out. He had never been with a woman like that before, and it made him smile at the thought of him actually being sprung. She did things to him that he had never experienced, and he hoped the pleasure was reciprocated. He went to his office, showered in his ensuite, and put on one of the many suits he had in the closet there. He loved coming to his salon early in the morning when no one was there, and it was quiet and serene. The sunlight showed through the enormous picture glass window in his office, giving him a fantastic view of Ben Franklin and the beautiful city skyline. Even at that early hour, the city sidewalks and streets were bustling with cars, corporate executives, and everyday people making their way to their jobs, schools, or homes. The city was alive early in the morning. But inside, Tailored To You, it was peaceful and quiet, just the way Clayton liked it. He rarely got a chance to be there that early, but when he did, he enjoyed the alone time. It gave him the opportunity to just think and strategize his next moves.

He turned on his cell phone to check any messages from the night before. He had turned it off when he had gotten to Regina's apartment so that he wouldn't be disturbed. He wanted all his attention to be given to her. He was still shaken up from Alisha's call and wanted to put all her bullshit on the back burner for now. He was happy that after being with Regina, all of his anxiety seemed to melt away. His phone started to Bing constantly. He saw that he had fifteen new texts and three voicemails. He decided to read the messages first. The majority were from Darrin, and there were about seven of them. He had sent him a message giving him the heads up about Alisha wanting to meet with him. "Yo, man, what's going on? I got your message. Hit me up when you can." There was one from Geneva, "Hi, shug. I'm going to Delaware for the day with my boo. If you need anything, let me know." Surprisingly, there was one from Naomi. "Hi, Clayton. I just wanted you to know the show's going great. I miss you, honey. Call me when you can." He realized he hadn't spoken to her in a few weeks, and she had no idea that their romance was over.

Ever since he met Regina, he had completely forgotten about Naomi. She was a sweet girl, and he enjoyed being with her, but he knew she wasn't the one. They really didn't spend a lot of time together because she was always traveling with her dance company, and Clayton didn't mind at all since he was only dating her for sexual benefits. Clayton knew he would have to break it off gently with her. He didn't want to be an asshole, so he decided he would do it when she came back to town in a month. He made a note to send her some flowers wishing her well on the tour. He then listened to his messages. "Hi, Mr. Taylor; this is Janice Brown from the North Carolina wellness center. I just wanted you to know we received your payment, and we have faxed your receipt to your business. Your uncle is doing better, but please give us a call to let us know when you'll be coming down for a visit. We look forward to hearing from you soon. Thank you." Clayton had sent twenty-five thousand dollars to them for the care of his uncle Mike and had already put in his calendar to visit him after the Gala and the salon grand openings. He hadn't been there to see him in over a year and knew his mother would be disappointed in him for not going to visit. He really hated going to that place because it reminded him of his childhood and the suffering he and his family went through. But Mike was family, and that was more important.

Just as the second message was about to play, he heard the motion sensor beep. That must be Francesca, he thought. She was an exquisite young woman he had met on his many trips to Brazil. Clayton had slept with her on occasion when he visited, and he grew very fond of her. She had told him how much she wanted to come to the States and start a career in fashion, so he paid the way for her to come back to Philadelphia with him and gave her a job till she got on her feet. She was so grateful to him and wanted to continue offering her sexual services, but Clayton declined. He explained that he had a lady and that she was only to be enjoyed by him when he was in Brazil. She understood, and he was glad. He gave her a job as a receptionist at the head of the salon because she was so beautiful, and he knew she would be able to entice male clients to his establishment. She had been working there for over a year, and he had seen a big uprise financially, and he couldn't be happier. "Mr. Clayton, good morning," she said in her thick Brazilian accent. "Good morning, Francesca. How are you today?" he asked, smiling. "I'm wonderful. I received an invitation from your friend Darrin to be a model at the Gala this weekend. Isn't that great?" She gleamed with excitement. He knew Darrin had been fucking her for about six months now and promising her he'd get her a modeling gig, so he was happy and relieved he had finally kept his word. Clayton introduced them at an employee party he had thrown back then and gave him the ok to peruse her. He explained how she was a hooker back in Brazil but that she was really trying to make it as a fashion model, and since he was in that business, maybe he could help her. Anything to get her off his plate. Darrin was more than willing to take her off his hands. He always joked he would never have too much pussy. "That's wonderful, Francesca. I know you're going to be great." Clayton told her, happy she was getting the chance to do what she loved. Yes, "that is great she smiled." Can I get you some coffee or breakfast before I open, she asked. "Yes, coffee would be nice," he said, wanting her to give him a few more minutes to relax before people arrived.

It was almost ten, and he wondered where the time went. "OK, should I get some for Ms. Geneva as well, knowing she will be getting to the shop soon?" "Uh, no, Geneva won't be in today. She's out of town," he remembered from her text.

Oh, right away, I'll be back she said as she turned on her Manolo heels and left his office. That gave him at least another twenty minutes to finish listening to his messages and checking a few emails. He realized he had skipped one of the messages when Francesca came in and decided to listen to it later. It was probably from a client or Geneva, he thought and figured it wasn't of importance. The last message was from his distributors for the event. He was pleased with how everything was coming together for the party, and Regina had been the icing on the cake for agreeing to be his date. He was excited to have her on his arm as he launched the biggest business deal of his career. Nothing could stop his success, he thought. Not even a shady bitch like Alisha. She had broken his heart, used him for her own personal gain, and tried to ruin his future, but he had won against all odds, and he was now looking forward to a happy, prosperous life and more wealth than he could possibly imagine.

When he turned on his computer, a reminder popped up for him to go over the guest list. He had a huge VIP listing and needed to make sure all his important guests would be seated properly. He had all the lists of people, including a few NBA stars and famous rappers from Philly, at his immediate table that seated twelve, and there were some actors and investment bankers he would sit with Geneva and Ray at a table a few feet away. Chef Ramsey was catering for the elite section, and he had some local chefs doing the rest. He had all the news media and magazine editors coming through, and he knew everything had to be on point. He was determined to get a full-page article in all the top ten magazines and at least a ten-minute spot on the news. He wanted everyone to know he was a success and a force to be reckoned with, and this was only the beginning. Tailored To You was going to be a global sensation. It was just a matter of time. His stocks were up, and he had a lot of brokers vying for investments. He was changing the game of beauty. Nothing could stand in his way except for Alisha and his past, and he was determined to take care of all that sooner rather than later.

34

THE SET UP

It was early evening, and Ethan had just finished working on some important contracts for the firm. When he reached for his phone, he saw he had several missed calls. He checked the voicemail and heard that Snake had been blowing his phone up. He had spoken to Evelyn earlier, and she let him know she was going to be in New York for the rest of the day, and he was relieved. He could finally catch up on some much-needed work. She was going to be longer than she expected, and that gave him some free time, so he decided to go down to his firm's library and give Snake a call back. "Hey, man. Damn, you act like somebody died or something; what's up?" he said when his friend answered the phone. "Look, bro, I've been hearing a lot of shit. I needed to make you aware as soon as possible." "What shit, Snake? Are you in trouble again?" Ethan asked with a nervous chuckle. "Naw, man. I'm not the one that needs his head on a swivel tonight; it's you." "Man, what are you talking about?" Ethan asked with more urgency. "Look, the twins came by the hood a few days ago, and they had a lot to say about their lawyer. It seems the bitch you are married to is planning a big move on them, and I needed to let you know." "Man, what the fuck you talking about? You must of heard some wrong shit. We are fine, ain't no shit jumping off. Besides, my wife doesn't even know them dudes, so chill," Ethan replied, annoyed at Snake for making the accusation. "Well, my nigga, they definitely know her and have a bounty on her head. They also know that your golden boy who owns the salons will be the master of ceremony at your event and said they had some unfinished business to settle with him. I didn't wanna pry and ask too many questions because we both know them niggas is wild and crazy, but I will tell you this: watch your back and your bitch 'cause your surroundings ain't safe." "Look, man, I appreciate the lookout, and I'm gonna try to get in touch with them before I go to the event this weekend. if not, I'll just talk to them there since I invited them and find out what the hell is going on." He was really starting to get angry that Snake was talking out of terms about his wife, and now he really needed to find out exactly what the twins knew about her. Thinking back to their first encounter, it did seem strange to him, but there was no indication that they knew one another. "Aight, bro, stay alert," Snake said before disconnecting the call. When Ethan hung up the phone, his mind was in a daze. Was everything Snake said true?

It hurt Ethan to his core to think that the love of his life could in any way be connected to the twins or would try to manipulate him and play him like a fool. But if that were true, he knew that was the game of the streets. Get them before they get you. "But why?" He thought. Worry instantly enveloped him after receiving the call. The whole conversation had him angry and confused. The words his childhood mentor spoke broke his heart. His entire life was beginning to shatter. All that he loved and worked so hard for had been transforming into a lie, a manipulation on the deepest level. Nothing was making sense to him. But he knew there was no turning back. His life and entire career were on the line, and nothing or no one was going to stop him from reaching the top. His life had been going wonderfully as he had planned until that day, so he knew he had to get to the bottom of things and make things right before the Gala. He decided he'd go visit his old hood. It was literally days before he would make the biggest deal of his career. Never did he imagine it would also be the day he would end up being betrayed or making the choice to kill a man that could potentially ruin his life. When he pulled up on the corner of Haverford Ave, a big smile grew on his face. He recognized a lot of the people on the basketball court. He shook his head and laughed at the familiar faces that still hustled and hung out there. He remembered hanging out with his old crew, sharing stories of back in the day, hitting a blunt and taking a few shots of Hennessy like they used to do when they were younger. It was also a teaching and learning moment for him to gain knowledge from his old heads that used to run the neighborhoods. And this particular night was no different. As he sat in the old, dilapidated playground talking to some of the young hotheads now running the streets, Snake pulled up in his classic Eldorado Cadillac that still looked showroom new. All the young guys got up to speak to him, for they always had respect for the pioneers who had started them in the game.

"Hey, brother, they told me you were sneaking around here trying to make some sense of my young soldiers," he said humorously. "Yeah, trying to school them on some proper street behavior so that they wouldn't need me in the future," Ethan replied to his friend. "Well, hop in and take a ride with me real quick," he said. Ethan got up and said a few more words to the young men who were sitting on the bleachers with him. He gave them a handshake and then got into the car with Snake. "What's going on, brother?" They greeted each other with a hug. "Ain't shit, man, just trying to make it day by day," Snake said, putting the car in drive and pulling away from the curb." Look, man, I'm glad you came by tonight. After our phone call, I figured you would slide through. I got something to rap to you about. I've always been straight with you, and you know I'll always have your back," Snake said in a serious tone. "Yeah, I know that man, and I know something is wrong," Ethan said to his friend, suddenly feeling nervous. He kept replaying the conversation in his head from earlier.

He had rarely seen Snake get serious and to the point so quickly. Something bad was going down, and he knew his friend needed him. Little did he know it would be him on the receiving end. "Look, man, as you already know, Jacob and James are on the move, and some shit about to go down that could fuck up your life royally," he said in a stern voice. "Fuck up my life? What do you mean?" Ethan asked anxiously. "You kept saying that same shit on the phone earlier," Ethan sighed. "Well, man, they got tipped off that Jacob's son was here in Philly making big moves and that they know if he's here, so is the bitch; they have been looking for that robbed them and killed their main hoe down south years ago. They know that he and the chick ran off together, and no one had heard from them since until an old friend from Philly reached out to one of the twins for some weight. He started running his mouth and told them how he kept hearing about this rich, successful dude in town that they wanted to run a lick on. He owned a big beauty salon and spa in the Center City and knew that a lot of famous people went there when they were visiting and that they kept a lot of money in the joint. They even had a layout of the place, thanks to the guy's nephew. He had worked there for a time doing janitorial work for the owner, and they got pretty close, so he was able to get a lay of the land and know where the safes were located. The longer the conversation went, the more the twins realized that this dude was talking about Clayton Taylor. He had no idea Taylor was Jacob's son. Well, long story short, when they got into town, the dude gave up all the information they needed about Taylor, and so after they got what they needed from the nigga they signed his death certificate. Needless to say, as much as they despised Clayton for the shit he had done to them, they were not gonna let some random street dudes rob or kill him."

Ethan sat in total shock and silence as Snake told the story. He was giving him the rundown of one of his biggest clients to date. He also was hipping him to the fact that the twins weren't really there to settle business with him. They may actually need him again to beat another murder rap. They never shared with him that they knew Clayton, and they damn sure never told him that he was Jacob's son. Ethan had disclosed a lot of information to them about his deal because he was trying to get them to invest, and they still never said a word. "Man, so what does this have to do with me besides Taylor being my client?" Ethan asked, growing concerned about his involvement with Clayton. "Are they gonna need me to represent them again?" Ethan asked, still shaken from what Snake had just told him. "Naw, brother, that's only half the story," Snake said as he drove around until they stopped and parked in front of Wine and Spirits on Delaware Avenue. "Hey, you want something out of here?" he asked before he turned off the ignition to get out of the car. "No, man. Fuck, I need you to finish telling me how this nigga Clayton is tied to me." "Stay calm, dude. I'm gonna finish filling you in. I just need a bottle to take the edge off, and I got a feeling that after you hear the rest of what I gotta tell you, you're definitely gonna need a drink, too." Snake got out of the car and went inside the store, leaving Ethan to think. "What on earth did Snake have to tell him?" he wondered. He checked his phone to see if he had any missed messages, but surprisingly, there were none. He checked his emails and saw that Regina had sent him the proposals he needed for Clayton to sign. Just as he was about to respond to her, Snake got back in the car. He had bought two-fifths of tequila and a pint of Hennessy.

"Damn, man, what you trying to do? Get us locked up for a DUI?" Ethan joked. "Naw motherfucker, the Henni is for us. The tequila is for my lady. She loves this shit and says it gets her horny." They both shared a laugh. Snake popped the cap on the Hennessy and took a shot, then passed the small bottle of libations to Ethan. "Alright, young brother, here's the scoop. So, back in the day when the twins used to have legit businesses, Jacob had a thing for a lady he was close to. She wasn't a street chick, which I'm assuming drew him closer to her. She was wholesome and honest, and he respected her. She was a hairstylist and always made the young girls look good around town. He always liked her, but they never got real close cause she had a husband that she was faithful to. Well, Jacob found out that her nigga was doing dope and was sleeping with prostitutes behind this woman's back. He let her know what a low-down nigga she was involved with, and it broke her heart. He knew that telling her he could catch her at a vulnerable moment, and he took a chance to get with her, and it worked. He ended up fucking the broad and getting her pregnant. When she told him she was carrying his seed, he told her he wasn't even sure if the baby was his and wouldn't do anything for her unless or until she left that no-good husband of hers. She was crushed, man, cause even though she slept with the ole boy, she did still love her husband and believed in her wedding vows." "Look, Snake, I don't give a fuck about the twin's harlequin romance. Ok, what the fuck does this have to do with anything that's going on with me?" Ethan abruptly interrupted. "Dude, would you shut the hell up and just listen," Snake said, annoyed.

"Alright, man, go ahead." Ethan took a swig from the liquor bottle to try to calm his nerves. "Ok, well, nine months later, she gave birth to a son, Clayton Taylor, and Jacob knew he was his seed because he looked just like him and his brother. He also went and took a blood test just to be sure. Well, he and the woman had both agreed not to tell her husband that she had cheated because she feared that would be the end of her marriage. It didn't matter, though, cause that nigga was so caught up in the streets he hadn't even cared that his lady was pregnant. Anyway, a few years later, his cheating ass got killed by one of his mistress's jealous boyfriends, so her son was left without a father either way. The chick ended up going for years without telling Jacob her old man was deceased or letting him see his son. When he finally saw her again, he found out she was alone and was barely making it taking care of their child and her brother. By that time though, Jacob and James were into the pimping and drug game, so Jacob knew he would never have the chance of building a real relationship with her or the kid. He did offer her money from time to time, but she refused to take it, saying she wasn't interested in his illegal money or activity. She looked for work around town, often getting odd jobs to make ends meet. As time went on, she ended up working for a street dude named Smitty, but it was at a rival pimp's whore house. He hired her to take care of his hoes, do their hair, feed them and help them take care of their kids. The dude Smitty knew Jacob had a thing for her a long time ago, but he had no idea about her son. He really only hired her to always try to have one up on the twins. Anyway, she would take her kids with her when she went to work and over time, her son ended up falling for one of the hoe's daughters in the house. He fell in love with the bitch and would do anything for her that she asked him to. The kids were inseparable for a while until the girl's mama failed to pay a debt to the twins, and she got put out. Her pimp, Smitty, had given her to the twins as payment. In his mind, the hoe was all used up anyway, so he had no use for her anymore. Well, the young girl and her mama no longer lived in Smitty's house, so it was hard for Clayton and her to see each other, but she had that nigga's nose so wide open he'd sneak over to the twin's block just to spend time with her. He was so sprung she had that ill nigga following her around like a puppy dog. Well, supposedly, she told him that she was being abused, and she convinced him to help her take out the twins so that they could run away together and live happily ever after. You know some fairytale shit," Snake said, shaking his head. "Well, a few years later, they robbed the motherfucking twins and killed that nigga Smitty too, for what he had done to the girl's mama. Ethan listened intently while taking another drink and then passing the bottle to Snake. Alright, homie, this is where it gets deep," Snake said before taking another swig from the Hennessy bottle. He knew he was finally getting to something Ethan wanted to hear.

"The girl this little nigga Clayton was so in love with was named Alisha. Alisha Saint James," he repeated. "Ok nigga, you said her name. Who the fuck is she supposed to be?" Ethan asked with anticipation. "Bro, that's your wife," he said in a low tone. "What? Wait! What the fuck are you talking about, man? My wife's name is Evelyn, not no fucking Alisha St. whatever you said," Ethan said with disdain. "Look, man, it's her. She has been changing her name and identity so many times over the years no one knew. The bitch lived in New York for a long time after the robbery and even had my nephew Kendall fucked up over her. I didn't get the connection before now because I never met her when she was hiding out in New York. I first laid eyes on the bitch when she started dating you. I had no idea she was the one running shit with my nephew. He always kept her on the down low." Ethan began shaking his head furiously. "Naw, man, there's gotta be some mistake. There's no way," Ethan said, refusing to believe his wife was this woman Snake said she was. "Look, bro, I know it's hard to take in right now, but you gotta believe I would never tell you anything to hurt you, man. For real," Snake said, placing his hand on Ethan's shoulder as he saw his friend begin to sob. He hated to see his homeboy cry. Ethan was like a son to him, and he knew giving him this information would destroy him, but he also knew it had to be told for his own protection. "Bro, my nephew came to me the other day and gave me the whole run down, and when he showed me her picture on Instagram, I couldn't believe my eyes. It was your wife. He came all the way here to let me know what she was planning. Man, she asked him to kill the twins for her. I couldn't believe it myself, but my nephew doesn't lie, bro, and it's a shame, but she still got her hooks in him, too. He is actually considering doing it."

Ethan had a look of disbelief and hurt on his face. His best friend had just told him that his wife had a hit out on two men he was doing business with and that she asked his family to do it. This all felt unreal to him. "Why the fuck would she ask your nephew to do something like that? Are they still fucking around or something?" Ethan asked, still in shock. Not wanting to face the reality that his wife of seven years could also be an adulterer. "Naw, man, it ain't nothing like that with them anymore. Apparently, she saw them niggas with you and was scared they were either gonna hip you to her bullshit and lies or either try to kill you. She knew Kendall knew the whole story about her past, and he told her that if she ever needed him, he would be there for her. She had told him who you were when the two of you first got married, and he gave her his blessing and wished her well. He later found out that you and I were tight, so he was cool. That's why he came to put me down with the plan so that I could protect you." "Naw, man, this can't be real," Ethan said, wiping his eyes. "Yeah, man, it is. I know it's a lot, but the shit is definitely real." The two men sat together in the car for the next two hours in silence, drinking the Hennessy Snake had purchased.

Ethan was trying hard to absorb all the information he had just heard. After some time, Snake finally broke the silence. He knew Ethan was trying to make sense of everything he had told him. And he needed him to know that whatever he wanted to do, he was down with it. Ethan had been loyal to him in the past and had even saved his life, so he had no problem reciprocating the favor. "Look, man, however you wanna play this is cool with me. You know I got your back, and I'm damn sure not gonna let nobody hurt you, he said to his friend." "Look, bro, I know I just need some time to let this sink in, ok? This shit really got me fucked up right now, and honestly, I don't know how to handle it." "Cool, just let me know," Snake said, making sure Ethan knew he had an army behind him if he needed one. Snake drove Ethan back to the playground where his car was parked. When Ethan got into his car, his mind was still racing. He couldn't believe all the shit Snake had just told him. His heart had felt like it had been ripped from his chest. The one time he thought he had finally found true love, it turned out to be nothing but a joke and a con. He couldn't believe that his wife had been so devious and that she had a murder-for-hire plot out on the twins. This was almost too much for him to take. But in the end, Ethan knew it was his life or hers.

35

CON GAME

On the drive home, Ethan decided to call the twins. He needed some answers and wanted them now. When he dialed the number of their hotel, James answered. "Hello," he said forcefully. "Hey, who's this, Jacob or James?" Clayton asked, unsure since they both sounded so much alike. "This James, who the hell is this?" he replied. "Oh, hey man, it's Ethan. Uh, are you guys busy? I was wondering if I could swing by and have a drink. I got something I need to talk to you guys about," he said, trying not to sound anxious. "Sure, man, where do you want to meet?" James replied. "I'll come to where you guys are, man. Ain't no point traveling nowhere far. We can meet at the bar in your hotel if that is cool with you," Ethan said. He wanted them to meet in a public place just in case they decided to do him in before getting to Evelyn. "Alright, man, how long you gonna be?" he asked. "I'm only about ten minutes away." "Alright, man, see you in ten." When Ethan hung up, he sighed heavily. He wasn't sure what he wanted to say to these assholes, but he knew he had to get to the bottom of what they were accusing Evelyn of.

He wasn't sure about Clayton's role or if he was in on the plot to have them killed, but he was praying they had been mistaken about his wife. He didn't want any of the things Snake had told him to be true. He loved his wife and wanted to spend the rest of his life with her. She had been one of the reasons he had worked so hard to be successful. The other was the promise he had made to his aunt and uncle. He had promised them that he would make a difference in his city. He would rise to the top and make them proud. He knew he had done a lot of things that they wouldn't have approved of, but he did what he had to do to survive, and if it wasn't for Snake and the rest of his boys, he wouldn't have made it this far. He busted his ass working hard and defending criminals for years, and he had the street smarts along with the book knowledge to make him a great attorney. His time had finally come to take the world by storm, and he refused to allow anything or anyone to get in his way.

When he pulled up to the twin's hotel on Twelve and Vine, he felt uneasy. He was sure they knew that Snake had told him everything that was going down. It was now time to confront them. He carefully placed his 38 caliber pistol in its holder on his leg and pulled his tracksuit pants over it. He wasn't expecting a shootout in the hotel bar of a Center City hotel, but with the twins, he couldn't be too sure. He parked his car half a block away from the entrance. He needed a few seconds to get himself together and figure out his next move. He kept trying to decide if he should just ask them outright about Evelyn and Clayton or if he should play it cool and let them tell him what he needed to know. Either way, the whole situation was fucked up, but he had to know the truth. When he got to the entrance of the hotel, it was lit. There was a bridal party in the lobby taking pictures and serval people sitting in the lounge chairs chatting and listening to the piano player enjoying the warm September evening. He walked in and headed towards the hotel lounge that was located near the back. When he got inside, he saw the twins sitting in a booth. He casually walked over towards them, hoping he didn't look as nervous as he felt.

"Hey guys, what's going on," he said as he shook their hands before taking a seat next to James. "Ain't nothing, man. What's going on with you?" Jacob replied. "You said you needed to rap to us about something, so talk nigga," James said. "Oh, yeah. Damn, brother, can a guy order a drink and get comfortable?" Ethan said, looking around for someone and trying not to react to James' comment. "Hello, gentleman, may I take your order?" the waitress said when she walked over to their table. Ethan was still a little buzzed from the Hennessy he had with Snake but needed another drink to build up his confidence. "Yeah, I'll have a shot of the 1842 neat he ordered. Would you guys like something?" he asked. "Yeah, give me an order of French fries and a Pepsi and bring my brother a hot tea," Jacob said to the lady with a smile. When she walked away, James looked at Ethan sternly. "Alright, now we ordered something, so what you got on your chest, you need to discuss," he said, sensing something odd about Ethan wanting to meet with them after his work hours. "Alright, look, I'm just gonna cut to the chase and ask you guys what's the deal with my client Clayton Taylor," he said, not wanting to bring Evelyn up in the conversation just yet. "What do you mean what's the deal? He's your client, right?

Don't you know all there is about the dude?" Jacob said with a chuckle. "Look, man, I spoke to Snake, and he told me some shit I'm finding kind of hard to believe. He said that this guy Taylor double-crossed you some time ago and that you all had a score to settle with him." He changed up the story to get their reactions, and he didn't want to let them know that he knew Clayton was Jacob's son and that he and his wife had robbed them. "That's what that nigga Snake told you, huh?" James chimed in. "Well, look, I don't know what else he said to you, but I hope he also told you to watch your back," James added. "And why should I need to do that?" Ethan asked. "Because it seems not only did you get caught up with that slimy motherfucker, but your pretty little bitch is also somebody we need to settle a score with," James said angrily. Ethan felt his blood start to boil.

He hated when someone called his wife, or any woman for that matter, a bitch. "Look, man, I don't know what beef you got with Clayton Taylor, but my wife Evelyn don't have shit to do with any of my business or yours," he tried to convince them. "She doesn't even know the guy, or either of you, for that matter." Jacob started to laugh. "Are you fucking kidding me? You mean to tell me that bitch ain't tell you about her and Clayton? Or us, for that matter?" He asked, surprised. "No, she didn't," Ethan said. "Well, I was pretty sure that that night she came to meet you and almost fainted when she saw us standing there outside of the hotel, it would have been the time to spill her guts and tell you the truth," James said, realizing Ethan might actually be in the dark about his wife. "The truth about what? Tell me what it is my wife really did! I need to know!" Ethan anxiously replied. The waitress walked over and placed their orders in front of them, interrupting their conversation. "Here you are. Let me know if you need anything else," she said kindly. "Thank you, darling," James said, winking at the pretty lady. "Look, man, your lady and that nigga Taylor are into us for a lot of money, and we're gonna get it one way or another," Jacob responded before placing a fry into his mouth. "So, this is about money?" Ethan asked. "Look, how much does she owe you? I'll be more than willing to pay her debt," he said, reaching into his pocket for his checkbook. "It ain't just about the money. She took away something from me that was worth way more than money," James replied in a loud voice. "Calm down, James. People are starting to stare," Jacob said to his brother, noticing the people around them looking. "Look, man, I ain't got time to be soft to this nigga about his woman. That bitch killed Kim, and I can't let her ass get away with that," he said. Ethan could see the hurt in his eyes for the first time as he spoke. For a brief moment, he almost felt sorry for him. He didn't know the woman he was talking about, but he could tell she meant a great deal to him. "James, look, I don't know what went down back in the day, and I'm really sorry man," Ethan said, trying to show some sympathy to him. "Yeah, well, sorry, ain't gonna cut it, brother. That broad did something unforgivable, and the day has come for her to pay," Jacob said. "Now, it can go down one of two ways: either you gonna be in on it or…" "Or what?" Ethan asked, shocked. Were these niggas asking him to set his wife up or, even worse, kill her? He suddenly felt sick to his stomach. "Look, you gotta make a choice and make it now cause this time we are not letting her or that nigga Clayton get away," Jacob said. "She has lied and conned you, too, man. This is what she's good at. Manipulating people and using them for her own gain, and we have proof. She doesn't care about you, man. She knew you were easy, and she played you just like she did that nigga Clayton and whoever else she got a hold of." Everything they were saying was starting to sink in.

As much as he didn't believe it, Ethan knew that these guys were telling the truth and they meant business. He didn't know what to do. His whole body felt null and void. How could he possibly entertain the thought of setting up his wife for them to kill her or even fathom the thought of killing her himself? He felt like the world was crashing down around him. He had been a pawn in Evelyn's sick game, and he was furious. But he also felt like a nut, knowing that all this time, the twins were playing him as well. It seemed like nobody had his back in this situation. "Alright. Look. I hear everything that you guys are saying, and I need some time to figure some shit out, ok? I'm asking that you don't make a move until I do," he said, hoping they would pause their plans. He had to get his mind together and come up with a way to nip all of this shit in the bud. "Ethan, you have always been straight with us and been one hell of a lawyer for us, too, man, and we need you. It would be a shame if you didn't make the right decision," Jacob said. "We can show you everything so that you can see we're on the up and up." He really did like Ethan, and they were gonna make a whole lot of money together if he played his cards right. Ethan downed his shot of liquor in one gulp and got up to leave the table.

When he rose to his feet, he felt his head start to spin. "Hey, guys, I'm gonna run to the restroom real quick," he said to them. "Sure, man, take your time," James said. He walked across the room to where the bathrooms were located and rushed into the stall. He had to vomit up all the liquor he had consumed. His stomach was in knots, and he felt sweat forming on his brow. He knew he was probably sick from all the drinks he had consumed because, truthfully, he wasn't a real drinker and wasn't good at holding his liquor.

But, truth be told, he also knew that finding out all the shit he did that night about Evelyn and Clayton and how his infamous career was about to be shattered was the real reason he was sick to his stomach. He almost regretted going to the hotel but was glad he did. He found out about his wife, and as much as it hurt him, it also hardened him and made him turn back to the person he was trying so hard to bury. He knew he used to be heartless and didn't give a damn about anyone but himself. He used to have a motto for the streets: Get Down or Lay Down, but he had left that man behind in his past because he wanted a fresh start in his life, and he thought Evelyn was just that fresh start and a new beginning. Now, he had to take off the mask of the good guy, and that troubled him. He just wanted to get home, close his eyes, and pray that this was all a dream. He threw some water on his face and went back out to join the twins. "Hey, man, you don't look so good," Jacob said to him when he sat back down. "Yeah, I'm not feeling so hot either," he replied. "Yeah, well, we called you an Uber to take you home because you shouldn't be driving in your condition," James said. "Thanks a lot, guys. I appreciate that," Ethan said. He was glad they had done that for him. He knew there was no way he could make it all the way to Bucks County in his state. They all got up and walked towards the hotel exit, each in their own thoughts. James was hoping to get the waitress's phone number while Jacob was thinking about his son, but all Ethan had on his mind was getting revenge on all those who crossed him. "Hey, man, we'll be in touch real soon," James said to him. "Payback's a bitch," he thought.

36
EVELYN

Evelyn sat back in her chauffeured black SUV, exhausted from shopping. She had easily spent close to thirty thousand dollars. She had gotten a few new handbags from Gucci and at least four pairs of shoes from Prada. But she spent the most on a beautiful black evening gown from Dior for the party she was attending with Ethan. She wanted to look absolutely stunning when she saw Clayton, and that dress hit the mark. It was a full-length strapless silk gown with embroidered crystals and diamonds surrounding the corset. It was beautiful, and she knew Ethan would be pleased. She made an appointment to have her hair and makeup done at the John Jacobs salon for early Saturday morning, and she had a masseuse coming to the house at noon to work out any stress or tension. She was getting well prepared for a wonderful evening. Evelyn pulled out her cell phone and dialed Clayton's number. She closed the partition in the car so that the driver couldn't hear her conversation. "Hello, you have reached Clayton Taylor. I'm sorry I cannot take your call at this time, but please leave a message at the sound of the beep, and if it's an emergency or business call, please call my assistant and leave a message. Thank you. Beep". She smiled, still loving the sound of his voice. "Hi, it's me again. Please call me so that we can talk. I'm taking care of our problem, and I just want to know how you are and…" Beep. The phone disconnected before she could finish her message. She wanted to talk to him before Saturday and let him know she would be attending his Gala so that it wouldn't be a shock when he saw her there.

She was sure he still didn't know Ethan was her husband. But she knew he probably wouldn't answer any more of her calls, so she would have to wait till Saturday to see him. The drive back to Philly was quick, and she was happy. She wanted to go home and soak in a nice hot tub before dinner and maybe even have a drink before Ethan got home. Having a few shots of Grand Mariner almost always relaxed her. When she walked into her home, the kitchen staff was busy at work preparing dinner. "Hello, Ms. Price. Nice to see you," Henrietta greeted her at the door and took her bags from her hands. "Henrietta, it's good to see you, thank you." Evelyn kicked off her shoes in the hall. She had walked the sidewalks of Manhattan for hours shopping. "Looks like you had a little therapy," she said, holding up Evelyn's packages. "Yes, and it was great," she said as she plopped down on the sofa in the family room. "Can you please pour me a drink?" She said to Henrietta as she put her feet up on the footstool. "Right away, Ma'am." Henrietta hurried over to the bar in the corner and poured Evelyn a big drink from one of the containers. "Here you are, Grand Mariner, neat," she said, handing her the sifter nearly full of the brown liquid. "Ahhh, that's perfect, Henrietta. Thank you."

She took a sip of the liquid gold, savoring the taste. She picked up the remote to the surround sound system and turned on the seventy-five-inch television mounted over the fireplace. She hadn't watched TV in the family room in a while and just wanted to relax. She turned to one of her favorite programs on the ID channel. "Henrietta, can you please run me a bath? I'll be going up shortly," she said to her housekeeper. "Yes, ma'am, right away," she replied and headed for the stairs with Evelyn's packages. She loved the way she took care of her. Henrietta provided Evelyn with a motherly figure she desperately needed. She comforted her and took care of her every need. She wished Candy had done that for her and that maybe she wouldn't feel so negative about having kids of her own. She wanted to give Ethan a baby and was even pregnant with Kendall child years ago, but she quickly aborted his seed because, at the time, she felt that neither of their lives was set up for raising a child. If only her own mother felt that way. But then she wouldn't be here living a fabulous life and married to a wonderful man, but also, she wouldn't be in the fucked up situation with the twins either. Evelyn sat on the couch, staring aimlessly at the TV, thinking about all the things that had transpired in her lifetime. Mrs. Price she quickly snapped out of her thoughts when she heard Henrietta saying her name from the stairwell. "Yes, Henrietta, what is it?" She was relieved to be taken out of that space. "Your bath is ready, ma'am," she said as she walked into the living room and picked up Evelyn's drink. "Would you like for me to freshen this up for you and bring it upstairs?" she asked, holding the glass. "Yes, that would be great." Evelyn turned off the TV and went upstairs to her bedroom. She looked forward to relaxing in the hot steaming tub full of bubbles. As soon as she removed her clothes and was about to step into the tub, her phone rang. Shit, she exclaimed. She had meant to turn her cell off when she went upstairs. She had already spoken to her husband, so she wondered why he could possibly be calling her back now.

"Hello," she answered, annoyed. "Damn, bitch, why the attitude?" she heard one of the twins say. Her hand suddenly started to shake as she held onto the phone. She knew their voices anywhere. "Hello," he said forcefully. "I know you there. Well, say something, bitch," he said again and chuckled. "How did you get my number?" Evelyn felt the sweat start to bead up on her forehead. "Your man gave it to me, but how about that don't even matter. I thought you'd be happy to hear from me," he said, his voice dripping with hate. "Why would you think that?" she asked, her voice trembling. "You looked so surprised to see us last time. I had to call to find out how it felt to see an old friend. I ain't seen you in years, baby girl. I thought you were dead or something or, at the very least, strung out on crack or wet." She could hear the cynicism in his words.

"Look, if you want the money back we took from you, I'll get it, ok? Just leave me and my husband alone." Tears started to run down her face. "Aww, hoe, this ain't about no money and you know it. You took something away from me, worth more than that. You and that punk ass nigga you use to hang with. You even tried to take our freedom, but you failed to realize me and Jacob are unbeatable. We looked for you for years and had come to the conclusion that you were dead, but as luck would have it, you married to our lawyer. Now ain't that a bitch," he said, laughing into the receiver. "Please don't hurt Ethan. He doesn't have anything to do with what happened between us. He's naive and totally clueless about street life. Please don't harm him," she pleaded. Her mind started to swirl as she thought about them taking Ethan hostage and doing harm to him or worse. "We not interested in that square ass dude bitch. He ain't the one that did us dirty; it's you we want, that's it. Oh, and that nigga Clay, is he still breathing?" he asked, referring to Clayton. "We actually wanna thank him for taking care of that nigga Smitty for us back in the day, even though he helped you rob us. If we run into him, we just might let him keep his life since we know you were the true mastermind and all," he said sarcastically. Evelyn gasped, surprised to know that Smitty was dead and that Clayton had killed him. He had told her that Smitty had a change of heart and decided to give them more money for the drugs than he had planned and that he was happy that they were leaving town together.

"Listen, I'll get you your money and even more if you want it, and I'll even try to recruit some women for you; please, just don't hurt my husband. Please. I'm sorry I can't bring Kim back; it was an accident. I didn't mean to shoot her," she cried as she thought of the only friend she had at the twin's whore house of horrors. "She was a loyal bitch, and it still breaks my heart that she's gone," he said, almost remorseful. "I know, and I'm sorry, twin. I'm sorry, I swear. Please just let me give you back the money we stole and leave us alone." She prayed he had a shred of empathy left for her since he was the one who gave her mother the drugs that killed her. "You just like that stinking ass whore mother of yours thinking I give a fuck about your apologies and tears." He could tell she was crying. "Does your man know what a conniving thieving bitch he's married to?" he asked. "Huh, bitch? Does he?" He yelled into the phone. She sat silently as he spoke. "Well, maybe he needs to know. Maybe he needs to start making funeral arrangements for your slimy ass," he said through gritted teeth. "Please, twin," she whispered, knowing that he was gonna kill her the next time. Wait for my call so that we can get our fucking money, and please don't try to leave town. I found out you got a lot to lose if you do; he laughed and hung up.

Evelyn's whole body trembled with fear as she thought about what he would do to Ethan. Maybe they had already gotten to him and told him about the awful crimes she committed. That's how they got his phone and her number. She was so frightened she couldn't think straight. She could barely see from the tears. Her insides churned with anguish. How did this all go wrong so fast? She didn't know if she should call Ethan or Kendall first. She wanted to make sure that her husband was ok, but she needed Kendall to know that the twins were gonna strike soon and to be prepared. Just as she dialed Kendall's number, Ethan entered the bedroom. "Babe, you in here?" he said cheerfully. "Oh my god, Ethan, you're here," she sighed as she ran into the bedroom and threw her arms around him. "Of course, what's wrong?" he asked, feeling her body shake in his arms. "I just missed you so much, and I'm glad you're home." She held onto him for a few more seconds before releasing him from her tight grip.

Yeah, I know I'm late. I had to make a stop before heading home," he said as she watched him somewhat stagger over to place his wallet and keys on the dresser. "Have you been drinking?" she asked as she wiped off the tears she shed from her eyes. "Yeah, I had a few drinks with those two guys you saw me with the other day, the twins. We had to wrap up a few things business, you know," he slurred. "Ethan, where is your cell phone?" she noticed he hadn't placed it down with his other belongings. "My phone, shit. I must have left it at the restaurant, but don't worry, my buddies will hold it for me," he said, feeling slightly inebriated. "How could you leave your cell phone?" she shouted angrily, knowing that's how those bastards got her number. "It's just a fucking cell phone. Will you calm down?" he was starting to get annoyed. And then you drive home drunk," she said, praying he didn't allow them to drive him home and know where they lived. "Of course I didn't drive home. I caught an Uber, babe. Stop getting so upset; it's not that deep." All he wanted to do was lie down. He didn't think his wife was gonna start snapping at him for having a few drinks with his clients.

Ethan climbed into the bed and looked at her. She had been standing there completely nude, and he started to get a hard-on. "Come over here and let me tap that ass," he said, grinning. "Take a fucking nap. You're drunk." Evelyn grabbed her silk robe that was on the bed, went back into the bathroom and slammed the door. She was angry yet scared shitless at the fact that her husband had just been out with the two men that wanted her dead. She went into the medicine cabinet and took out two Motrin. She went back into the bedroom to give the pills to Ethan and ask him some questions about the twins, but he had passed out. He wasn't really a drinker, and Evelyn knew he couldn't hold his liquor. "Damn it," she said as she heard him snoring lightly. "I guess my interrogation will just have to wait till the morning," she said aloud. She had finally decided to get into the tub, but all the bubbles had disappeared, and the water was cold. She turned on the hot water, then reached for her phone and noticed she had a text from an unknown number. It read "HAVE MY MONEY SATURDAY NIGHT!!!" She knew it was from the twins. She dialed Kendall's number again, and he answered on the first ring. "What's up, beautiful," he said. "Saturday night, my problem needs to go away," she said and pressed the end button.

She was furious when she hung up the phone. She thought about how it would all go down. All she had to do was make sure Kendall knew where she would meet them. She wanted Him to be on the go and start spraying their asses before she could even step foot out of the car. Those niggas had to die, and she knew Kendall wouldn't let her down. When it was done, he would plant some money and a few bricks in the trunk of their car, then the cops could just chalk it up as a drive-by, possibly between drug rivalries, and it would just be another unsolved mystery in the city of brotherly love. Yeah, her plans were solid, and she knew Kendall was thorough, so everything would play out perfectly. Evelyn finally began to relax and smile. This could all happen before the party, and she could enjoy herself with her husband. She was relieved that in two days, she was finally gonna have some peace, for her Saturday couldn't come soon enough. "Tick, tock," she thought and slid down further into the warm soapy water.

37
DENIAL

The big night had finally arrived. The start of a new beginning. While Ethan stood looking at himself in the full-length mirror of his bedroom, he started to feel nervous. He had represented major clients before, but for some reason, tonight felt different. It felt like he was finally making it. Getting the recognition he deserved. The next Johnnie Cochran. Over the years, he worked hard to be successful, and tonight, he was getting his just due. He was going to become famous all over the world. Ethan Price, world-renowned attorney. He liked the sound of that as he said it in his head. He smiled at his image in the mirror. "Damn, brother, you finally made it to the top," he said out loud as he gave his tux one more glance over. Everything was perfect for Ethan. He had completed all the paperwork and contracts needed for Clayton's other locations, he messengered all checks and documents over to the courthouse to be filed, and he even managed to wrap up some of the other cases he had, including the one for Mrs. Brooks's son.

He knew that Snake would be grateful, and he made a point to swing by the old neighborhood later in the week to check on her son before going to LA for some business meetings. Every now and again, he needed to connect with his old neighborhood. He never felt like he was too good for his hood. He looked over at his nightstand and decided he would wear his bus-down Rolex, which his wife had purchased him for their anniversary a few months back. Maybe that would make her smile since he had noticed how strangely she had been acting since the night before he had come home tipsy. That next morning, she grilled him about the evening and made him promise not to hang out with the twins alone again. She said it was unprofessional and gave him a bad look, especially due to their gangster reputation.

Ethan had been worried sick after visiting Snake and the twins. The whole conversation he had with them still made him angry and confused. The words his childhood mentor spoke broke his heart. His entire life had been shattered. All that he loved and worked so hard for had been a lie, a con game, and a hustle on the deepest level. Nothing made sense to him. But he knew there was no turning back. His life and entire career were on the line tonight, and nothing or no one was going to stop him from reaching the top. Evelyn was right about her assumptions about the twins, and Ethan knew because of her ties with them, they were deadly. He hadn't told her about the information they gave him about her or Clayton, and she had no idea that he had invited them tonight. He figured the best place to line them up would be at the GALA when he reintroduced her to Clayton as well. It was a big risk putting them all face to face like that, but Ethan knew this was how the game had to be played. It was hard for him to keep his cool, but he was determined to get revenge. All he had to do was play the nut they all thought he was, and when the shit hit the fan, take anyone out that stood in his way. As he sprayed on his Bond No. 9 cologne, he heard Evelyn in the dressing room. He stuck his head inside just as she slipped her gown over her perfectly round ass. "Damn, baby, I can't believe how incredibly beautiful you look," he said as he felt his manhood start to rise. Despite the hatred and loathing he felt, there was no denying she still turned him on. She turned and smiled at her husband lovingly. "Aww, thank you, babe, you're not looking too shabby yourself," she said, admiring him in his tailor-made Paradox tuxedo. "I think we're going to be the best-looking couple there," he said as he walked over and grabbed her by her waist. "I agree," she said as she gazed into his eyes.

Evelyn really loved her husband and wanted to protect him in any way she could. She felt like he had gotten in way over his head dealing with the likes of the twins, but she felt good to know that after tonight, all their problems would be over. Evelyn planted a kiss on Ethan's cheek and gently pushed him away. "You'd better let me finish getting dressed before we won't make it to the party," she said with a chuckle. "Alright," he said as he swatted her playfully on the backside. "But please try and hurry, babe; we're already running late," he said as he rushed back into the bedroom to get his wallet and keys. When he picked up his cell phone, he noticed he had several more missed calls from Snake but decided he'd call him later after the Gala. "I told Regina to send the car for us at seven, and it's already seven twenty, so I'm sure the driver is waiting patiently," he said as he looked back into the dressing room to see Evelyn putting the final touches to her makeup. "You look amazing, darling. Now hurry up," he said jokingly. "Ok, I'm almost ready," she said as she did a final spin and then realized she should tinkle while she was at home because she hated using the restroom out in public. "Honey, please give me a few more minutes," she pleaded to Ethan as she grabbed her beaded purse and headed back towards their En-suite bathroom. "Ok, but please hurry. I'll be down in the den making a few calls," Ethan replied.

He decided he would listen to a few of his voicemails while he had the chance since Evelyn was taking forever. When Ethan picked up his phone again, he saw he had voicemails, so he listened and realized it was one from Snake. He decided to give him a call when he noticed that Evelyn was going to be longer than he expected, so he went to his den to give him a call back. "Look, bro, I know a lot of shit is going down tonight, and I need to make sure you are one hundred percent on point." Look, man, I appreciate the lookout, and I'm gonna try to get in touch with them before I get to the event. If not, I'll just talk to them there and find out what the hell is going on." Snake was well aware of everything going down, but he didn't want to alarm his friend. "Thanks, brother. Just know I'm a call away. I'll be in touch, peace." When Ethan hung up, he had a strange feeling in his gut. He knew that nothing was settled the night he met them at the hotel. He was trying to make sense of everything Snake had told him, but he couldn't. He tried reaching the twins but kept getting their voicemail, so he decided to just wait till they arrived at the ballroom to try and clear up any misunderstandings they had with him or his wife. He had heard the stories back in the day when he first started representing them but would never have thought their situation would be in his own backyard, so as a precaution, he made sure to have some of his young boys on standby. As Ethan went to leave the den, he decided to retrieve the gun he had hidden in the wall safe just as a precaution. He knew he had a pretty good relationship with the twins, but he also knew the street code. If there was some beef that couldn't be resolved, he knew things could get ugly and go left, and he wanted to make sure that he was strapped. He placed the steel in his lower back underneath his jacket, where it couldn't be seen. He wasn't there long before his wife would finally join him in the foyer ten minutes later. When he walked out, he saw her standing there looking absolutely stunning. "Wow, babe, you look gorgeous," he said as he planted a soft kiss on her cheek. "You don't look so bad yourself," she said, admiring her handsome husband.

She was wearing the lovely emerald and diamond necklace he had bought her earlier in the week, as well as the eighteen thousand dollar gown she had gotten in New York on her shopping spree. She looked more beautiful than any runway model during fashion week. He still couldn't believe that this fantastic woman would be or could ever have been involved with ruthless gangsters, nor could she have ever robbed anyone or committed murder for that matter, he thought. They had it all wrong, and he was determined to set everything straight if that was the last thing he did. Ethan was unaware of how extremely nervous she was about seeing Clayton and how much it mattered that she looked her best. She still wasn't sure exactly how he was going to react to seeing her on Ethan's arm, but she was just going to take her chances on him being cool. She hoped she would have the opportunity to speak to him alone before Ethan got a chance to make a formal introduction, but she wasn't sure. Her husband never really told her about his meetings with Clayton or even becoming his attorney, but at least she knew that deal was legit. There was no way Clayton figured out Ethan dealt with the twins in any way because she knew for sure he would have never done business with him. Both of these men were in the dark and didn't even know their lives were at stake. When they stepped out of their home, the wait staff, as well as the limo driver, started to applaud the stunning couple. "You both look wonderful," Henrietta said as she leaned in to give Evelyn and Ethan a hug. "Have a beautiful night," she said as they climbed into the silver Bentley waiting for them in the driveway. "Honey, this is going to be a night you are never going to forget," Ethan said as he took his wife's hand in his. Little did he know that statement would reign truer than either could have ever imagined.

38
REGINA

Regina couldn't be more excited. The big night was finally here. Tailored To You's main event Gala and Regina felt like she would burst. She had butterflies in the pit of her stomach, and she felt like a princess in a fairytale. She had found the most beautiful evening gown at a quaint yet stylish boutique on South Street and a pair of Manolo's to match. She was all set for the Gala. Clayton had set up an appointment for her to come by the salon that morning for a complete makeover and had even had a chauffeured town car available for her the entire day in case she needed to run some errands. She felt so special. She had never been to the Bellevue before but had made several reservations for the firm's out-of-town clients in the past, so she knew it was a fancy place. She was happy he had given her the extra ticket to bring her cousin Monica along so that she wouldn't be so nervous among the socialites and elite by herself.

She knew he would have to mingle with his guests and make his presentations, so he wouldn't be able to be by her side for most of the night. At least now, she would have someone to talk to and gossip with. As Regina got dressed, she couldn't help but feel joy about her good fortune and how lucky she was to have met Clayton. He was everything she had ever dreamed of, and she finally had found real happiness. He was a dream come true. Her life had been filled with so much pain from her past, but now it was filled with joy. She didn't feel afraid anymore. She wasn't constantly looking over her shoulder for James or Jacob, and she actually felt safe now that she was with Clayton. She was starting to get a little nervous as she glanced over at the clock. It was already six o'clock, and Monica still hadn't gotten there. She picked up her phone and was about to dial her number when she got a FaceTime call. Bitch where the hell are you? She asked, irritated that Monica hadn't arrived yet.

"Girl, I'm down at the roundhouse. That nigga Kenny went and got himself locked up and called me to post his bail," she said hesitantly. "Are you fucking kidding me? You chalking me for some no good ass nigga, Monica?" Regina asked, hurt and angry her cousin wasn't going with her to one of the most important nights of her life. "I didn't think it would take this long. Apparently, he had a warrant, so he gotta see the judge before they'll let him go." "I don't believe this shit. You know what? Don't even worry about it. I will go by myself. Thanks for nothing," Regina said as she hung up and threw her phone on the bed. She felt a tear start to run down her cheek. "Get it together, Regina, you're a grown-ass woman," she said aloud. "You don't need your immature cousin to chaperone you to your man's event." She went into the bathroom to check her makeup. She looked stunning as she blotted her lips and reapplied her lipstick. Regina went back into the bedroom and slipped into her gown. The delicate fabric felt like a cloud against her skin. She had never worn something so expensive. She eyed herself in her full-length mirror and almost cried. She had never felt so beautiful. She slipped on the leather and rhinestone heels and felt ten feet tall. They were the perfect height to be eye-to-eye with Clayton. She wanted to be by his side at an equal level. He was such an important, powerful man, and she wanted everyone to know he was with an equally strong, powerful woman. "You go, girl," she said to her image in the mirror.

She double-checked the contents of her small rhinestone clutch, which matched her shoes perfectly. "I think I have everything," she said as she walked into the living room and grabbed her keys. It was now seven fifteen, and she knew the car was gonna arrive at seven-thirty to pick her up. She decided to drink a shot of tequila to relax her nerves since she still had a few minutes. Her legs shook as she walked back and forth in her apartment. She assumed it was the heels since she wasn't used to wearing shoes with such height. They had to be at least a ten-inch heel, and that was out of her normal. The highest she would do was a five or six-inch for work, and that was only on days she felt like being sexy. This was all so new to her. Just as she finished the drink, she heard the buzz on her intercom. "Ms. Allen, your car is waiting for you." "Thank you, Carlos. I'll be right down," she said through the monitor. Regina gave herself a once over in the mirror, grabbed her purse and shawl, took a deep breath and went down to her waiting car. Clayton had told her he was gonna send her a stretch Limo so that she and her cousin could have lots of room and be comfortable. Unfortunately, she was alone and would have to enjoy all the luxury by herself. "You look great," the door attendant said as he escorted her to the car. "Thank you, Carlos. I feel great," she said, flashing him a smile as he escorted her outside.

The chauffeur was standing there in an all-black tuxedo with a matching hat that he tipped as she walked over. "Good evening, Ms. Allen," he said as she approached the door. "Hello," she said, blushing and feeling like royalty. "I'm Scott, your driver, and if there's anything you need, please don't hesitate to ask," he said. Once inside, Regina let out a gleeful giggle. She was still whirling from the experience. When the driver got into the car, he rolled down the middle partition and asked if she would like some champagne or wine. "Yes, that would be great," Regina said, grinning. "It's to your right, madam, chilling in ice." She looked over and saw a gold bottle of Louis Roederer Christal in a silver bucket, along with two long-stem glasses. She removed the beautiful glistening bottle, popped the cork and poured the silky smooth liquid from the bottle into the champagne flute. As she sipped on the fruitful, delicious libation, she felt the bubbles start to tingle in her mouth. The taste was divine. "Excuse me, Ms. Allen, will you be making another stop to pick up another passenger?" Scott asked over the intercom of the limo. "Actually, no. I'll be traveling alone," Regina said, slightly annoyed as she thought about Monica standing her up. "Very well, we will be heading straight to the hotel, then."

As they drove along the city streets, Regina stared out the window. The city looked so beautiful and serene; she thought as she admired the buildings lit up and the city skyline. She felt relaxed from the champagne, but her heart raced as they approached the hotel. Nearing Chestnut St., she glanced out the tinted windows to see that Broad Street was packed. Luxury town cars and limousines lined both sides of the huge street. As the car approached the valet, Regina could feel her heart pounding. She was finally here. She saw Clayton standing outside, greeting his guests. She wondered if he was outside waiting for her to arrive. He looked wonderful in a midnight black tailored tuxedo designed by Gucci. His beard and hair were perfectly cut as it glistened under the lights of the hotel. There was a red carpet trailing from the curb to the entrance and two large, beautiful golden statues of life-size combs and sheers on both sides. Regina watched as lovely women adorned in the most exquisite gowns and handsome men in expensive tuxedos exited limos and town cars to shake his hand and attend the hottest event in town.

Millionaires and celebrities alike would be there, and Regina felt like the princess of the duchess, knowing she would be in the arms of one of the most powerful, successful men in Philadelphia. "Miss Allen, we are approaching the entrance. Are you ready to exit?" Scott said, interrupting her thoughts. "Uh, yes," she said as she took the final sip of her champagne and clinched her purse. She felt her body trembling from the excitement and said a silent prayer that she wouldn't slip or fall out of the car. When the limo came to a stop, a tall, slender valet driver approached and opened the door. "Good evening, ma'am, and welcome to the Bellevue Hotel." He reached for her hand and carefully helped her out of the car. "Thank you," Regina said, giving him a small, shy smile. When she got out, paparazzi swarmed her, taking pictures from all angles. She felt like she was at the Grammy Awards. As she walked the red carpet, photographers and reporters shouted, asking her name and what her association with the event was. Just as she was about to speak, she felt an arm gently caress her waist.

It was Clayton. "You look absolutely stunning," he said, then softly kissed her on the cheek. "Mr. Taylor, is she your romantic interest?" she heard reporters say to him. "This is Regina Allen from Price and Associates, and any other information you are seeking will be disclosed inside later this evening," he said as he and Regina made their way inside the grand hotel. "Wow, thank you for rescuing me. I had no idea what to say to them since I've never been on a red carpet before," she said, flustered from all the cameras flashing. "It's quite all right, beautiful. I was actually outside waiting for you to arrive so that I could protect you from all that," he said, pointing towards the crowds outside. "I figured it might be a bit overwhelming. Where's your cousin?" He asked, looking back to make sure he hadn't left her stranded outside. "Oh, she bailed on me at the last minute," Regina said, slightly embarrassed. "Don't worry about it. I'm glad you're alone so that I can have you all to myself by my side tonight," he said as he removed her shawl and handed it to the coat check valet. "I know you are going to be busy talking to investors and business people, and I don't want to be in the way," Clayton Regina said, not wanting to interfere with his business dealings. "Are you kidding? As beautiful as you are and as stunning as you look in that dress, I don't want you out of my sight," he said, grinning as he looked her over. "Well, by your side I shall be," she said as she took his arm, and he escorted her into the main ballroom.

When they entered, everyone started to applaud. Regina looked around and recognized a lot of his staff members, as well as some clients and associates from her law firm. She didn't see Mr. Price but knew he would definitely be arriving soon. She also knew tonight would be the night she would finally get to meet his wife, Evelyn. As they made their way over to the bar area, Regina noticed how elegant and chic the ballroom was set up. There were large crystal chandeliers hanging from the ceiling with beautifully decorated tables lining the outer perimeters for dining. To the left of the bar was a huge dance floor, and beyond that was a stage with five chairs and a podium. In each corner of the room, there were tables filled with Tailored To You products and large framed photographs of Clayton's salons and employees from each city. There was a huge projection screen behind the stage that Regina assumed Clayton was going to use to give his presentation. It was almost eight, and the gala was well underway.

When they got over to the bar, his Assistant Geneva was sitting there having a cocktail. "Hey, Regina. Girl, you look gorgeous," she squealed as she jumped up to give Regina a hug. "Thank you, Geneva. You look pretty amazing yourself," she said as she admired the lovely rhinestone and sequin gown Geneva wore. "Yes, honey. Designed and made by Clayton's best friend. He also created all the uniforms the staff is wearing, as well as my fiancé's tux. Oh, where are my manners?" she said as she grabbed her man by the arm. "Regina, this is my Boo, Ray. Ray, this is Regina Allen; she is our company Attorney and Clayton's lady," she said, smiling hard. Regina wasn't aware that Clayton had told people she was his woman, but it made her heart skip a beat. "Hello Ray, it's a pleasure to meet you," she said, extending her hand to him. "What a lovely bracelet," Regina heard a woman's voice say behind her. When she turned, she saw Clayton smiling next to a beautiful woman adorning her own exquisite jewelry. "Hello, darling," the woman said as she reached out to hug Regina. She was shocked at the woman's aggressiveness. "Oh, hello," she said, confused about who the woman was. "Sweetheart, this is Isabella, my very close friend," Clayton said. She placed two kisses on Regina's cheeks. She wore a lovely long gown adorned with Swarovski crystals and rhinestones. It was flesh-colored, which made her appear that she wore nothing but gems. She looked exquisite, and that intimidated Regina a bit. "It's a pleasure to meet you," Regina said as she extended her hand that she wore the bracelet Clayton had given her. "Clayton has told me all about you, and I must say, his admiration was spot on," she said in a thick, exotic accent.

Clayton then placed his arm around Regina, as he could see she was looking uncomfortable. "Isabella, please have some champagne," he said as he stopped a waiter walking by with a tray of bubbly. Clayton handed her a glass of the sparkling liquid as he watched Regina eyeing her carefully. He hadn't gotten a chance to tell Regina about Isabella, so she had no idea who she was. "Baby, this is the talented designer who created your bracelet for me," he said, trying to get control of the situation and putting Regina at ease. She was surprised at her feeling of envy for this woman she didn't even know. "Really??" She said, feeling silly at her jealousy. Clayton had her feelings and emotions all over the place, and she instantly felt protective when she saw this beautiful woman close to her man. "The bracelet is gorgeous," she said, holding onto her wrist. "So are you," Isabella said, smiling. "Well, darling, I must go mingle now and see if I can conger up some new business," she said as she seemed to glide away from them toward the dance floor. "She is intriguing," Regina said to Clayton as Isabella walked away. "Yeah, she's very exotic, and she's a really wonderful person. I can't wait till you get to know her. I'm sure the two of you are going to be good friends," he said with a grin as he watched Isabella entertain the room. He knew her aura was strong, and every man in the room wanted her attention, but he was quick to put Regina's mind at ease. "She's a very attractive woman, isn't she?" He asked. But surprisingly, as of late, she only has eyes for other beautiful women," he said with a smirk. "Really?" Regina asked, stunned. "You would never have guessed she played for the other team," she laughed. "Besides, I have the most beautiful woman right here with me," Clayton said as he leaned over to kiss Regina softly on the lips. "You know exactly what to say to me," she said, smiling lovingly at him.

39

GAME CHANGE

When Ethan and Evelyn got into the car, he couldn't shake the feelings he had. The more he thought about the night, the more he grew angry and frustrated. He was in a trance and never heard Evelyn calling his name. "Ethan, are you all right?" she said as she reached out to caress his cheek. "Yes, I'm fine, darling. Just thinking about the presentation is all," he said, trying to sound calm. He was actually starting to feel sick as he thought of all the events that had been happening the last few weeks. His wife had been acting strange and sometimes downright crazy when she knew he was working with the twins and sometimes even Clayton. She never wanted to join him for dinner or meetings when invited, and whenever he brought them up in conversation, she seemed to grow furious at even the mention of their names. Everything was becoming clearer to him as they drove towards the city. "What else was he missing," he thought. He knew he never really did a lot of research on Evelyn because he was in love, and he believed everything she told him. The stories were so convincing that there was no way any of them could have been a lie. She was too refined and professional to be from a hick town in the south. She was so well connected and had millions of dollars.

When they first started dating, they would sit for hours, and she would cry, telling him about her childhood and how she missed her mother and how if it wasn't for her grandparents, she wouldn't be the woman she is today, successful and determined. Ethan could see the hurt and pain in her eyes as she spoke, and there was no way her past life wasn't true. He kept trying to convince himself. He never really asked too many questions because she willingly shared more than he had expected. He felt like she was sharing her true life with him, and he wanted to do whatever was possible to protect her. Besides, he had been so caught up in trying to settle his debts and become successful in his own right that he had neglected to see warning signs that were apparently right under his nose. Had he been a pawn in this game all along? His mind was racing, and his heart was beating at a rapid pace. "Darling, are you sure you're ok?" Evelyn asked again, feeling his palms start to sweat. "I'm just a little nervous, is all," he said. "This is the biggest night of my life, our life," he said as he gently squeezed her hand.

He then had a thought. "Listen, I'd like to stop by the office for a moment and make sure I have everything needed for the presentation. I want to make sure everything is in order. You wouldn't mind, would you, love?" he asked in a soft tone. "Of course not, E. I know how important tonight is for you, and any preparations you need to make are fine with me." For her, it was the perfect excuse to have time to contact Kendall and make sure everything was going as planned. "Randolph, please go by my office before heading to the hotel," Ethan said to the driver. "Right away, sir," he replied. They rode in silence the rest of the way, each in their own thoughts. When they pulled up to the high rise, all seemed unusually quiet. The building was dark except for a few office lights of some interns who were not fortunate enough to be invited to the Galla of the Century. "Would you like to join me inside?" Ethan asked his wife as he exited the car, hoping her answer would be no. "No, dear. I'm actually going to have Randolph drive me to the closest CVS for some aspirin. I feel a slight headache brewing and want to get ahead of it so that I can enjoy the evening. I'll call you when we get back, ok?" she replied. "That sounds great," he said relived.

He wanted to try to reach the twins one more time before arriving at the Gala to find out what was going on and knew it would be difficult with his wife being there. Before he closed the car door, he leaned in and kissed her passionately. "Wow, what was that for?" she asked, surprised. "I love you, Evelyn," he said and closed the door, not waiting for her response. He watched as the car pulled away from the curb, and he entered the building. While waiting for the elevator, he redialed the twin's numbers. As he rode up to the thirty-fifth floor, James answered his phone. "Damn, man, getting a hold of you guys seemed impossible," Ethan said nervously. "Yeah, well, now you got me. What's up?" James asked. "I was hoping I could talk to you and Jacob about what you may have planned tonight." When he got off the elevator and walked the corridor towards his office, he noticed the door slightly open and light coming from the reception area. "James, you there?" he asked as he got closer to his office. "Yeah, I'm here," James said, letting out an evil laugh.

When Ethan entered the room, he saw James sitting at Regina's desk in front of his office. "Wow, what are you doing here?" Ethan asked, slightly surprised and nervous to see the twins in his office. "Well, we were hoping to see you too, champ," James said, grinning. "We tried calling you but kept getting your voicemail, so we decided to swing by here to see exactly what our money was being invested in. This is quite a place," he said, turning around in the chair. "Oh, Jacob is using your executive bathroom, if you don't mind," he said as he got up and walked over to Ethan. "Of course I don't mind. Are you kidding?" Ethan said as he started making his way to his office with James following. When he walked over to his desk, he noticed the picture of his wife had been removed from its frame.

"Look, man, I wanted to talk to you guys about my wife." "Ahhh, that's exactly what we wanted to talk about," Jacob said as he exited the bathroom, drying his hands on one of Ethan's Ralph Lauren towels he had in there. "Hey, Jay. How are you?" Ethan asked nervously. "Aw, man, can't complain, was just admiring the beautiful things you got going on in here, is all," he replied. "Ok, enough with the bullshit; where's your pretty wife? I was sure we would get the chance to finally see her tonight," James said, getting aggravated. "She's waiting for me down in the car. We're on our way to the Galla. Remember I invited you guys?" Ethan said. "Oh yeah, the big party is tonight." "Yes, and I wanted to have a few words with you guys before we got there to make sure everything was cool. The way we left things the other night, I feel like we didn't come to an understanding," Ethan said nervously. "Well, my friend, everything is not cool. We seem to still have a problem. Actually, two problems, your bitch and that son a bitch, Clayton," James said angrily. "Wait, nigga, don't disrespect my wife like that," Ethan said angrily. "Your wife? Don't disrespect your wife? Did you hear this uppity nigga, James?" Jacob said, laughing. "Fool, did you forget what we told you and who or what you married to?" "Yeah, I know what you said, and I'm still trying to wrap my head around the whole thing, so please excuse me for still having love for her, damn. We have been together for over seven years," Ethan shouted. "That bitch is a lying, conniving thief and a killer. She robbed us of a lot of money, and she and her little boyfriend Clayton killed my bottom bitch!" James said spitefully as he gripped Ethan by the collar. "Man, you gotta be lying. Evelyn could never do anything like that," Ethan said as tears started to stream down his face. "She could, and she did. We told you we have been looking for that bitch for years, and thanks to you, she's been delivered to us on a silver platter. She's nothing but a whore, a sneaky lying ass whore that convinced you she was somebody else. Her name ain't even Evelyn or whatever she told you her name is. It's Alisha Saint James, and she's the daughter of a stinking dead whore named Candy from North Carolina. I've got all the facts right here," James said as he threw a manila envelope onto Ethan's desk.

Ethan fell down into his chair and listened as the twins continued their story, shattering his dream and image of his beautiful wife whom he had loved. They showed him pictures and documents of court appearances and newspaper clippings of her and her face, a face he had never seen but recognized. With each word they spoke, it felt like his heart was being ripped from his chest little by little. They told him of how she had set them up with Clayton, stolen millions worth of drugs and money from them, and shot a young woman who was supposed to be her friend. He knew about the robbery from years past. It was big news that went national, but he had no idea the woman he fell in love with years later could be involved. He was now coming to realize she was heartless and cold. Everything she had ever told him was a lie. She took the stories of her past and dressed them in a different package to manipulate him and use him for her own personal gain. He had given her his heart and trust and told her he would protect her. He couldn't comprehend all that the twins were saying, but they had proof, and he knew it was all facts. His mind raced as he thought of all the lies she told. Her so-called business ventures, about how she acquired her fortune, are all lies! And Clayton, that son of a bitch he knew all along. He intentionally hired him to represent him so that they could take him down. They planned the whole thing. They would use him to make them millions and kill him. Everything was starting to come into focus for Ethan. Everything the twins had told him the night he met them at their hotel and all the proof they had tonight sealed the deal. He knew what he had to do. He had to take that bitch down as well as her lover.

With each word the twins spoke the angrier Ethan became. "What the fuck!?" he yelled as he slammed his fists on his desk. "I'm gonna kill that bitch!" he screamed. "No, my friend, you gonna leave that to us," James said as he patted

Ethan on the back. "I know you're hurt and all, but we want that privilege to put a bullet right between her eyes," Jacob said. "Besides, we want all the money she stole from us." "Well, look, we can go downstairs. Bring her up here and make her talk," Ethan said, rushing towards the door. "No, man, chill," James said, grabbing him by the arm. "Relax; we got her right where we wanted her. She thinks that you are blind and dumb to everything that's happening, and her plan to get rid of us is solid. The bitch is stupid and has no idea that she is playing right into our hands. I need you to stay cool; we have everything under control." Just then, Ethan's phone rang. "It's her," he said out loud. "She's back from the store, and she's waiting for me." "Well, you don't want to leave your lovely wife waiting now, do you?" They said as he grabbed his keys and headed towards the elevator. "Hey, don't forget it's all under control. Just do your part and stick to the plan," Jacob said to Ethan as he entered the elevator. All Ethan could think about was Evelyn and how the woman he loved just weeks ago was now someone he wanted dead. "Till death do us part," he said aloud as the elevator doors closed.

40
FOCUSED

As soon as the car pulled away from the curb, Evelyn dialed Kendall's number. She had been trying to reach him all day but couldn't get in touch with him. She needed to make sure that he was in the location to take care of the twins and that everything was going as planned. "Randolph, please drive to the closest CVS," she said, relieved Ethan had to make a stop by his office. "Sure thing, Ms. Price," he answered obediently. He knew to never ask any questions when it came to Evelyn and Ethan. Even though he had been her lover for the past five years, he knew his place and that she was the boss. After two rings, Kendall finally answered. "Hey, baby," he said when he picked up. "Really, Kendall now is not the time for that shit," Evelyn said, frustrated. "Where are you?" She asked with urgency. "Damn, why such a shitty attitude? Tonight's the night I'm where I'm supposed to be," he replied in an aggravated tone. "I'm sorry, I'm just nervous and want this shit over and done with as soon as possible so that my life can go back to normal, is all," she said, trying to calm down. "I'm making the call at nine." "I know, A. I've got everything under control. You just do your part and get them niggas in place. I'll take care of the rest. Me and my boys are already on Locust Street waiting. Them assholes ain't gonna know what hit them," Kendall reassured her. "Ok, ok, I'm sorry. I'm just stressing right now, and my husband is acting weird tonight," she sighed. She sensed something was wrong with Ethan, but she didn't have time to worry about him, or what he was going through because she was too worried about Kendall doing the biggest favor she could have ever asked of him to commit murder.

Her driver took her to the CVS located on the corner of Fifth Tenth and Spruce Street, just a block away from where Kendall was posted waiting for the drop. She couldn't really see anything because of all the traffic and people on the streets, but she felt confident he was there waiting. Randolph went inside the store for her to get the Motrin as she requested, and she sat back and poured herself a drink from the bar inside the car. She needed to calm her nerves and stay focused on the plan. She also knew she was just minutes away from seeing Clayton again after all these years. She was still feeling anxious about their reunion but was sure that it would go well. Clayton did love her once, and she felt like all they had gone through together in the past would soften him enough to at least still be cordial. Since her husband was now his attorney, she was hoping that one day, they could wind up becoming friends again. Randolph entered the car with a small bag containing her pills, and she quickly popped two, washing them down with the tequila she had been sipping on. "Let's head back to pick up Ethan," she said, feeling relaxed from her drink. "Right away, Mrs. Price," the driver said and headed back to Ethan's office. When they arrived out front, Evelyn called to let him know she was back. "I'm outside, sweetheart," she said sweetly into the receiver. "Ok, I'll be right down, getting on the elevator as we speak," her husband replied and hung up. She had hoped wherever he needed to handle was done and that he'd get back in the car with a better attitude than when he left. She knew how much tonight meant to him but knew her husband was a brilliant lawyer and could face anything. He had defended the most hardened of criminals and closed some of the biggest company deals in Philadelphia history as well as in several other states, so she knew this deal would be a breeze tonight. She could understand his reservations, though. This merger was going to make him a multimillionaire and set his career on fire. He was going to be the most sought-after attorney in the country. Evelyn was proud of him and knew this was his dream of a lifetime. This is the place he always wanted to be, and she felt happy that she was there with him for it all. As soon as Kendall took care of the twins, she could finally relax and enjoy being Mrs. Ethan Price. All of her worries would be over, and she wouldn't have to constantly look over her shoulder for trouble. And she was gonna be able to finally stop taking those fucking Zanies that always had her feeling like she was in a trance. Yeah, life would finally be simple and happy. A life she had always dreamed about. Little did she know it would all be just wishful thinking.

41

FACE TO FACE

As Regina and Clayton stood there sipping their champagne, they noticed the spotlights start to circle the room and gleam over to the entrance. All eyes were on the attractive couple that walked into the room. The lighting made it hard to see, but Regina knew it was Mr. Price and his wife, Evelyn. "It looks like your boss and his wife are here," Clayton said, trying to focus on them through the bright lights. "Yes," Regina said excitedly. "I finally get the chance to meet his wife," she said, also wondering what her boss would say about her being there as Clayton's date. Regina felt a tinge of excitement flow through her as they got closer to the entrance. Clayton squeezed her hand as they approached the enchanting couple. He was looking forward to meeting Mrs. Price as well.

The closer they got, the more the couple came into view. Regina held onto Clayton's arm, and suddenly, she felt his body start to tremble. "Babe, are you ok?" she asked, wondering why he tensed up so suddenly. Before he could answer, Ethan and Evelyn walked in their direction. "There he is," Ethan said happily as he reached out to shake Clayton's hand. He had been looking around as he approached them and was so happy at the way everything had turned out. He never even noticed the angry look on Clayton's face. He was so focused on the crowd and the beautiful scenery that was surrounding them. He couldn't wait to give the presentation for Tailored To You. Despite all that was happening, he very much intended to close this deal. "So, man, you excited?" he asked Clayton as he looked around the room at all the celebrities and guests. "Yeah, couldn't be happier," Clayton said, almost in a trance but never taking his eyes off Alisha. As Evelyn stood there, she could feel beads of sweat start to form on her forehead. She was terrified to finally be standing there in front of Clayton, and it was almost like a dream. She hadn't seen him in over twenty years, and he still looked great. Besides his now chiseled body, everything still looked the same. His handsome face, the smooth texture of his skin and even the scar over his right eye he had gotten when they were kids.

She felt her heart race as she noticed the hard, glaring stare he had on her. He looked as if he wanted to reach out and strangle her right there in front of everyone. She dropped her eyes and looked away from him. He had no idea that Ethan was her husband, so she knew his mind was swirling, wondering why she was with him. She had never gotten the chance to tell him that his big business deal was with the man she was married to. Ethan noticed Regina standing next to Clayton, holding his arm, and smiled. "Hello, Miss Allen, don't you look lovely," he said as he leaned over to kiss her cheek. "Thank you, Mr. Price," she said, blushing from his compliment. "Everything looks amazing," he said, still not noticing the piercing glare Clayton was giving his wife. "Oh, excuse my manners. Clayton, Regina, I'd like you both to meet my lovely wife, Evelyn," he said as he placed his hand on her lower back. You could see Clayton's expression turn from anger to confusion. "Honey, this is the incredibly talented, successful Clayton Taylor, owner and creator of Tailored To You Enterprises, and my assistant, Regina Allen," he said proudly. It's a pleasure to meet you both, Evelyn said, shifting her eye contact to Regina.

Clayton never took his eyes off her. It was as if he was under a spell. He was standing face to face with Alisha, the girl that broke his heart and the bitch that ruined his life. He could feel his blood start to boil. "I'm so happy to finally meet you," Regina said, extending her hand to Evelyn. "I've heard so much about you, and the picture on Mr. Price's desk doesn't do you justice," she said, admiring the beautiful woman on her boss's arm. "Well, Miss Allen, I've heard nothing but great things about you, too," she said, trying hard to cover her nervousness. "My husband always brags about what a great legal assistant he has." The two women exchanged smiles. Clayton never uttered a word as he continued to glare at Alisha. There was an awkward silence for a moment before Ethan chimed in. "Uh, Miss Allen, may I speak to you for a moment about the presentation?" He was assuming things felt strange because Regina was there as Clayton's date and she nor he ever told him. Ethan wasn't paying attention to the deadly stares from Clayton or the fidgeting of his wife. He wanted to get Regina alone to reassure her that it was okay;

she was there with his best client. He was so focused on the billions of dollars that were circulating the room and wanted to make sure she had her head in the game. Besides, he wanted to leave Clayton and Evelyn alone together to get a feel for their reactions towards one another. "Sure, Mr. Price. Honey, will you excuse me?" she said to Clayton as he still had his eyes locked on Evelyn. "No problem, luv," he said as he slowly moved his gaze from her and took Regina's hand and kissed it. "I'll be right back, darling. I need to make sure everything is on point for later," Ethan said to his wife as he kissed her on the cheek. "Get acquainted with Clayton. I'm sure you gonna want to book a spa day or something at his salon," he said jokingly as he turned to walk away, and Regina followed.

Clayton watched as they went to the bar and immediately moved in closer to Alisha. "Bitch, are you kidding me?" Clayton said through clenched teeth, going in on her. "Evelyn? That's your name now? And you're married to my attorney?" He was livid. "Clayton, please calm down. I didn't know my husband was your lawyer. He just told me a few days ago. I swear," she said, rushed, trying to calm him down so he wouldn't cause a scene. "Listen, can I just talk to you privately?" she pleaded, looking around and noticing they were standing close to other guests who might hear their conversation. "Talk to me? You can't be for real, Alisha. Or is it Evelyn? You called me over and over for the last few days, telling me the twins were back, but you conveniently left out that I was doing business with your husband. You slimy, no-good bitch." "Honestly, Clay, I didn't know," she said, calling him by his childhood name. "Alisha, I could kill you right now and never think twice about your conniving ass," he said angrily. "I know, I know you're angry and have every right to be, and I'm sure you have so many questions. Just please give me the opportunity to explain," she said, shuddering. "What the fuck do you want from me, Alisha? Huh? What?" He said with tears starting to form in his eyes. "Why do you keep coming into my life to ruin it, huh?" He asked, then noticed they were surrounded by guests and realized he had to try to keep it together.

He saw people starting to look over at them, and he knew he had to stay calm. "Clayton, please just hear me out. We have a serious problem right now, but I'm taking care of it tonight. I just need to talk to you, please," she begged. "I told you I have absolutely nothing to say to you, and I swear if I find out that you or your husband are trying to take me down, I will kill the both of you," he said in a venomous tone. "Clayton, Ethan doesn't have a clue about my past or you. He is only focused on this new business deal. I promise you he's on the up and up. No shady cons whatsoever," she said. "So, he doesn't know he's married to a lying, conniving, thieving ass killer then." Alisha hung her head in shame at him, bringing up what she had done in her past. "No, I left all of that behind me and started a brand new life with him, I swear. But there is a bigger problem I need to tell you about," she said hesitantly. "What, Alisha? What the fuck do you need to tell me since it's not that you are my fucking lawyer's wife, and you're trying to destroy me?" She paused before she began to talk. "Well, it seems that Ethan hasn't been very honest with me or told me everything about his past either. I found out a few days ago that he had a business deal with the twins some time ago, and that's why they are here in Philly. They saw me with Ethan and now know I'm his wife. They know we both are here in Philadelphia, and they want revenge." "What?!?! What the hell are you talking about, Alisha?" Clayton raised his voice, causing some of the guests to turn around and stare at them again. Clayton's heart began to race, and he felt it tighten. He grabbed her by the arm and led her near the entrance. He had to get her outside so that they could talk freely. He hoped he didn't get the attention of Ethan or Regina.

Just as they were about to leave the ballroom, he saw the twins walk up to the front door. "What the fuck are they doing here, Alisha?" He asked, shaking and motioning towards them. "I don't know, Clayton, I swear. Kendall was supposed to get rid of them," she responded frantically as fear covered her skin like a blanket. "Who the fuck is Kendall? What the hell is going on?" Clayton felt a tight knot form in his throat. He reached behind his jacket but didn't feel the handle of his 45 pistol, which he kept on him at all times. He had decided to leave his piece in his car since this was a formal event, and he didn't imagine some bullshit like this would happen on the greatest night of his life. He had tight security and protection for all his celebrity guests and knew Darin had some muscle strategically put in place as a precaution, but this situation of running into the twins wasn't even a thought. He felt like he was caught naked and unsure of his next move. As the men entered the ballroom, Ethan noticed them from the bar and left Regina standing where they had been talking about the night's events. He walked towards them, grinning. "You guys made it before the presentation." He was happy they were on time. "This is great," he said, shaking the known killer's hands.

The twins came through the double doors wearing matching identical grey tuxedos and cowboy boots. Their gold chains sparkling on their chests. They were just steps away from Alisha and Clayton. "Jacob and James Spears, I'd like for you to meet the one and only Clayton Taylor," Ethan said, turning to face Clayton and his wife. "Oh, and this is my lovely wife, Evelyn, whom you didn't get a chance to meet last time." Regina squinted to see who her boss was talking to. It was a little hard to see through the spotlights and cameras flashing. She was assuming it was another entertainer gracing them with their presence. She moved a little closer, and when she focused harder on their direction, she couldn't believe her eyes. There stood the men she had been running from for years. The men who tried to kill her and make her abort her child. The men that she watched torture women for fun. She felt the blood drain from her body. She couldn't believe she was in the same room with the notorious Twins. She had turned white as a sheet as she stared at the two familiar faces. She felt like if she tried to turn and run, her legs would buckle beneath her. How could this be happening, she thought. Her stomach started to knot up. She felt lightheaded and sick. She was scared to move.

Clayton glanced around the room, looking for Darrin. He knew he was strapped and ready for any drama that would pop off, but he was never prepared for this kind of chaos unfolding right before his eyes. It felt like Clayton's world was crashing down around him. The twins were here at his gala, and he was not prepared with his backup or heat. He was vulnerable and scared shitless. "I am so happy you guys actually showed up, man." Ethan was obviously greener than a blade of grass, Clayton thought. He had no idea what was happening right under his nose. "This is like a dream come true," Jacob said, looking over at Clayton and Alisha. "I told you guys it was gonna be fire," Ethan said, grinning from ear to ear. "Clayton Taylor, it's a pleasure to finally meet you, man," Jacob said, extending his hand. "Finally?" Clayton asked, feeling the anger rise in him. "Yeah, Ethan here told us about this big business deal he has going on with the richest mutherfucker in town and how he was gonna make a shit load of money. So, you know, me and my brother couldn't resist meeting you," he said smiling sinisterly. Clayton stared at them with daggering eyes. "Yeah, well, Ethan here didn't inform me of additional guests that would be arriving," he said harshly. "Well, shame on him for keeping us a secret," Jacob responded. "And who do we have here? Hello there, darling," he said, turning his attention to Evelyn, who stood there frozen like a statue. "Hello," she said in a whispered tone. "So, you're Ethan's wife, huh?"He asked, almost amused. "Yes, nice to meet you." Her voice cracking with each word. "You two look so good standing next to one another. I thought this was your girl," he chuckled as he nudged Clayton's shoulder. "No, she belongs to me," Ethan said, taking Evelyn's hand. He noticed it was cold and clammy. "Would you guys like some champagne?" he asked as a waiter walked by with a full tray of sparkling wine. "Naw, we good," James said, finally speaking. He had been scooping out the room, taking inventory of his surroundings.

"Well, how's about we go mingle and see what kind of money is out here, then?" Ethan said, hoping to close some major deals with the A-list guests that were in the room. "Sure thing," Jacob said as he started to follow behind Ethan. "James, you coming?" he asked as he watched his brother move toward Clayton and Alisha. "Yeah, I'll be right there. I just want to say a few words to the man of the hour." As he walked up to them, he could see beads of sweat on Clayton's forehead and Alisha damn near in tears." Don't look scared now, mutherfuckers. Your time is coming tonight," he whispered to them. He grinned and walked towards his brother and Ethan, who were waiting for him. The lights were dimmed, and the music was somewhat loud in the lovely ballroom, so Ethan couldn't see the fearful looks they both shared and the words that James spoke. "Omg, Clayton, what are we gonna do?" she asked as tears rolled down her face. "We have got to get the fuck out here," she said, panicked and afraid of what the twins might do to them. "Get your shit together, bitch. Those assholes are not gonna kill us in a room full of celebrities and the press. They ain't that stupid," Clayton responded. "Oh God, Clayton, I don't know what we're gonna do," she said, crying softly.

Just then, Regina walked up, looking dazed and confused. "Clayton, what's going on?" she asked him, noticing Mrs. Price crying and him looking visibly shaken. She herself was on the verge of a breakdown and needed the comfort and protection of her man. She was able to get over to them without Ethan or the twins noticing her. She had to leave but wanted to talk to Clayton first. "Who were those two men that just came in?" she asked, knowing full well who they were. He turned to her and placed his hand on her cheek. "Listen, baby, this night is going horribly wrong. I can't explain it now, but I promise you I will. I'm not gonna let anything happen to you, ok?" he said, trying to sound reassuring. "Clayton, there's something I need to tell you," she said with so much anguish and urgency in her voice. "Baby, please, can it wait? I really need to get Mrs. Price some air. She is not feeling well, and I promise as soon as I come back inside, we can find somewhere to talk," he said. "Well, why can't you tell her husband to come take care of her, Clayton? I really need to talk to you now. It's really important," Regina said, almost in tears herself. He turned and grabbed her by the shoulders. "Regina, I need you to listen to me, ok? Mrs. Price will be fine. She just needs some air. Will you please go over with Mr. Price and tell him to set up for the presentation? As soon as I come back inside, I'll talk to you." He was trying anything he could to get Regina to leave them alone so that he could talk to Alisha in private. "I love you, baby, and I'm gonna tell you everything just as soon as I come back inside," he said and took Evelyn's arm and led her out the door, leaving Regina standing there, not knowing what to do. The twins nor Ethan saw them exit the ballroom.

Regina felt nauseous. She knew she couldn't go to the other side of the room where Mr. Price was because he was over there with the twins. She felt her heart racing. She didn't know what to do at this point, and she was panicking. Her whole body trembled with fear. She wanted to run out the door, but Clayton was out there, and he would instantly know something was wrong. She thought maybe she could just mingle with the crowd and make her escape when Clayton and Mr. Price went on stage. How could her man, the one who vowed to protect her, leave her like this? She thought. She could be dead within minutes, and he would have never known why. He was more concerned with caring for her boss's wife. Regina glanced around the room, looking for Clayton's friend Darin. She knew he carried a gun, and maybe she could find some protection with him since her so-called man was too preoccupied. She needed help to feel safe. She was about to be face to face with killers, and this time, she couldn't hide.

42
TRAPPED

When Clayton and Evelyn got outside, the cool air felt good as it hit their faces. They were both relieved that the paparazzi had left, and there were only a few people standing outside smoking cigarettes and chatting. They walked to the other side of the entrance so that no one inside could see them. "What the fuck!" Clayton let out an anguished scream. Evelyn started throwing up on the side of the wall. "Bitch did you set me up?" Clayton asked, confused and furious. "No, I told you I didn't; I had no idea they were coming inside," she said, wiping her mouth with the back of her hand. "What the fuck do you mean you didn't know they were coming inside? You have exactly ten seconds to tell me what the fuck is going on, Alisha, or I swear to God, I'm gonna fucking kill you now," he said as he grabbed her by the throat. Clayton, please listen," she begged. "I hired someone to kill those two bastards tonight. They were supposed to make it look like a gang rivalry, and we'd be rid of them forever. I don't know what happened, Clayton, I swear. They were supposed to be dead a few blocks away. Look, I'll show you," Alisha said as she reached into her purse to get her cell phone. She wanted to call Kendall so that he could let Clayton know about the plan. "Who the fuck are you calling?" Clayton asked as he paced the sidewalk. "I'm calling the guy that was supposed to handle those niggas inside the party." When she looked at her phone, she saw she had several missed calls. She tried calling back, but the number kept going to voicemail. "Well? What the fuck happened?" Clayton asked anxiously. "I don't know. The phone keeps going to voicemail." She kept trying to call repeatedly.

While she kept dialing the number, she noticed a flurry of police cars speeding by down broad street, sirens blaring. Evelyn felt a knot form in the pit of her stomach. She had a gut feeling they were on their way to 16th and Locust Street, the location where she knew the hit was supposed to happen with Kendall. "I think something bad happened," she said, feeling panic. "Oh, god, no," she cried as she continued dialing Kendall's number. Next, an ambulance sped by at the same speed as the police cars. "Oh no, no, no," she said over and over, knowing something bad must have happened to Kendall. She realized there was a voicemail on her phone, and she quickly listened to the message. She heard Kendall's voice shouting, "Get those mutherfuckers now," and then she heard two shots, and the line went dead. Tears rolled down her face as she wept for her former lover. "He didn't succeed," she said quietly as Clayton stood there watching her weep. "What the fuck do you mean he didn't succeed!?" Clayton yelled. "I think they hurt Kendall," she cried. "No, shit. Bitch, them niggas probably killed the whole crew that was supposed to be taking them out. This is insane. What the fuck are we gonna do?" He said as he punched the brick wall of the hotel. "We have to get our loved ones out of there," Alisha said, starting to head back to the entrance. Clayton grabbed her by the arm. "And just how the fuck do you plan on doing that, huh? No one knows what the fuck is going on besides them and us, and if we start some shit in there, they are definitely gonna finish it. My whole life and career are on the line, and I'll be damn if I'm gonna let you ruin it again. Like I told you, there is no way they are gonna jeopardize their life or freedom by doing something to us here in the open in front of hundreds of people and the news media, so calm the fuck down and let me think of something," he said trying to get control of the situation. "We have to get ourselves together and go back in like nothing ever happened, you hear me?" he said to her. Evelyn wiped the tears from her eyes, applied gloss to her lips, and then smoothed the front of her dress. "Ok, Clayton," she said, trusting him like she always had. Whenever she lost control, Clayton was always there to protect her. She knew he would handle it just like he had before, but this time, he was no longer in love with her, and she wasn't the girl he wanted to save.

When they walked back into the party, they noticed that Ethan and *Geneva had* the room's attention. They looked relaxed as they spoke, giving the crowd an overview of what was Tailored To Your operations. Everyone seems to be enjoying themselves. They noticed the twins standing in the corner, talking to each other, playing it cool. Clayton scoped the room, looking for Regina. She was nowhere to be found. He had to find her and get her to leave the party just to be sure she would be safe. There was no way he could tell Geneva since she was on stage with Ethan but hoped that nothing would go down to put anyone in harm's way. He had no idea what was gonna happen to him or Alisha or anyone there for that matter, but he did know for certain what the twins were capable of and knew no one was really safe. He tried to make his way over to Darin to let him know what was happening, but he was on the other side of the room, speaking to the staff and getting them ready for the show. When Ethan turned around to address the other side of the room, he noticed Clayton making his way near the edge of the stage. He assumed he was getting closer to being intro-duced. "Well, ladies and gentlemen, without further ado, allow me to introduce the star of the show, Mr. Clayton Taylor." Everyone in the room stood and applauded loudly for Clayton as he had no other choice and went onto the stage.

As he approached Ethan, he watched the twins make their way over to Alisha. He felt the blood start to rush to his feet. The sweat started to run down his neck in his tuxedo, and his hands felt cold and icy. He was exposed, and his right-hand man wasn't aware of his situation. He was certain he was about to be taken out by ruthless killers. He had been running from those bastards for the last twenty years, and they finally got him. It was hard for him to see in the crowd as he scanned the room to see where the twins were located. The spotlight was shining directly in his eyes. He hadn't seen that James had Regina tightly by the arm with a gun secured in her back, and he didn't see Jacob standing behind Alisha with the same kind of heat on her. When he put his hand up to his face to try to get a better view of the crowd, he heard Regina suddenly scream. The crowd started to look around as the room became chaotic. People started trying to figure out why a woman was screaming at the top of her lungs. Clayton jumped from the stage and ran toward his woman. The commotion was building all around. Ethan knew it was time for him to make his move. He pulled the gun he had concealed in his tux and pointed at Clayton. He pulled the trigger and shot at him three times, one hitting him in the back. The crowd started to run as panic filled the room. Men and women ran toward the exits and ducked under tables for shelter.

As Clayton hit the floor, he saw Alisha fighting Jacob for dear life for his gun. Everything seemed to be happening in slow motion. It was mayhem happening all at once. Clayton began to crawl towards Regina when he saw James point the gun at her head. All of a sudden, he saw a flash; his ears started to ring, and he felt himself falling into a black hole. Everything went dark, and his body started to go numb. He couldn't hear or see anything. He felt like he was floating in midair. Sounds completely mute. "What the fuck is happening to me?" he thought. Was he dying? Was he already dead? He couldn't speak or move, and he was losing consciousness. The whole ballroom had exploded, and the floor had caved in, taking down everyone and everything that was still standing. He couldn't hear or see anymore, and he felt his lungs immediately start to fill with smoke and blood. The last vision he saw was the love of his life with a gun pointed at her head, and her last sound was her piercing scream. "Wait, how was I shot?" His mind started to race. He then realized that Ethan had shot him. "What the fuck?!" His lawyer had shot him in the back. "What the hell was going on? What would possess this mutherfucker to shoot him? His thoughts were racing a mile a minute. Was he dreaming? This couldn't be real. Was it his demise to die this way? Where was Alisha? Did Jacob get the chance to put a bullet in her? He thought he saw her fall, but he wasn't sure. Was she lying there amongst the trash and rubble like he was fighting for her life, too? This bitch had created this shit storm. He silently hoped that the twin would take her out but felt pity for her as well. Why the fuck did Ethan shoot him? Where was Regina? He brought her into all this danger. This was all his fault. Where were his friends Geneva, Darrin, and Isabella? He hoped they made it out.

He couldn't keep a straight thought in his head. His mind was moving rapidly. It felt like every bone in his body was broken, and he was slipping away slowly. He thought of his uncle Mike being in that facility alone with no family left to care for him. He had failed him, he failed his mother, and most importantly, he failed himself. All his dreams of putting the past behind him were over. This was his payback for all the mistakes he had made, for all the promises he had broken, for all the sins he had committed. This was his reality. God was finally getting even. He felt like he was in a dream state. "This must be my transition from life to hell," he thought. There was no way he was going to heaven because of all the terrible things he had done. This was his final chapter of life. He couldn't breathe, he couldn't see, he couldn't hear, he couldn't move. It was as if time had suddenly stopped, and everything around him was fading. His heart was beating slower and slower with each second that went by. It was almost over for him, and there was nothing he could do about it.

43

BITTERSWEET

It was all happening so fast. Evelyn thought she, too, was in the same dream. She watched her husband point the gun at Clayton. She felt the bullet enter her stomach. It was like still frames of a picture. It didn't feel real to her. She knew she was fighting Jacob for his gun, and when she looked over, she saw Ethan pointing a gun at Clayton. She refused to put his life in danger again. It happened as if in slow motion. She flung her body towards Clayton to try and shield him. Ethan pulled the trigger three times. Two landed on Clayton's back and the other on her. When she fell to the floor, she felt her body floating in the air. All she could see was white smoke as she drifted downwards. She seemed to float for hours. She saw her mother reaching out, trying to save her, but she couldn't reach back. Candy's face was clear in her vision like an angel. She was fighting to get to her, but it was no use. Her arms were stiff. They felt like heavy boulders weighing her down. She heard Kendall calling her name, but she refused to answer. How could he let her down? She needed him. He promised he would always be there for her, but he failed. She trusted he would always have her back, but he lied. She saw Kim's face with tears in her eyes, and when she reached out to wipe them, she vanished. She wanted to console her, tell her she was sorry, and ask for her forgiveness, but it was too late. Kim was the only real friend she ever had. She loved Kim, but she killed her. How could she be so ruthless and evil to the one person that was like a sister to her? All the people she lost, all the people she ever loved, were in her mind's eye.

Then she saw Clayton. His face was full of rage and anger. She kept trying to look away, but she couldn't. She had to make it right for him. She had to take the bullet for her first love. She had to save him the same way she had saved her many years before, but she had failed. She watched him fall, too. She watched his life end in a fleeting moment by the hand of her husband. Ethan had looked her in the eye as he pulled the trigger and watched her jump in front of Clayton, but he kept pulling the trigger. All three were meant for him, but Evelyn took one directly in the stomach. She felt her skin burning as if someone was holding a torch to it. She felt salty tears roll down her cheeks as she tried to inhale. She couldn't see around her, and she had a deafening and piercing ring in her ears. Suddenly, she hit the bottom floor of the ballroom with such force that it felt like every bone in her body was shattered. Everything around her had exploded. She was in excruciating pain and couldn't move. She was in shock at all that unfolded within minutes.

Everyone and everything that mattered to her was gone. The men she loved, her mother, and her friends, and she at that moment realized her own life. She had tried to be a good woman and live her life right after all the terrible tragedies she had suffered and put others through. She had done wrong but felt like she had paid her dues and was finally living right. She had tried her best to make things right with all the people in her life, and she wanted to finally get closure with Clayton. That meant the most to her, but she knew she would never have the chance. She was dying. Each breath she took, she knew, was her last. She felt her heartbeat start to slow down as blood steadily flowed from her body. As she coughed, she felt the mucus and blood escape her mouth. She knew she was drifting away. "God, please forgive me," she whispered as she felt her soul start to rise from her. She was in excruciating pain, and her head and heart were pounding. Within seconds, she took her last breath before losing consciousness. Alisha Louise St James was presumed dead. Her life was over, and all she had sacrificed died with her.

44
MISTAKES

As Regina regained consciousness on the clammy, dampened concrete floor, her thoughts were racing. She opened her eyes and tried to focus. They felt like tiny chips of glass had cut into them. The old, dilapidated room encased her as she tried to visualize her surroundings. When she looked up, she could see that the floor had caved in on her as broken wood and marble tiles still fell from above. She had fallen a whole floor down. The distinctive odor of rats and rusty nails filled her nostrils as she started to inhale frantically. A shudder and chill went from her feet up to her head. She was panicking as her body started to tremble with fear. She wanted to get up and run but felt paralyzed. A tight knot formed deep in her throat from the smoke that filled the room. It all seemed surreal to her. She needed to know what was going on, where Clayton was and if anyone else was still alive. She tried to collect her thoughts and make sense of everything that happened. She couldn't see anything in the darkroom, and the only light that was shown was from the upper-level ballroom. "Where was everyone?" she thought. Her vision was still blurred from the dust, but she could smell a ghastly stench in the air. It was eerily silent except for the crack-ling of wood burning and the sirens of an ambulance in the far distance, and she silently prayed it was on its way to save her.

She thought of the explosion and how it had been so strong the floor caved in. Everything had happened so fast. The party was so beautiful, she thought, and then they showed up. She tried to get to Clayton, but he left her. How in the hell did they know she'd be there, how did they find her, and how on earth did they know Clayton and Mr. Price? How did those bastards get to her? She couldn't believe how lucky she was to still be alive. She lies still, trying to listen for any human sound. There was nothing but flames nearby, but she knew she couldn't have been alone. She moved her arm slowly and could feel the shard of glass beneath it. It cut into her skin like a razor, and she felt a warm liquid flow down her arm. She knew it was her blood. She lay listening for a few more seconds before deciding to try and sit up again. Her body quivered violently. As she pressed her palms into the glass and rubble on the ground, she winced while pushing herself into an upright position. Her head started spinning, and a sharp pain shot up the right side of her body.

She was disoriented and confused as she squinted her eyes and looked around. Her head was throbbing, and her heart was pounding out of control. She reached down to feel her legs and realized she was covered with broken pieces of glass, debris and the same warm liquid that ran down her arm. "Oh, God," she cried, realizing she was covered in blood. Was it hers? Someone else's? She couldn't gather her thoughts to remember. As she sat there, panic overcame her smoke-filled lungs quickly, and she knew she had to find an escape. "I gotta get outta here," she kept repeating over and over in her head as she felt tears forming in her eyes. She tried standing but was in so much pain she couldn't. She had no idea if her legs were broken from the fall and the wood and glass that lay on top of her, but she knew she couldn't stand on her feet. She was in excruciating pain. She began feeling around the floor for something, anything she could use as a crutch to stand. The street light didn't provide enough light to help her see.

Salty tears ran down her cheeks as she crawled around and felt her body grow weaker. She frantically searched the floor with her hands, using what energy she could muster when she came across a large bulky object that felt like a body. It scared the hell out of her, and she fell back onto the floor and screamed. "Hello, please, somebody help me, please," she yelled at the top of her lungs into the darkness. "Please, God, somebody help me," she repeated as she began to scream louder, only to hear her voice as an echo. "Oh my God, oh my God, who could this be?" She thought, terrified and shaking feverishly. Regina felt sick to her stomach. She reached over again to feel the lifeless body of a man she knew had to be dead." How did this happen?" Regina cried out as she tried to sit up again but couldn't. She slumped back down into the trash and debris and began to cry harder as she tried to make sense of everything that happened. Why did this happen to me!?" She cried. How did she get caught? She had tried so hard to play everything right, but the devil had caught up to her.

She finally began to accept the fact that she just couldn't escape. Her body was getting weaker from losing so much blood, and the smoke seemed to get thicker each time she inhaled, and she saw no way out. Her head was spinning, and as she drifted in and out of consciousness, her thoughts went to her daughter. Nyla had no idea what she and her mother were going through. She always made it appear like they were playing a game, moving from state to state, never staying in one place for too long, as deadly as it may be. She only had her mom to care for her, and if James found her, how would she survive? He was sick and twisted, and he didn't care for anyone's life except his own. He had no thought of protecting his daughter's life if it meant ruining his. Regina knew there was nothing she could do to help her now, so all she could do was wait for her fatal demise and silently pray her daughter would be safe. She had given her a locket with a small key inside and always told her that if ever something happened, she would find the box she had hidden for years for her daughter's survival. It contained a letter explaining everything: one million dollars in cash, keys to a condo she had purchased in Maryland and evidence of her father's crimes. It was an insurance policy for her daughter in case of the inevitable. Regina just hoped she remembered all she had told her.

She had no clue that the night would turn out like this. She thought she was finally safe, finally happy. Her life was truly turning into the fairytale she had dreamt of. But in reality, it was all an awful nightmare. Where was the man she loved? She watched as he tried to come to her rescue but saw Ethan Price pull a gun and shoot him. She couldn't believe her eyes.

Why did her boss shoot Clayton? There was no way to wrap her mind around that thought. There were so many unanswered questions in her head. She kept trying to fight to stay awake to stay alive but felt herself drifting. She closed her eyes tightly and prayed for a miracle.

45

IT AIN'T OVER

In the distance, Clayton could hear the sirens from the ambulance. He thought he may actually be saved from this terrible situation. The room was immensely dark and filled with smoke, and his vision was still blurred, but from his clogged ears, he thought he heard the sound of a woman's voice calling out for help. Was he imagining this, or could there really be someone still alive from the powerful explosion? He was surprised that he was still breathing. His whole body was numb, but he could feel the heavy weight of wood and marble from the floor above, pinning him down. He lies there fractured and broken, waiting to be rescued or waiting to die. He wasn't sure which. He lay still for what seemed like forever but never heard the voice of the female again. In fact, the only sounds he could hear were the crackling of fire and water gushing from the sprinklers above. He was hoping someone had called the police or the fire department because the explosion had to have been heard for miles. It came from out of nowhere. Everything happened so quickly. Clayton kept seeing the flash like that from a camera.

He remembered he was crawling, trying to make his way over to Regina to save her. "Damn it, Regina," he thought. He had risked the life of the woman he loved after so many years of heartache. He jeopardized everything. Wait, why was he crawling? Fuck he had been shot! That's right, he had been shot by Ethan Price, his lawyer, his friend, that bitch Alisha's husband. Why in the hell did he shoot him? And then he remembered Alisha jumping in the way, trying to shield him. Why on earth had she done that? Did she know her husband was going to do him in? Was this all part of her plan? But then he thought it couldn't be because she had been shot too. Maybe he double-crossed her just like he had done to him. There were so many questions swimming around in his head. But he didn't have an answer for any of them. All he knew for certain was that he was lying on the dank, dark basement floor of the Bellevue Hotel, surrounded by fire smoke and presumably dead bodies. He couldn't see anything, but given the headcount of partygoers in the room, he was sure the number of fatalities was high.

The Gala had been a huge success. Bringing in top designers and hair artists from around the world. He had noticed big company execs from Paris and Monaco and other famous countries around the globe, and they were all there for him, Clayton Taylor. Celebrities and Fashion icons, top models, and the industry's most elite magazine editors attended the biggest party Philadelphia had ever thrown. He had finally made it. He was the man of the hour. His mother would have been so proud of him. He had big dreams, and they were finally coming true. And it made him feel even better knowing that he was going to have a family to grow with him.

He was falling in love with Regina and her daughter and wanted the next big venture in his life to be making her Mrs. Clayton Taylor. He envisioned popping the question down on one knee and her saying yes. He envisioned a big, beautiful ceremony on the Nile of France with hundreds of guests there for the celebration.

He couldn't wait to share special moments with his new step-daughter, showering her with love and the attention she deserved. He wanted to make them both happy. Regina shared some of the turmoil she faced in her past with him, and he wanted to show her that her whole life didn't have to be filled with sadness. He was going to protect her and give her all the things she deserved in life. But now it was all just a fantasy. The love of his life was dead. He watched as the twin pulled the trigger that was aimed at her head. There was no way she could survive a gunshot wound to her temple. He started to sob, thinking of what could have been with her. His whole life was shattered by the explosion, just like that in a blink of an eye. As he lay there trying hard not to inhale the smoke-filled air, he felt his chest tightening. He closed his eyes and prayed. He asked God to forgive him for the sins in his life, all the terrible mistakes he made and for not fulfilling the promise he made to his mother. He knew that he had donated enough money to the hospital for the care of his uncle, but he never wanted him to spend his whole life there. He had plans to bring Michael with him to live wherever he had finally decided to lay down roots. He wanted him with him by his side, caring for him just as he watched his mother do for many years, but now, he was dying, leaving him all alone.

He lay there for what seemed like forever when he suddenly heard voices up above. "Hello, is anyone there?" He heard a man's voice yell out. For a split second, he thought he was hearing the voice of God and was starting to become content with the fact that he was dying, then quickly realized it was coming from the main ballroom. "Hello, can anyone hear me?" the voice said again. "Down here. I'm down here," Clayton began to yell frantically. He was being saved. He couldn't believe it. God had heard his prayers. The fire and rescue team were there, and he thought I just might get out of here alive. He looked up and could see the firemen clad in big jackets and hoses. It was like the fog was lifting, and he could finally see. He tried sitting up but was in too much pain. His body was stiff. I'm down here he yelled out again, hoping they heard him this time. He wasn't sure how long they had been calling out, but he was so happy they didn't stop trying. "Ok, we're getting a ladder to come down to save you," he heard one of the firefighters say through the hole in the floor. "Just hang on, and we'll be right there. We've found another survivor," he heard him call out. "Hurry, please. I've lost a lot of blood, and I can't move," Clayton said. "Just hold tight," the man said as he lowered a large ladder down into the floor.

He hurried down to Clayton and saw that he was covered with debris. "OK, sir, please try to relax and stay calm. We have to get this marble and wood off of you, and then we can get you out here, okay?" He then yelled out to another firefighter to come help. Clayton could hardly inhale. He was in so much pain. It felt like every rib in his chest was broken. He watched as the men lifted huge pieces of flooring and glass from his body. He could see another fireman lowering what looked like a gurney down to the other men in the basement. "Ok, sir, we're gonna try and lift you and get you outta here," he said as he and another fireman slid a large piece of board underneath Clayton's body. When they lifted it, he let out an excruciating scream. His body felt like it was on fire. He felt like he had been run over by a semi-truck. Just try to relax. "We're getting you outta here, sir," the man said to him again reassuringly. He felt his body being rolled onto the gurney and then being slowly lifted into the air. "Hey, Bob, over here, there's another woman, but she's barely breathing, he heard another fireman say from the other side of the room. He couldn't see clearly everything that was going on around him or the people, but he did catch a glimpse of the men placing a body onto a board just like his on the floor. Could it be Regina or Neva or maybe even Alisha? He silently hoped. He was almost certain now that he wasn't losing his mind and that it could have been any of them calling out to him as he lay there bleeding, but his body was so badly injured there was nothing he could do.

When he reached the top, he tried to focus on all the commotion that was happening. He was desperately trying to see if any of his staff or friends were among the hundreds that lay there injured. Dozens of police firemen and even the bomb squad were on the scene trying to figure out what was going on. There were several bodies covered with sheets, and he knew instantly those people had been fatalities. The emergency services had gotten several calls from surrounding businesses and homes saying that the hotel had been in flames. They dispatched units from all over the city, unaware of the horrific tragedy. Once they had gotten Clayton safely on the top level inside the ballroom, a medic came over and began asking him questions. "Sir, can you hear me?" the lady paramedic asked him. Clayton's vision was still slightly blurred, and he could hardly hear her voice from the ringing in his ears. "Sir, can you tell me your name?" he managed to hear her say. "Yes, I'm Clayton. Clayton Taylor," he said weakly. "Ok, Mr. Taylor, we're gonna get you to an ambulance," she said as she placed an oxygen mask over his nose and mouth.

There was someone else on the other side of him, hooking him up to an IV as they began to roll his gurney toward the front entrance. He glanced around, noticing people propped up next to walls and the makeshift stage. They were covered in blood and cuts. Some had masks over their nose and mouth, providing oxygen to help them breathe. He saw several EMTS administering aid to the wounded. Just before they exited, he saw Ethan standing by and talking to one of the police officers. He looked shaken but not badly wounded. Clayton felt his body start to shake again. He frantically tried to sit up while his screams were muffled by the oxygen mask on his face. Ethan!!!! He tried yelling out over and over but couldn't be heard as they whisked past him. Once outside, he was placed inside an ambulance. He kept frantically trying to remove his mask because he needed to tell the police not to let Ethan get away. He had shot him! He knew he had to have something to do with what happened, the explosion itself, and he made a vow he wasn't going to rest until Ethan was dead.

He suddenly felt his body starting to go limp. Another paramedic had injected something into his IV, and he felt like he was floating. Before he could try and ask what they had given him, he felt his eyes close, and he passed out. The ambulance was on its way to the hospital and just in time. They were diagnosing him as being paralyzed from the waist down and in need of a blood transfusion to save his life. He was slipping away fast. Luckily, the hospital was only a few blocks away. When they pulled into the emergency room driveway at Jefferson Hospital, everything was frantic. There were patients all around the entrance and inside, waiting to be treated. As he began to gain some consciousness, he noticed several people from the party all around looking disheveled and disoriented. He still had the mask over his face, but his vision was becoming clearer again. His eyes frantically searched the faces of the crowd. He needed to lay eyes on Regina or Geneva or even Darrin. He needed reassurance that they were ok. He needed to know if they survived.

The EMTs quickly rushed him over to the desk, where he overheard them telling the ER doctors that he lost a lot of blood, he had two bullets lodged in his side, and he had a collapsed lung and had no feeling from the waist down. They thought his spinal cord could have been shattered from the fall. He needed X-rays and a spinal tap and should be rushed to an operating room immediately. He was in bad shape, and he knew the doctors would have a hell of a fight to keep him alive. He felt his head start to spin as they rushed him down what seemed like several hallways before making it to the elevators. Fear overtook him as he thought about them, saying his spin had been crushed. The reality of it all was he may never walk again. He was going to end up a cripple but felt like he was better off dead.

46

BACK FROM THE ASHES

When Ethan thought about what happened he was astounded. He couldn't believe there was an explosion. The magnitude of it was forceful and it was timed perfectly. As soon as he introduced Clayton, and he walked up onto the stage he remembered pulling the trigger and watching him fall. He had also watched his wife try to protect and shield that nigga as he unloaded the bullets from his gun. For him it was all about survival and staying on top and whoever he needed to destroy in the process then so be it.

It especially hurt Ethan to his core, though, to know that the love of his life had tried to manipulate him and play him like a fool, but deep down, he knew that was the game of the streets. Get them before they get you. He was a little dazed and confused as everything seemed to be moving at such a fast pace. He looked around and saw paramedics and fire-fighters putting people on gurneys and assisting the wounded. He didn't see his wife, the twins or Clayton, and he wondered if they were all dead. His mind was going in circles, and his head was pounding. He remembered parts of what happened, like going onto the stage to introduce Clayton and pulling the trigger of his gun. He had been determined to kill Clayton for ruining his life, and he was gonna put a bullet in the head of the twins as well, but that didn't go as planned. He wanted to even give Evelyn one last chance to come clean about everything she was involved in, and if she didn't, then it was gonna be lights out for her too. But she risked her life for Clayton. He still loved her with every fiber of his core, but he was tricked by her lies and betrayal, and he was gonna set things straight once and for all. The twins had been running his life ever since he helped them with their first case, and just when he thought he could finally walk away with his debt paid, he found out that all the people in his life were part of a grand scheme to try and destroy him. Never did he imagine that his wife, the woman that he loved and cherished, would be involved with those street niggas and one of the biggest Salon and spa moguls in the country.

He really thought Clayton was his friend, someone he could trust. He was ready to build an empire with him and make them the richest men in Philadelphia. It hurt him to find out that all this time, this man had conned him along with his wife and that she had been connected to him all along, but he needed to know why. He needed to figure out their plan. He had so many unanswered questions. He was devastated that she had jumped in front of the bullet that was meant for Clayton. His soul ached each time he thought of her being shot. He had to find her. That was all that kept running through his mind. Ethan squinted through the haze of smoke and debris, trying to get a good look at the people in the room. He had to find Evelyn and try to get her to safety. He knew she had been shot because he witnessed her take the bullet from his gun, but he needed to know if she was dead or alive. As he rose to his feet, one of Philly's finest approached him.

It was Officer McCloud, a policeman he knew from the third precinct. "Hey, man, are you all right?" he asked, concerned, recognizing Ethan right away. "Yeah, man, just dazed, is all. I can't believe this shit. I don't know what happened. One minute, I was on the stage introducing my client, and the next thing I knew, a bomb went off," he said, pretty sure the cop was unaware of his involvement in what happened. He searched the floor, but the gun was nowhere to be found. "Yeah, everything is crazy around here, man; so many people are giving different accounts of what happened. My chief is questioning the guests now. Well, the ones that can actually speak, to try and figure everything out," the officer replied. As he listened to the officer, his concern grew. He prayed that no one remembered him pulling a gun before the explosion. "Yeah, I'm looking for my wife, Evelyn Price. I need to know if she's ok," he said, trying to sound frantic and change the subject. "Do you know if they have taken anyone in an ambulance or treated anyone by that name?" Ethan asked, genuinely concerned. "No, I'm not sure, but I'll do what I can to find out," the officer said reassuringly. "Thanks, man, I really appreciate it; I need to find her to make sure she's ok," Ethan responded.

As the officer walked away, Ethan was relieved as he continued to scour the room for Evelyn. His eyes scanned every part of the room when he caught a glimpse of a woman standing near the doorway that resembled his wife. His heart began to beat fast. Was he dreaming? For a brief moment, he thought it was her standing there elegant and alive, but he realized this woman was older yet still as beautiful. She was dressed in a lovely silver beaded evening gown, and her hair was swept up in a bun with curls cascading down into her face. She was the spitting image of the woman he met years ago. She'd stood about five feet nine with an hourglass shape. Her clothes were expensive and well intact, with no scorches or damages. Ethan knew she couldn't have attended the party but knew if she had, he would have remembered seeing someone so lovely. She stood there so calm and poised, and he wondered who she was.

He got up from the edge of the stage and slowly walked in her direction. She didn't appear to be bothered by the commotion that was going on around her. As he got closer, it was almost like looking at a picture of Evelyn. She had every striking feature of his wife, and it was almost scary. "Excuse me, miss, are you ok? Are you looking for someone who attended the event tonight? A loved one?" Ethan asked, unsure of what to say and not wanting to blurt out that she resembled his wife. "Actually, no, I didn't attend, but I heard it was quite a bang," she said amusingly. "I am looking for someone; I'm looking for several people, in fact," she said slowly as she gazed at him. "Well, are you hurt? Do you need medical attention? Is there anyone I can help you find your husband or escort?" he asked, trying to get more information. "No, I don't need your help. I'll find who I'm looking for on my own," the mysterious woman replied as she turned and began to walk away. "Wait, who are you, miss? What's your name? Ethan asked her as she headed towards the doors. "Monique St James, but you can call me Candy, suga," she said as she went out onto the Philadelphia streets and disappeared.

47

GHOSTLY PRESENT

Evelyn regained consciousness in the back of the ambulance on her way to the hospital. She had tubes and needles trailing up and down her arms. She heard the paramedics saying she had severe trauma to her abdomen from the gun shots and smoke inhalation. Her vision was blurred but she could see the images of the people working on her. "Hello, ma'am. Can you hear me?" She heard the woman say when she saw her flutter her eyes. "She's waking up," she said. "Just relax, your on your way to the hospital," a man said in the background. The sirens from the ambulance were deafening to her ears. She could barely hear what they were saying to her, and each time she tried to speak no words came from her mouth. Her entire body felt rigid and she felt a burning sensation around her stomach. "If you can hear us, blink your eyes," the woman said to her. Evelyn did as she was told. "Can you wiggle your fingers?" They asked her, and she did. "Great, she doesn't appear to have any spinal damage, but she's loosing a lot of blood," the male paramedic stated. "We're almost there, just hang on," they kept saying as she watched them adjust her IV and apply pressure to her midsection.

The ambulance seemed to be moving in slow motion and she wondered how long she had been unconscious. She thought she had died, taken her last breath, but she had only passed out. Her injuries were severe but not life threatening. She felt lifeless and empty. She started to cry, feeling the tears stream down her face. How had she survived? Why on earth was she still living and breathing even barely? She was at peace with dying, going to meet her maker. To see her mother again. All the terrible things she had done in her life she felt had finally caught up to her and she wanted her death to be payback.

But now she was being rushed to the hospital in critical condition. She didn't have any fight left in her and she didn't see a reason to go on. Everyone in her life was gone and she had nothing left to live for, assuming they died in the explosion.

Even her husband had turned against her. Ethan had shot her and, as much as she wanted to believe it wasn't intentional, she saw the look in his eyes and knew he wanted her dead too. But she couldn't understand why. She thought he loved her. She wanted to spend the rest of her life with him and had even decided that once the twins were out of her life she would give him babies. She knew that meant so much to him and she wanted to finally make him happy. Ethan had meant more to her than any of the men she dated in the past. He accepted her flaws and all. That was why she married him. She had shared some really intimate feelings with him and opened up in ways she never thought she would. He made her feel safe and protected, and she knew she would eventually tell him the ugly truth about her past. But just hours before he pointed a gun at her first true love, Clayton, and she jumped in front of the bullet. She sacrificed her own life for someone else, something she had never done before: putting someone else before herself.

Evelyn knew she had been cold and heartless to the men in her past, but not with Ethan. He made her feel alive, and she loved him even more because of it. Evelyn wanted to make a change in her life, and once she got rid of Jacob and James Spears, she knew she could start again and be the wife Ethan longed for, someone he could truly be proud of. But now, her nightmare was happening all over again. She hadn't escaped the lies and the destruction she had caused. Evelyn was alive and had to face every demon that existed in her world. She finally heard the ambulance pull into the emergency room entrance and all the paramedics inside scrambled to help her. They checked her vitals again, blood pressure, heart rhythm and pulse to verify she was stable. They removed her from the ambulance and frantically wheeled her inside. Evelyn looked around trying to see if she recognized anyone from the party, but there were no familiar faces. In fact, the hospital seemed unusually quiet. No one was hurrying around to care for anyone and there was no police presence there asking questions about the explosion. Evelyn looked confused. Where was everyone? Where were Ethan or Clayton? Why wasn't she seeing women in ball gowns or men in tuxedos holding bandages to their heads or comforting their spouses? Nothing seemed right to her. This couldn't have been the hospital everyone from the Gala was taken too, there was no way. Her mind started racing. She had to find out what was going on. Why was she taken to a different hospital from everyone else? She wanted to take the oxygen mask from her face and ask questions, but her arms were shackled down to the bed. A doctor walked over to her gurney just as the nurses reached the receptionist desk. "What do we have here? Black female, 5'11. Gun shot wound to the abdomen, concussion, contusions, bruising to the left rib, large gash to the left side of the face, some second degree burns to the right arm and possible dislocated shoulder caused by a fall." He read the chart from the nurses and proceeded to order Demerol and a sedative to help with her pain. "Hello, Ms. James. I'm doctor Lawrence, chief of staff for the University of Penn Hospital, and I'll be taking care of you." He spoke in a monotoned voice. "I've ordered you something for the pain and, as soon as it starts to work, we're going to send you off to surgery to try and repair some the damage you've sustained," he said. "If you can hear me and understand, please bat your eyes." Evelyn did so as well as nodded her head. "Good. We should have you up on your feet in no time, just try to relax and know you're in good hands," he said, as he patted her shoulder before walking away.

Evelyn felt a sense of relief after listening to the doctor tell her that she would be ok. She realized that as much as she thought she wanted to die, she actually didn't. Maybe there was a reason she was still alive, she thought. She knew she had to find out if Ethan or Clayton were still alive and what happened to Kendall. "Wait," she thought, "did he call her Ms. James? Why not Mrs. Price?" She quickly started to panic. Lying there, she could feel the drugs flow through her veins, and she felt her body getting heavy. An intern came and rolled her gurney to one of the rooms down the hall. She felt cold and thirsty and wanted to ask for an extra blanket, but he never removed the mask from her face. She could see him hooking up her monitors and replacing her bag of fluids. He never spoke a word to her as he went about his duties. When he was done, he left the room leaving the door cracked open slightly. Evelyn started to feel lightheaded but still had some sense of her surroundings.

She heard a man and woman outside her door talking and she strained to hear their conversation. "Do you think the medication we gave her was enough?" she heard the female say. "Yes, it was just enough to keep her comfortable and ease some of her pain. If we give her too much, she'll go into shock, or even worse, a coma, and Mrs. Morgan would be furious. She said she just wanted her heavily sedated, not drugged. Do you understand that, Theresa?" She listened as the male spoke. "Yes, I was just asking because they both stated that they didn't want her in too much pain, but they also didn't want her to remember anything that happened after she got here," the woman replied sarcastically. "Well, she couldn't have it both ways. Giving her too much propofol could easily stop her heart, and the last thing that bitch wants is her little angel dead," the man said in a sneering tone. As Evelyn listened to the couple she felt her heart racing and tried to figure out who on earth they were talking about. She felt tiny beads of sweat starting to form on her forehead and her breathing became arctic. Who in the hell was Mrs. Morgan and why was she giving orders about her care? Evelyn tired again to move her arms but they were tightly secured by the restraints. She needed to ask questions and find out what the hell was going on. Her body was growing weaker by the minute. She knew whatever drug they had given her was starting to work. She felt her eyes fluttering as she tried desperately to fight off the effects. After a few moments, her body felt paralyzed and she couldn't move. Her vision was blurred and she could barely see. She heard her walk into the room slowly, almost cat-like. She felt a warm hand stroke her face gently. She imagined she was a child again, being comforted by the one person she loved the most. "Alisha, sweetie, can you hear me, baby? The woman's voice said softly in her ear. "Alisha, baby, can you hear me?" Evelyn smiled at her mothers voice.

She liked this dream, it always made her feel safe. She imagined her mother wrapping her arms around her and caressing her, and she started to cry. Tears flowed from her eyes as she thought about Candy. Then, suddenly, she felt the grip of nails around her throat and she tried to wake up from her horrible nightmare. She gasped for air as the hand grew tighter. She squirmed and tried to fight, but couldn't. Her hands were still in restraints. She tried calling for help but her mouth was duck taped shut. She managed to open her eyes fully and focus on the person trying to take her breath. She couldn't believe who she saw. It was Monique! How on earth was it her? When the woman saw her open her eyes, she released her grip and stepped back. She had a sinister grin on her face as she watched Evelyn gasp for air. She reached over and ripped the tape from her mouth. Evelyn was in shock. "How the hell are you alive? I thought you were dead," she said to the woman. She felt her body trembling with fear.

"You thought or you hoped?" The woman said mischievously. "No, baby, I'm not dead, I'm actually more alive than I've ever been," she continued. "I've been resurrected and brought back as your savior," she laughed. Evelyn couldn't speak. No other words could come out of her mouth. She couldn't believe it, Monique Shantel James was alive. CANDY was back!

48

IS THIS THE END...

The explosion had been unexpected, and everyone in attendance never knew what was coming. The twins had set out to get even with all that had crossed them. When they saw Clayton, Alisha, and Regina all in one place, they felt as if they had been served a buffet platter. They were going to finally settle the score with each one of them, and thanks to Ethan, it was possible. When James walked up to Regina, he felt a surge of dominance over her. "This bitch left me," he thought. "I made her into the woman that she was and had given her any and everything she could have ever asked for, and she took my daughter and left me." He felt anger and hatred start to build within him. "You thought I'd never find you, didn't you, bitch?" He said to her through clenched teeth. He wanted to choke her right there in front of everyone, but he didn't want to cause a scene. He wanted to take her out to a back alley and put a bullet in her skull for betraying him.

In his mind, she had become enemy number one the night she'd killed Snake's girl and fled. He thought she would be his soldier and stand tall with him forever. "I want to see my daughter," he said to her, gripping her tightly by the arm. As much as he despised her, Nyla was his world, and he would die for her. "Never will you see her again," Regina replied angrily. "You put us through hell and tried to turn her into a ruthless killer like you," she said. "Well, ain't that funny, 'cause if memory serves me correctly, you too are a murderer, bitch. We all saw you pull the trigger on Crystal that night," he said with a smirk on his face. "I was protecting my child and saving Jacob's life in the process," Regina said as tears started to stream down her face, ruining her makeup. "That girl was going to shoot them, and there was nothing I wouldn't have done to protect my daughter," she continued. She looked around the room, trying to spot Clayton in hopes that he would notice her confrontation with James and come to her rescue. Or maybe Mr. Price would see the terrified look on his wife's face as Regina did.

Jacob had made his way over to Evelyn and seemed to be having an intense conversation with her as well, and she wondered why. What on earth did the twins have to do with her boss's wife? She saw he had a gun jammed in her side and thought he was going to shoot her. Maybe she would scream to cause a commotion, and Regina could get away. "What was happening?" she thought. How was she connected to these men? Regina knew that James wouldn't hurt her in front of all those people, but she wasn't sure what Jacob would do at that moment. Yet she was still terrified of what they had planned. Her mind was racing as she thought of Nyla and what he was planning on doing when he saw her. Was he going to harm her in any way? Would he try to convince her to turn on her mother and send her to jail? She wasn't even sure if she remembered that awful night. She had tried so hard to shield her from those terrible times of her past. The twins knew that his daughter and Regina were the only people who could connect him and his brother to Snake and Crystal's murder, and as far as she knew, the case was still unsolved. She, too, could be facing a lifetime behind bars if any mention of that night was revealed. Not only was she protecting her daughter, she was protecting herself.

When Regina tried to pull away from James' grip, the lights dimmed, and she saw her boss walk onto the stage. He never noticed Jacob standing with his wife with a piece in her back. He was about to introduce Clayton Taylor, and the room erupted in applause. Everyone stood and watched as Ethan Price talked about Clayton's accomplishments and success thus far, and the models and Hair stylists of Tailored To You paraded the stage in fits designed by Darrin. It was a beautiful scene as everyone was fixated on the performance. No one was aware of the terrifying scene happening right under their noses. When Ethan finished the presentation, he called out Clayton's name as he was making his way towards Regina. He then stopped and went onto the stage as the spotlight shone on him in the crowd. He had a distant look on his face as he walked up the three steps to join Ethan. All attention was on them when suddenly, out of nowhere, Ethan pulled out a gun and started shooting! The crowd was in disbelief. The models and presenters fled the stage in horror. Everyone started trampling one another, trying to get to safety. Regina watched as her boss fired a shot into the man she loved as well as his wife. Evelyn had managed to break loose from Jacob when she saw her husband pull out the gun. She ran towards Clayton, trying to push him out of the way, but ended up taking a bullet herself.

The whole moment seemed to play out in slow motion. Screams rang throughout the room in the midst of the commotion. Regina tried frantically to get to Clayton, but James wouldn't let her go. She felt as if a bullet had struck her as well. As everyone scattered and ducked from the gunfire, Jacob ran over to where they stood. "Man, we gotta get the fuck outta here! Come on!" he yelled to his brother. He grabbed him and started heading towards the back entrance. "This ain't over, bitch," James said to her before following his twin. As soon as Regina took a step towards Clayton, she felt a tremble, and the entire main floor of the hotel blew up. It sounded as if a million explosives had gone off, sending people's tables and chairs flying into the air. The floor was collapsing, and the foundation of the room was crumbling. Fire and smoke were starting to surround her, and she could hardly breathe. She saw men and women falling into a dark, dismal hole as glass shattered around her. She heard cries for help as the plaster burned and melted from the walls. She tried desperately to get to the entrance, but people were running and trampling her. She fell onto the piece of floor that was left trembling with fear. The smoke was so intense she couldn't see. So many people were running for their lives around her, but she wasn't able to stand. She tried desperately to gain her footing when she felt someone grab her and pull her into the black hole. She felt like the fall would never end. She started to scream as debris toppled her. A large floor joist had hit her in the head with such force it knocked her out. Regina took one last deep breath, and everything went black.

49

WHEN THE SMOKE
CLEARS

Regina was in a state of shock. She couldn't believe she had been rescued. In her mind, that moment when the beautiful ballroom went up into flames and the floor disappeared beneath her was the end, and she was dying, but as she woke and saw she was hooked up to several different machines, she then realized she was in the hospital. Help had finally arrived, she thought. She didn't know how long she had been there or how severe her injuries were, but she knew she was safe and would see her daughter again. She breathed a sigh of relief. It all seemed surreal to her that night, seeing the twins and watching Clayton get shot. Everything was a horrible nightmare.

At that moment, Regina heard voices enter the room. She couldn't see their faces, but she heard their voices. They walked over in her direction and seemed to be examining her, but she wasn't sure. "The patient still seems to be uncon-scious," she heard a man say. "Her brain is showing no signs of a normal sleep-wakefulness cycle, and she doesn't seem to respond to any touch or sound," he continued. Regina laughed as the two men spoke as if she wasn't in the room. She has suffered severe trauma, and her vitals aren't high enough to wake her yet," she heard the other doctor comment. "Wake her? Wait, what the hell are you talking about?" she said in her thoughts. She was lying right there in bed listening to every word they spoke, but she was in a medically induced coma, and they couldn't hear her from her subconscious. "Yes, I'm aware from her chart, but I did see some signs of eye flutter a few days ago, so there is still a chance for her," the doctor said. She felt herself screaming, but no one could hear. She didn't know what day it was as if she had suddenly felt released in a time. It was like she was on the outside looking into her own body. "I'm in a coma. Omg, what is happening?" she began to scream again. "Have the nurse administer another 5 CCs of Demerol. We'd like to keep her as comfortable as possible." "Sure thing, Dr Wexler. Oh, will you be calling her family this week to give them an update on her progress? You know if you don't, her fiancé will have the chief of staff up here in a heartbeat again." The two men shared a laugh. "I'll have Nancy or Patricia do it. God, you would think the man owned the hospital the way he keeps security at her door and requires information on a consistent basis. She's not queen fucking Elizabeth, you know?" the older doctor said to the younger resident. "That is true, but after going over the police report and seeing everything that happened, I can understand why they need her protected. Besides, the FBI needs her as a potential witness." "Well, they better pray to God she wakes up soon," the younger resident replied.

Regina couldn't understand what was happening. Who was her fiancé, and who the hell was she a witness for? Had James come to the hospital and told them she was his soon-to-be wife? And where was Nyla? She was scared he had gotten a hold of her and taken her back to North Carolina. All she could remember was the night of the party, and even that seemed to be a blur to her right now. She had been so disappointed that Clayton didn't protect her when she needed him most. He promised to protect her, and he didn't. She was face to face with James, the father of her child and the man that ruined her life. She could still feel the tight grip he had on her arm when he walked up to her at the party. "I can't believe my eyes," James said as he got close to her. "Bitch, I've been looking all over for you. Where is my daughter?" he asked as he stared at her. Her whole body shook with fear, and she felt her heart beating violently in her chest. "James, she is safe, and why do you even care?" Regina said, her voice trembling with each word. "What the fuck do you mean? She's my daughter, bitch, and I have the right to see her, and I care about how you're taking care of her." What do you mean, see her? Why on earth would you want to see her now?" she said. "Because she's my child, and I have that right. I should have broken your fucking neck the night you left, bitch. You're lucky the cops was coming 'cause that's the only reason you were able to get away." "You made me a murderer and almost killed me, and it was the grace of God that got me away from you," Regina said, starting to cry.

Her thoughts reminded her of that awful night in North Carolina. Regina had been coming downstairs late one evening after putting her daughter down to bed when she overheard James arguing with someone. It was one of his workers, Turk. He was trying to explain to him why he was short with his cut of the money, but James was not trying to hear a word he spoke. "Look, mutherfucker, this is the third time you came up short with my money, and I'm not gonna be played like no sucker out in them streets, you hear me?" she heard James say to him. "Look, twin, I can't help it. Its slow out there, man. Them niggas ain't spending like they used to," Turk tried to explain. "Nigga, it ain't the fucking point how much you sold, it's about how much you turning into me," James responded his words laced with anger. "Look, man, I got to stay up while I'm out there hustling yo shit for you and your brother, and sometimes I need to take a break and handle mines, so I dip into the profits every now and again," Turk said arrogantly. He didn't seem to have any fear telling James that he was skimming money off the top or sampling the product from time to time. "So, nigga you telling me you getting high on my shit?" James asked, moving closer to the man. Turk was in his late thirties and had a slender build. He had about two inches of height over James, but he wasn't physically matched. "Naw, man, I'm not saying I smoke yo shit; you know I get down with the herb, but I trick with the coke every once in a while, with a few of the girls out there working just to release some steam," he said starting to become nervous as he watched James get closer to him. "Oh, so you telling me you take my product and give it to them hoes on the street so they can suck your dick, that's what you telling me?" he asked him again, moving in a little closer.

Regina stood in the hallway, watching the exchange between the two men. She felt her body start to quiver because she knew something was about to happen, and she knew it wasn't gonna be good. She watched as James lifted his shirt out of his pants, making it easier to reach the piece he had tucked away behind his back. "Look, man, I know my money is a little light some nights, but damn, cut a brother some slack," Turk nervously said. James didn't like anyone to play with his money, and Regina had seen him make examples of a lot of people in the past who tried him. "Ok, well, we're gonna handle this shit tonight 'cause apparently, you think this shit is a game," James said as he pulled out his 9mm Glock and pointed at him. "Yo, twin, please, man, what are you doing?" Turk jumped back and started to beg for his life. "What am I doing?" He said sarcastically. "I'm about to let off some steam, nigga. Ain't that what you said? I'm just gonna do it a little differently than you do, that all," James said, shoving the gun in Turk's face. "Please, twin, please, man, I'm sorry. I'll get you yo money, man. Please don't kill me," he pleaded.

Just then, Jacob came through the door holding a woman by the arm. It was Crystal Turk's girlfriend. He flung her towards him as he stood there terrified. "I found his bitch hiding out in one of Smitty's crack houses. The bitch was in there selling our product," Jacob said to his brother. "Get the fuck outta here. So you telling me this nigga was stealing our shit and giving it to his bitch to sell and make money?" "Yup, that's exactly what he was doing," Jacob said, looking at Turk and his girl cowering in the corner. Crystal was a pretty, petite girl who stood about five four with a cinnamon complexion, and she couldn't have been older than nineteen. Regina remembered seeing her at the dances when she would come to visit Val for the summer. She was always in a dude's face running game, and she was always hustling. She was the plug for the young kids who smoked weed in the neighborhood, and she always dealt with the local drug dealers because they would take her shopping and keep her in the latest gear. "So, how long you and this nigga been stealing my shit?" James asked her. "Mr. James, I don't know shit about Turk stealing from you. He just told me that we could come up from a stash he had, and he would give me fifty percent of the profit. I ain't know nothing about the coke being yours, I swear," she said, her voice trembling with each word.

Turk started to cry as Crystal snitched on him. "Look at this bitch ass nigga crying," Jacob said as he sat on the sofa laughing. "Don't cry now nigga. You fucked up, and now you gotta pay the price," he said to them. Regina stood frightened, wondering if the twins were gonna kill them in cold blood right there in their living room. She had seen them beat people up many times, but she had never actually seen them kill anyone before, and she was terrified. She had a small child in the house, and she hoped James would consider that before making that fatal choice. "Take y'all fucking clothes off," she heard James say to the hopeless couple. They did as they were told, and tears streamed from their eyes. He then walked over to the mantel, where Regina kept several large jars of scented candles. He lit two of them and waited for the scents to permeate the room, then he walked over to Crystal and pushed her down onto the floor. "You picked the wrong nigga to go into business with, bitch," he said through clenched teeth, then poured the hot wax onto her naked skin. She let out an agonizing scream as the hot liquid burned her. "I'm sorry, twin. I'm so sorry!" She kept yelling as he continued to scorch her skin with the wax. He then took the other candle and brought it over to Turk. "Drink it, mutherfucker," he said to him as he shoved the candle toward his mouth. "Twin, please, man. I'm sorry, man, I'm gonna pay you back. I swear," he pleaded, but his words fell on deaf ears. James was enraged, and there was no stopping the torture he was about to inflict on them. "Drink it!" He yelled as the man took the candle from his hands and placed it to his lips.

Regina watched as the twins tortured them for what seemed like hours, beating them each time they had to repeat a command. Jacob walked over to Crystal and grabbed her by the hair. He then hit her so hard across the face that the rings on his fingers knocked out two of her teeth. She lay there shivering in a fetal position, weeping. Turk tried crawling over to her when James kicked him on the side of the head. Blood gushed from his mouth as he retreated back to the corner. "Don't try to console each other now, nigga. It's your fault this bitch is here. You pulled her into your trap, and now you both gonna take that trip to hell," James responded. Jacob walked over to a closet, pulled out large sheets of plastic, and laid them out on the floor. "Get yo dirty stinking asses on the plastic," he shouted at them. They slowly rolled onto it, still crying and pleading for their lives. Jacob then pulled out his gun and handed it to Turk. "I want you to blow this bitches head off for snitching on you, nigga," he said to him. "Twin, please, I can't, man. Please, give me a chance to get you your money, man, please," Turk begged. "It's too late for that, man. There's no way I'm gonna let you walk out of here. Are you fucking serious? You betrayed us, nigga, and ya girl ratted you out quick. So, you know she wouldn't think twice about speaking our name." Crystal sat there sobbing uncontrollably. "Please, God, please don't make him shoot me, please," she repeated over and over. "Neither one of y'all was sorry and calling on God when you was stealing our money, was you?" James asked as he mugged her towards the floor. "Take it, nigga. Take this piece and put a bullet in this bitches head." "That's payback," Jacob said, amused at the situation. "I can't do it," Turk cried. "Well, I'll do it for you," James said, getting frustrated, and he shot Turk in the head. He fell dead from the single bullet. When Regina saw him pull the trigger, she let out an agonizing scream. Both twins turned to see her standing in the hallway, trembling. James walked towards her and grabbed her by the throat.

Regina had terror in her eyes. She had never seen James so angry. His eyes were bloodshot, and he had an expression of hatred and evil on his face. "What the fuck are you doing here!? Why the fuck would you watch me take care of my business?" he asked her angrily. James, please, I'm sorry. I only came down to get a snack for Nyla. That's all," Regina said, trying to convince him that she had just gotten there. "Don't fucking lie to me. I know you saw what just happened," he scowled. "No, James, I didn't. I swear," Regina cried. From the living room, Regina heard Crystal wailing as Jacob continued to kick and beat her. She looked up and saw the familiar face. "Regina, please help me," she heard the young girl yell out at her. James then released his tight grip from around her neck and pulled her into the room. "You know this thieving ass bitch, Gina?" he said to her. "Kind of not, really," Regina said, not knowing how to answer him. She looked down to the floor and saw the girl bleeding from the mouth; her skin blistered from the wax. Her face was black and blue, and one side of her eye was swollen shut. Tears welled up in Regina's eyes as she looked at the battered and beaten girl on the floor and the body of her dead boyfriend. "How do you know her, bitch?" James asked Crystal. "I used to see her with Val, her cousin, sometimes that's all," she continued to sob. "Is that true, Gina?" he asked. "Yes, James, I don't really know her," Regina answered quickly. "Well, then you shouldn't feel bad about splitting this bitch wig," he said angrily. "What? What the hell are you saying? I don't have a beef with her," Regina said, scared of what James was asking her to do. "Well, I do. The bitch stole from me, from us. She took food out of our mouth, and she didn't give a damn about doing it, so you shouldn't care about taking her life," he said. "I want you to put a bullet in this bitch's skull. You are a part of me and my family, and you gonna have to pull your weight." "James, please, I can't kill her. I can't kill anyone. I'm not a murderer, please, James; I'm the mother of your child. You can't make me do this," Regina cried. Jacob sat back, staring at Regina almost sympathetically. "James, man, don't get her involved with this bullshit, man. She ain't built for that," he said. "The bitch was built to spy on us and see what happened," he shouted. He then turned to Regina and grabbed her by the back of her neck. "Well, since you're not brave enough to do it, maybe I'll go get my baby girl to handle it," he said, dragging Regina towards the steps.

"James, no, don't go near Nyla, please, please," Regina began to scream.

He dragged her up the steps to the second floor, where their eight-year-old daughter slept. Regina fought violently to get out of his grip. When they reached her room, he shoved her into the door. "You are gonna obey me and get my daughter since you are so fucking scared to handle my business," he said, seething. Nyla opened her eyes and saw her mother crying on the floor. James walked over to the sleeping child and picked her up. "Daddy, what's wrong with mommy?" she asked innocently. "She's letting someone steal from us, baby," he said, kissing her on the cheek. "Mommy, why are you letting someone steal from daddy?" she said to her mother. "Please, baby, mommy is gonna handle it. Please, James, put her back to bed. I'll do anything you ask," Regina said, trembling and defeated. "Well, let's just see how you handle it, honey," he said as he left the room, taking Nyla with him. Regina scurried to her feet to follow him down the steps.

When they reached the living room, Crystal was still lying on the floor naked and bleeding heavily. Jacob had continued to torture her repeatedly. She was barely clinging to life when they entered the room. "Look here, the bitch is still breathing," James said humorously. "Yeah, she tough as nails," Jacob said, laughing. "Well, it's time she takes her final nap," he said, reaching for the gun in Jacob's hand. "James, please, please, I'll do it," Regina begged him as she watched him hand the gun to his daughter. She saw the confusion and bewilderment in her child's eyes. "Do you know what to do with this, baby?" he asked his daughter. "Yes, daddy, it's cops and robbers toy," she said innocently. "You got it half right, sweetheart. It's for the robbers and cops, but it's not a toy," he said, explaining the gun to her. She held the gun, looking at it intently. "James, please give it to me. God, please don't make our daughter do this!" Regina said hysterically. "I'll do whatever you want, please," she continued to beg. Amused by the situation, James reached for the gun from his daughter when she pointed it at him. "Bang, bang, daddy," she said as she pointed the barrel at him. "Angrily, James tried to grab the piece from her hands and slapped her across the face." "Don't you ever point a gun at me! Are you fucking crazy?" he screamed at his child. Regina then jumped onto James' back and began violently striking him across the head and face. Jacob rushed over to break up the fight between the two, taking his eyes off Crystal, who was still crouched on the floor. As he struggled to break them apart, they were all quickly silenced by the sound of a shot of Jacob's gun.

When they turned around, they saw Crystal holding Nyla by the neck with the gun pointed at her head. She had managed to get a hold of the gun when the little girl fell to the floor from the hit by her father. She knew this was her only chance to get out of that house of horrors alive, and she wasn't going to hesitate to put a bullet in this little girl's brain. "Bitch, you don't want to do this," James said to her as he watched his daughter begin to cry. "Mommy, please tell her to leave me alone," she squirmed, trying to release the woman's grip on her. "Ok, baby. Crystal, please let my baby go, please. She has nothing to do with what's going on. Please, I beg of you, give me my baby," Regina said. "You must think I'm fucking stupid I let her go; I'm as good as dead. I'm sorry, Gina, she's gotta be my way outta here," Crystal said, barely able to see out of her swollen eyes. "You can leave, I promise. James, tell her she can leave. Just let Nyla go," she cried. "Yeah, bitch, you can get the fuck outta here. Just give me my daughter," he said, easing closer to them. "Stay the fuck back, twin, or I swear I will blast her," she said with a shaky voice. "I need some clothes so I can get the hell out of here," Crystal said, still on the floor naked, holding the defenseless child. "Ok. I'll get you some clothes, and then you gotta let my baby go," Regina said as she searched the floor for Crystal's clothes. When she reached down, she saw the clothes that Turk wore and saw he had a twenty-two pistol in a holster taped to the inside of his shirt. "He must have carried it for protection on the streets," Regina thought. She quickly slid the small weapon under her shirt as she picked up the jean shorts and tee shirt Crystal was wearing when she was brought to the house. She walked closer to Crystal and her daughter. "Here's your clothes. Please let my child go," she begged, watching tears flow from Nyla's eyes. "I told you I can't. That crazy nigga gonna kill me as soon as I do," she yelled. She rose to her feet, bringing the girl up with her. I need you to help me put on my clothes she said to her as she began to release her grip. As she did so, Nyla managed to break free and run towards her dad. "Fuck!" Crystal screamed and pointed the gun at the little girl's head with her finger on the trigger. She was about to shoot when she saw Regina pull out the twenty-two and fire. The bullet landed right between her eyes, taking her out instantly. It felt like time stood still and she was moving in slow motion.

Regina had never fired a gun before, but watching someone trying to harm her daughter was something she was not going to stand for. She would have taken anyone out that brought her harm. Nyla held onto her father for dear life, crying hysterically. Jacob started clapping. "Well done, sis, you took that bitch out," he said, cheering and giving Regina praise. He seemed unbothered by the fact that Crystal had his Neice hemmed up with a gun to her head, ready to shoot. Regina felt her knees grow weak as she watched Crystal's body hit the floor. She ran to her daughter and scooped her up in her arms. "Are you all right, baby?" she asked as she hugged her tightly and sobbed. "Yes, mommy. I'm just scared. Is daddy gonna hurt us?" she asked, frightened. "No, baby, everything is gonna be fine," she whispered to her daughter as she headed for the stairs. "Clean this mess up," James yelled out to her as he and Jacob started rolling the two dead bodies up in the plastic that was on the floor. They had to dispose of Crystal and Turk quickly before someone came looking for them. They took each body out of the house through the back door and put them in their van they had parked in the alley.

Regina listened as she heard them start the engine and pull off into the night. She quickly started gathering clothes and personal belongings for her and Nyla. She knew this was her chance to get out of there and go as far away as possible from James. She had been saving money for over a year just in case she had to bail James out of jail or pay for medical expenses, and she had accumulated quite a bit, close to three million dollars. She never thought she would have to use that money for an escape plan. Regina quickly grabbed the two suitcases as well as the small aluminum safe with the cash inside and placed them in her car. She then raced back into the house to get Nyla and some food for them to eat on their trip. She wasn't sure where they were headed, but she knew she couldn't stay in that house any longer. The twins had crossed the line and put her and her daughter in danger. For Regina, there was no turning back. She was now a murderer and on the run. From now on, her life would be forever changed.

50

FORBIDDEN GAMES

The downtown streets of Philadelphia were chaotic. Police fire and rescue vehicles stretched for miles. People were frantic, searching for loved ones. There were several fatalities and hundreds injured. Local news vans and radio stations anxiously tried to make their way through the barricades with little to no luck. Cars and surrounding buildings had been damaged from the broken glass and bricks that shot from the foundation of the building like cannons. The explosion had been so forceful it could be felt for miles around the city. Flames lit up the sky like fireworks on the fourth of July. Helicopters were circling the air, trying to get a bird's eye view of the damage. The scene was one of D-Day destruction and mayhem. Sirens blared from every direction. Pedestrians and medical personnel scrambled to get the injured to safety. The city was under a state of emergency. Private investigators, the FBI, local police departments, and utility companies were all on alert. They suspected the city could be under attack. Philadelphia had never had an explosion like this before, and there were suspicions it could possibly be a terrorist attack.

No one was sure, but the mayor of the city had done a press conference to let the city know how determined he was to find out. In a far corner of the cut, Snake and Kendall stood at the broad and chestnut street, watching as the beautiful Bellevue hotel went up in flames. Each was in their thoughts, but both were wondering if anyone had survived. "Hey, Unc, when am I gonna get my paper from you?" Kendall asked Snake. "Damn, man, chill. I told you I had everything under control. I just needed to get rid of them fucking twins and make sure that bitch made it to the hospital safe and sound, and then I'd collect my money and break you off," Snake replied, annoyed his nephew was sweating him about his payoff. "Look, man, I worked long and hard finding that slimy bitch and getting her to fall for me and setting up this whole charade for you niggas. I just want to be sure my payday is coming, that's all," Kendall responded. "Listen, we both walking away from this shit with more money than we could ever dream up. We did our part, and even though it took years to follow through, this was the grand finale," Snake said, pointing to the hotel fire a few blocks away. "Yeah, man, that shit is pretty sweet," Kendall said, smiling. "We did a great job. I feel bad for my soldier, though. It's a shame he got caught up in this bullshit, but hey, even the greats fall sometimes," Snake said, thinking of Ethan. He had hoped that by filling his mind with some of the truth about Evelyn, it would make him walk away, leave the bitch where she stood and let her face the consequences of the mess, she made with the twins, but he knew Ethan loved her too much and would try to protect her. He never knew this was a con from the beginning, and Snake knew that if he wanted to make it out alive, he had to stay ten toes down and go along.

Even though the hotel was in flames and pretty much everyone was dead, Snake knew the war wasn't over. It was only beginning. "Come on, Unc, let's get the fuck outta here before somebody comes over here and starts questioning us," Kendall said as he saw police making their way in their direction. Yeah man you right we've seen what we needed to let's get the fuck outta here he said as the two men disappeared into the darkness.

EPILOGUE

As the private jet finally began to descend at Philadelphia International Airport, the air was thick with fog. The flight seemed to last for hours since the pilot couldn't touch down right away due to congested airspace. The two passengers on the flight were a bit antsy to embark the plane. "I hope our ride is waiting for us when we arrive," the beautiful woman clad in expensive clothing and diamonds said. "Don't worry, darling. He said he'd be there on time just as we discussed, and I doubt he'd disappoint us," her handsome escort replied. "Good, we only have a few hours, and I would hate to miss such an extraordinary event. I heard there's going to be some important guests in attendance," she chuckled as she sipped on the expensive champagne she had in her hand. As the plane touched down gently on the runway, she looked out of the window and noticed a silver Bentley parked at the end of a red carpet on the tarmac. "Finally," she sighed as she sat down the glass of sparkling libations and grabbed her Birkin bag from the seat in front of her. She reached into her purse and sprayed on her Billion perfume before standing to exit the plane. As she and the gentleman on her arm approached the waiting car, she could see the skyline of the city through the clouds. "Philly still looks the way I remembered it," she said with a smile. The driver popped the trunk so that he could place their luggage safely. When he bent down, he removed a tarp to expose what was already inside. As he did, the woman let out a joyful squeal. She looked into the eyes of the handsome stranger and smiled. "Be careful with that dynamite, darling. It's not quite time for the tick, tick, boom!

To be continued…

THE PHILLY SLANG WORD DICTIONARY

Jawn- person, place, or thing

Drawn- you doing too much, extra

Papi Store- the Puerto Rican store

Square- nerd or naïve

Bumpkin- innocent, childlike

Green- unaware, passive

Trick- someone a prostitute uses for money

Vic- victim

Pimp- someone that solicits others for profit

Young boul- a young person

Old head- an older person

On spin- a wavy hairstyle

Drippy- very fashionable, stylish

Ree up- purchase of a large quantity of drugs

Thurl- on point, smart, quick on your feet

Bodega- owner-operated Cuban or Puerto Rican corner store

Peeps- close friends or relatives, your people

Fire- great, wonderful, amazing

Herb- marijuana, weed

Wifey- girlfriend, main lady

Bottom bitch- your most money-making prostitute

Zanies- Street name for Prescription drug

Daddy- another name used for pimp or boyfriend

Ho- prostitute

Brick-a Street name for a kilo of cocaine

Stay tuned for more street slang coming soon.

DEDICATION

Forbidden is dedicated to the most important person in my life…
My MOM.

I can't wait to see you again in heaven, to tell you all that has happened
to me…

Even though I know you're watching, smiling down and seeing the
woman I became to be…

I can feel your love and spirit, I carry in my heart every day…

Your laughter and your smile, that fills my heart along the way…

I look for your approval of the choices that I make…

And I pray to God each day, especially for my mistakes…

This journey has been sad and lonely without you, and oftentimes
I cry…

But you left me an angel to look after me sometimes I wonder why…

I hope that you are proud of me, as I travel this road, I remember…

You will always be my beautiful forever, my dear loving TENDA…

Thank you for giving me courage, strength and Virgo Confidence!! I love you, TENDA Linda…

Your Daughter, D.

Thank you.

How do you begin to thank all the wonderful people in your life? For me, that would be a whole other book with that title. Thank You. I have been privileged to experience exceptional people along this journey of Forbidden, whether it was before or after I put pen to paper. So, I felt in my heart to show my appreciation to some.

My children- Ride or Die! Omg, where do I start?

James- words can't explain the love and appreciation I feel for you. Countless times, I made you read my book, and countless times, you always agreed. Thank you for giving me advice and encouragement all the time! I could not have stayed so focused if you had not been there cheering me on. And thank you for helping me with the street lingo too much of the time, lol.

Nyla- you are me, and I am you (inside joke, lol). We are so much alike, and I feel like our minds are synced. I love you so much and all the way. Thank you for always being there when I needed an idea or a twist for my story. And I appreciate and love that you always support my dreams. You made me believe I could do it. And now there is no stopping me!!

I started writing this book twenty years ago and started and stopped so many times to watch you both grow into the most incredible people god has put on this earth. You inspired me each and every moment, and because of you, giving me a chance to grow, I was able to bring my characters to life. Thank you for being my Muse and keeping me updated on the culture. I'm actually hip now! Lol, I love you both forever.

J. Speaks- whatever career I wanted to have, you supported me. If I told you I wanted to be an astronaut, you would find out how much I needed for the rocket ship. You have always pushed me to be better. From the first day, I told you I wanted to write a book, you encouraged me. Thank you for always supporting my dreams, and I hope I have made you proud.

Michael C.- words can't describe how you have supported me. And the funny thing is you did most of it with sarcasm and love, lol. Thank you for being my little big brother and continuing to give shade so that I can keep creating amazing characters. I love you for life.

Mama Teresa- ok, so nobody knows that the first sentence about forbidden was heard by your ears! You have been there since day one, and you have always encouraged me and told me I would be great. I love you with all my heart. Thank you for stepping in and being one of God's angels to watch over me.

Tyisha H.- my tootie newnies. (if you know, you know) girl, I couldn't have gotten this book right without you. Thank you for the long nights, for calling for your advice, and for telling me how I overanalyze everything! Lol. And all the support and praise you give. You have given me the drive and passion to create my stories, and I will love and appreciate you forever.

Sekret B-(boo boo Kitty) The whole world stops! Carry on…. we were destined to be a part of each other's lives. You read the rough draft of Forbidden in its infant stage and asked if I was already a famous author! OK, What?! LOL, I will never forget the praise you gave to me. (Yeah, y'all read it right, PRAISE!) Being of a younger generation and enjoying my story lifted me to cloud nine. Thank you for supporting me and breaking me out of my comfort zone. I do so many amazing things now (creatively) because of you! You helped me create and bring all things forbidden to the world, and I can never repay you for all you have given to this book! BILLION Baby coming soon…

To my Sistahs- ok, grab your cups, and let's get to sipping!

Adrienne- giving God the glory for your wisdom. Thank you for being an ear when I wanted to give up! (Which was every other day lol) thank you for the honesty (sometimes brutal) that I needed to hear on more than one occasion, but most of all, thank you for being a friend (I know you singing The Golden Girls, lol). You accepted me with all my flaws, and with every crazy idea I ever came up with, you supported me, and I could not be more blessed to have you as a Sista!!

Bette- she is the reason why I carry an umbrella! (Private joke lol) no, but in all seriousness, you have truly been a shoulder to lean on. When we first met, you were my cheerleader from day one. Even though you didn't believe me when I said I was a writer until I sent you my rough draft, lol. I appreciate the support you've always given me. You challenge me artistically and motivate my senses. You taught me not to sweat the small stuff, and when there's too much on my plate, go take a nap! Lol, thank you for always showing up for me, even when I'm too stubborn to ask. You will always be my best pettiest best friend. Love you to pieces.

To everyone else who tolerated me when I was frantic, panicked, crazy, happy, excited, and glad, I thank you. Forbidden was a long time coming, but stay tuned. There's more to come. Be Blessed. Oh, and to the Haters, Nay Sayers, and doubters- People often asked me how I would feel if my book never became a bestseller? My response is: I guess I'll never know!

Forbidden Secrets… stay tuned.